The Back Page

Other Booklist Publications

Reid's Read-Alouds: Selections for Children and Teens, by Rob Reid

The Back Page

BILL OTT

with a foreword by Joyce Saricks

AMERICAN LIBRARY ASSOCIATION

Chicago   2009

Bill Ott worked in libraries in Washington State for nearly 10 years before coming to *Booklist* in 1980 as Adult Books Editor. He was promoted to Editor and Publisher in 1988. In addition to *Booklist,* his reviews and essays have appeared in numerous publications, including *American Libraries,* the *Chicago Tribune,* and the *New York Times Book Review.* He has contributed chapters to *Crime Fiction and Film in the Southwest* (2001) and *Florida Crime Writers* (2007). In 2004, he received the James Friend Memorial Award for Literary Criticism from the Midland Authors Society.

The paper used in this publication meets the minimum requirements of American National Standard for Information Sciences—Permanence of Paper for Printed Library Materials, ANSI Z39.48-1992. ⊚

Library of Congress Cataloging-in-Publication Data
Ott, Bill.
   The back page / Bill Ott ; with a foreword by Joyce Saricks.
      p. cm.
   Collection of essays which originally appeared in the author's column in Booklist.
   Includes bibliographical references and index.
   ISBN 978-0-8389-0997-3 (alk. paper)
   1. Books and reading—United States—Miscellanea. 2. Books—Reviews. 3. Fiction genres. 4. Booklist—Anecdotes. 5. Popular culture—United States—Anecdotes.
   I. Title.
Z1003.2.O88 2009
028'.9—dc22

                                                                    2009012813

ISBN-13: 978-0-8389-0997-3

Printed in the United States of America
13 12 11 10 09   5 4 3 2 1

CONTENTS

GENRE FICTION

LIFE AT *BOOKLIST*

LIFE BEYOND BOOKS

QUIZZES

INDEX

FOREWORD

Confessions of a Back Page Junkie

FOR MANY OF US IN the library world, Bill Ott's "Back Page" column is the highlight of every *Booklist* issue. The new copy arrives, and we flip the back cover open, just to make certain the column is there. Always lively, sometimes irritating, sometimes affirming our own thoughts—but consistently expressed in a manner far beyond our own writing skills—the Back Page offers piquant observations about our world of books and publishing and popular culture. We may read it first or read reviews first, saving the column as our reward, but we like to make certain it's there, ready for us when we can savor it. There are dark days, however, when we flip open the magazine only to discover that—horror of horrors—"The Back Page is on vacation." On vacation? He has some nerve! The wait for our next fix, for some of us, just isn't pretty.

At long, last addicts like me can relive the pleasures of the Back Page column whenever the need arises. Collected here in one volume are the best of Bill's Back Page, a satisfying mix of curmudgeonly humor, insightful analysis of some of the more abstruse publishing issues (e.g., the pulps), paeans to the great and not-so-great but certainly memorable literary lights, and nearly impossible quizzes that have sent us to our computers and the shelves. A bargain at any price!

Bill joined *Booklist* in 1980, and in the late '80s, he started writing the Back Page as "filler" on that undesirable page that preceded the index. But his column quickly became the last word on innumerable topics. For me, the column was the staple of every other Monday night on the desk. My colleague Lynn McCullagh and I would take turns poring over and then discussing Bill's column. Or on those glorious occasions when he had a quiz, whoever got it first would quiz the other. (Of course, the quizzes were often so hard we had to share the work!) For years, many of us have badgered Bill about publishing the columns. I confess that I personally had an ulterior motive: I have long believed this book would be the perfect stocking stuffer for several hard-to-please names on my Christmas list. Finally, the wait is over.

Like his own favorite, *Schott's Miscellany*, Bill's columns range across the world of popular culture, language, and publishing. Where else today can you read about diagramming sentences (with illustrations, no less, and a decidedly political stance)? Surely I'm not the only one who must credit Bill with introducing me to a wealth of useless knowledge (that animal crackers were first marketed in 1902 and Hershey's Kisses debuted in 1907—important stuff like that). Bill gleans these nuggets and others like them from various books of trivia that cross his desk. Although he claims that he falls on such books in desperation, lacking a topic for his column, he clearly knows his audience. I have been known to rush to the shelves to peruse many of these titles—and I even own several. (Some became Christmas stocking-stuffers in lieu of this long-awaited volume!)

While I'm a sucker for the quizzes, it's the essays that most clearly demonstrate Bill's broad interests and wit. The four sections of essays— "Books and Authors," "Genre Fiction," "Life at *Booklist*," and "Beyond Books"—provide scope for his clear thinking and incisive commentary. Not surprisingly, the majority of the essays fall within the first two sections. He is, after all, writing in a journal devoted to books. But the topics range widely within the confines of these sections (and favorite topics like golf and baseball often appear unexpectedly throughout). For example, we can share his dismay over his failure to read Stendhal and participate in his pleasure in Anthony Powell's 12-volume *Dance to the Music of Time.*

"Books and Authors" offers his inimitable take on *Peyton Place* as a cultural phenomenon, on J. K. Rowling's pronouncement about Dumbledore's sexual orientation, and on misspent youths (his own and memorable ones from fiction). Who else could take the fact that there seem to be more children's books on jazz than on trucks and turn it into a riff on trucks-in-literature that leads from James Crumley and other western crime writers, to an essay on drinking and driving and the role of the truck in the West. Not to mention the Japanese "noodle western" *Tampopo* with its own truck-driving hero, Goro, in a modern-day eastern version of *Shane.*

In "Genre Fiction," readers can share Bill's passion for crime fiction and some of the stars of the genre. He writes invitingly about some of his favorites—Michael Dibdin, George Pelecanos, Magdalen Nabb, John le Carré, Ian Fleming, Michael Connelly, Carl Hiaasen, Ross Thomas— and his appreciation provides the best possible introduction to these authors, who sometimes become our favorites, too. It's impossible to miss his enthusiasm for the pulps and the art of pulp covers, not to mention noir detectives and crime novels, the darker the better. These are obsessions, really, and Bill has written about that, too: "Columnists need obsessions, even addictions. We simply couldn't keep turning out 900 words on a regular schedule if we weren't allowed to indulge ourselves every now and then." Luckily, he makes his obsession with pulps, crime novels, and noir interesting enough to share. Who else would class Thomas Hardy's *Jude the Obscure* as a noir novel, I ask you?

"Life at *Booklist*" makes me want to join the group for coffee. Not to say anything, of course, because who would venture to talk books with this crowd, but just to sit and listen to their conversations, which must be fascinating. One can just hear them attacking the *New York Times Book Review*'s list of the best American fiction for the last 25 years! And their list of suggested alternative titles certainly rivals that in the *Times* and, from my perspective, is a lot more relevant and interesting. And who wouldn't have loved being involved in the decisions about what to include in the Booklist Century list, 100 years and 100 titles. The title of that essay, "Blood on the Tracks," says it all.

Finally, in "Life beyond Books" we get a glimpse beyond Bill's public persona. Here we discover how his passion for crime fiction got him out of jury duty, the adolescent trauma responsible for his aversion to crafts, his mixed reactions to a trip to the White House, and his reflections on political realities of more recent vintage.

Last but not least are the quizzes, the crown jewels of the Back Page. For some of us at least. This may be where we meet the real Bill Ott—the no-more-Mr.-Nice-Guy Bill Ott—because the quizzes are devilishly hard and, thus, endlessly appealing. Not to mention endlessly amusing, as are their premises: How many columnists can segue from dentists in literature to a three-part quiz about movie stars playing writers in movies? We can all be grateful that Bill is just that kind of guy.

All this makes for thought-provoking, entertaining reading. Like the best readers' advisors—and Bill is a natural, although he'd probably deny it—he writes so engagingly about books and authors that we readers find ourselves powerless to resist his recommendations.(However, I must admit that so far he has not been able to tempt me with a golf book, but there are years—and columns—to come.)

My years of readers'-advisory training prevent me from outright "recommending" this collection, despite my respect for Bill and my own pleasure in his columns. We readers' advisors have learned to *suggest*, rather than to *recommend*. On the other hand, I do strongly suggest that the blend of humor, humanity, intelligence, cantankerous musings, and wit, leavened with a curmudgeon's outlook, makes this a book that offers a variety of satisfactions—for the intellect as well as the funny bone. This is a book that will appeal to a wide range of book lovers. And while readers' advisors also don't offer guarantees as a rule, I can, in fact, offer one with this title: you won't be disappointed with a "Back Page is on Vacation" notice. Not even once.

—Joyce Saricks

PREFACE
Booklist, the Back Page, and Me

A FEW DECADES AGO I worked at Timberland Regional Library in Washington State. After a couple of forgettable years as a serials librarian—I recall mainly sending missing-issue claim letters to EBSCO—I was promoted to book selection coordinator, a dream job, really, because I spent the majority of my time reading book reviews, not only in *Booklist* and the other library review journals but also in the various general-interest magazines that had book sections. I liked the reviews fine, but I especially enjoyed the chance to wander away from strictly job-related content and indulge myself with author interviews, essays, or even the literary quizzes that appeared occasionally in the *Saturday Review of Literature*. What a great boondoggle, I thought, reading an interview with James Baldwin or Norman Mailer and getting paid for it!

Years later, after I had become editor of *Booklist*, I thought of my former self, exulting in what felt like the guilty pleasure of reading interviews and taking quizzes on the job. Why not let my fellow slackers indulge themselves by reading *Booklist*? After all, *Saturday Review* had long since gone under. So *Booklist* began to publish author interviews and more reflective essays on books and writers to complement the reviews that will always be our bread and butter.

About the same time, I was approached by our advertising representative with a problem: our advertisers weren't particularly interested in buying space on the inside back cover of *Booklist* because there wasn't anything special on the last page to draw readers' eyes. How about a column, I asked? Maybe I could do some quizzes like the ones I used to read in *Saturday Review*. And so the Back Page was born—out of a desire to give book selectors something silly to do with a few minutes of their time, on the one hand, and out of a base need to serve Mammon, on the other hand.

I very much doubt that the hardy band of librarians who founded *Booklist* in 1905 would have had much sympathy for either of the two motivations behind the creation of the Back Page. They took the mission of a selection tool very literally, defining the magazine as a "current buying list of recent books with brief notes designed to assist librarians in selection."

Not much room in that charge for quizzes or columns about how books got me out of jury duty or why I hate Mickey Mouse. But times change, and just as public library book-selection philosophies have changed over the years, so have our notions of what a book-selection journal should contain. Why not appeal to our lighter sides, even our utterly frivolous sides, every now and then? Somebody has to do it, so why not *Booklist*? Or so I convinced myself when I began writing the Back Page.

That this little column has lasted more than 20 years continues to amaze me, but realistically, I think it owes much of its longevity to the rise of readers' advisory services in public libraries. Thanks to RA librarians' need to constantly learn more about books and authors, it's no longer frivolous to read columns about genres or even to take quizzes about dentists in literature. I started out hoping to make it easier for slackers like me to waste time on the job, and I seem, at least in the eyes of some, to have wound up providing what might charitably be called a marginal service to hard-working librarians.

My first indication that the Back Page might be serving something like a utilitarian function came when Hazel Rochman introduced me to legendary YA librarian Mike Printz, after whom the Michael L. Printz Award for outstanding YA literature would be named. I was pleased when Mike told me he enjoyed the Back Page, but I was shocked when he added that he often used the columns in his work with students and teachers. I still don't understand exactly how he managed that, but I'm not complaining.

Understand, though, that I haven't abandoned my original mission: I'm still out to help bookish types avoid doing real work. Maybe someday a self-admitted layabout will write me a fan letter. In the meantime, I'll keep writing.

Books and Authors

GOLDEN AGES

IN EARLY DECEMBER 1980, after I'd been working as *Booklist's* Adult Books Editor for about four months, I made my first trip to New York to visit publishers. The plan was to introduce myself and spread the word that we were going to jazz up our coverage of adult books by doing our reviews further in advance of publication and by starting something called "Upfront," a special section devoted to reviews of high-demand books. My assistant editor and I divided a list of some 30 publishers in half and were planning to see as many as eight library marketing directors a day during our two-day trip.

Frankly, I was petrified. Having grown up on the West Coast, I knew nothing about the publishing industry (except what I'd read in books like Rona Jaffe's *The Best of Everything* and Herman Wouk's *Youngblood Hawke*). I knew virtually nothing about New York, either; that was painfully obvious from our itinerary, which had me scurrying downtown and then back uptown countless times. Naturally, I was late for most of my appointments. What I remember most about that trip was the offices; there were still quite a few trade publishers ensconced in their fabled midtown digs, before the exodus downtown had begun in earnest. So there I was, sitting in a waiting room above the classic Scribner bookstore on Fifth Avenue, musing on whether Hemingway had ever sat in the same chair.

I thought a lot about that trip recently as I was reading Al Silverman's *The Times of Their Lives: The Golden Age of Great American Publishers, Their Editors and Authors* (St. Martin's/Truman Talley). This anecdotal history of trade publishing since World War II makes absolutely compelling reading for anyone interested in the people who made books in the latter half of the twentieth century. Silverman, the longtime editorial director and then president of the Book-of-the-Month Club, knew everybody in the glory years and has refreshed his memory by interviewing all the surviving A-list editors and publishers and hundreds of their employees.

As I worked my way through the book, one trend emerged forcefully. Silverman defines his Golden Age as running from 1946 to the late 1970s and early '80s, "before the era of publishing ossification had begun." And, in interview after interview, his subjects comment on how it all went bad

3

in 1980. Clearly, I had nothing to be intimidated about back in December of that year. The good old days were over, and the bad new days had begun, timed almost perfectly to me taking my first wide-eyed strides down Fifth Avenue—just like the poor kid in the movie *Atlantic City*, who comments on the view of the ocean from the boardwalk. Burt Lancaster, glancing back at the ocean, shakes his head sadly and mutters, "Yeah, that used to be some ocean."

But even if I missed it, it was still some ocean, as Silverman makes abundantly clear. This is one of those books you can open anywhere and start reading. Within a few paragraphs, you will have come upon an anecdote that you want to repeat to whoever happens to be nearby. For example, who knew that Alfred Knopf, in his first job in publishing, working for Doubleday in 1913, wrote what may have been the first "reader's guide" in American publishing history: an 18-page evaluation of Joseph Conrad's novels published as a promotional pamphlet to accompany the release of Conrad's *Chance*? Knopf, we learn a few pages later, came to be known among his employees more for his curmudgeonly behavior than for his literary acumen. Critic Stanley Kauffmann, who worked briefly for Knopf before being fired, describes the publisher as having "as close to no taste in literature as a leading publisher could have." Maybe they never talked about Conrad.

Perhaps the best part of Silverman's story is the books themselves. Nearly every editor he interviews has a story about the book that launched his or her career. Take Tom McCormack, who turned St. Martin's into a major force in American trade publishing. McCormack talks about trying to build St. Martin's list on book-buying trips to England but being rebuffed by agents who preferred to deal with Random House or Doubleday. Then one agent slipped him a dusty tome called *If Only They Could Talk*, by a Yorkshire vet named Herriot. McCormack thought it was a little thin by itself, but when Herriot agreed to meld that book with another of his unknown works called *A Vet's Life*, a whole new book was born. It was called *All Creatures Great and Small*.

That kind of serendipity just keeps popping up in the stories of how best-sellers came to be. Tony Schulte, the new Chicago sales rep for Simon & Schuster in the mid-1950s, runs into an old army buddy hawking peanuts in front of Comiskey Park. The buddy's name is Shel Silverstein. Ken McCormick, at Doubleday, is forced to call Alex Haley and tell him that Nelson Doubleday is afraid to publish *The Autobiography of*

Malcolm X, even though McCormick had signed him to write it. Partly out of guilt, McCormick agrees to give Haley a $40,000 advance on his next book, which eventually became *Roots*.

OK, that's enough about publishing's Golden Age. Let's get back to me. One more thing about that trip I took to New York in December 1980. I was staying at the old Americana Hotel on Seventh Avenue, and one of my fellow guests was a young man named Mark David Chapman. On the evening of my last day in New York, Chapman shot John Lennon. Golden Ages crumbling wherever I turn.

Booklist, September 1, 2008

WHAT I READ ON
MY OCTOBER VACATION

"VACATIONS ARE A TIME to catch up on your reading."

So said Joyce Saricks in her October 1, 2004, "At Leisure" column. In my case, that's a little bit like a dentist declaring that vacations are a time to catch up on some crown and bridge work. For me, though, there is a significant difference between the reading I do when I'm working and the reading I try to do when I'm on vacation. My rule is a simple one: on vacation, I don't want to read anything I will need to review after I get home. Pressing deadlines (Are there any other kind?) often force me to violate this rule, especially on shorter trips, but on the rare occasions when I'm out of the office for more than a few days, I make every effort to try my hand at "leisure reading." So, after finally overcoming my various travel phobias and committing to a nearly two-week trip to Italy, I moved on to the vexing question of what to read.

Naturally, I looked to Joyce for help. After all, it's not that often in my life when I have occasion to choose what to read. Usually, there's a pile of books for review on my desk or bedside table, and the only selection involved is picking the one with the nearest pub date and having at it. Fortunately, in that October column, Joyce provides plenty of tips for vacation-bound readers. She wisely counsels that we should try to anticipate what our mood is likely to be on the trip and choose books accordingly. But, of course, our moods are anything but predictable, so Joyce also advises to take lots of books fitting various moods.

I tried my best to follow her advice but ran into several problems. First, there were space considerations. Knowing there would be four of us loading bags into a smallish rental car to drive from Milan to Lake Como, I consciously took a relatively compact suitcase, leaving only my carry-on bag for books. Thanks to the new airline rules about liquids, I had a little more room in my carry-on than usual, since I was forced to leave the bottle of Jack Daniels at home. Still, I would only be able to fit a few books in the bag, nowhere near Joyce's suggested 12 for an 11-day trip. I do agree completely with Joyce's advice to take paperbacks only. I think it's also a good idea to curb your enthusiasm. As much as I'd like to read Proust someday, I'm realistic enough to know it's not going to be in Italy, when I'm feeling a little sleepy after a big lunch and plenty of wine. (Remember James Stewart in *Mr. Hobbs Takes a Vacation* dutifully lugging his copy of *War and Peace* out to the beach but never getting beyond the first paragraph?)

I'm a big advocate of reading novels set in the places you'll be traveling to, but last spring, in the course of putting together *Booklist*'s "Hard-Boiled Gazetteer to Italy," I pretty much caught up on my Italian mystery reading. And literary fiction doesn't really fit my vacation state of mind, partially because of what I call the shopping factor. I'm not much of a shopper myself, but when you travel with a major-league shopper, as I do, you spend a lot of time waiting for your partner to move from store to store. I don't mind the waiting as long as I'm armed with something to read, but the book in question must be easy to dive in and out of— qualities you rarely find in literary novels. Though not exactly germane to the topic of vacation reading, I must point out here that I found the shopping in both fashion-mecca Milan and in the various villages on the shores of Lake Como sadly deficient in a most-important area: the man-chair. When I sidle into a women's apparel store, I'm immediately looking for this all-important accoutrement, and I'm happy to report that the majority of U.S. stores have come to see the necessity of providing at least one man-chair or, even better, a man-couch. In Italy, unfortunately, I was too often left to read a couple of pages while leaning on the outside of a building or sitting on a curb—all the more reason why the book has to be something you can dive into. For me, that almost always means crime fiction.

OK, crime fiction fits my physical requirements, which go a long way toward determining my mood, but I'm still back to the basic question: Which books? Naturally, I waited too long to make my choices, ruling out trips to either bookstores or libraries. That meant I was limited to what I could find on my shelves at home, and naturally, I couldn't find the one thing I was sure I wanted to take: the first couple of installments in David Hewson's terrific crime series set in Rome. That was a blow and a bad one, but it led me to a concept: early volumes in series I've only started to read in midstream. Now I was on to something: I grabbed a couple of Magdalen Nabbs, from her Inspector Guarnaccia series set in Florence, and then, moving away from Italy, opted for *Booked to Die*, the second in John Dunning's Cliff Janeway series starring the Denver bookseller, and Michael Connelly's *Lincoln Lawyer*, the only recent Connelly that I didn't review for *Booklist* myself. The Connelly is well over 500 pages, so I talked myself into going with only four books, knowing that Joyce wouldn't approve.

I promised myself I wouldn't review any of these books, and I'm not going to do it here, either. I will say that each fit my mood of the moment just fine. I read them all in various angles of repose, from leaning on Fiats in Milan to lounging on the decks of ferries chugging across the placid waters of Lake Como. And, yes, Joyce was right. I finished the Connelly the night before flying home, prompting a panic attack over what I would read on the plane. The Gods were smiling at me, though, as I was able to find a Donna Leon I'd never read at Malpensa Airport in Milan (Why would anyone name an airport Bad Thoughts?). The trip home was saved (except, of course, for the fat guy in front of me whose seat was in my lap for nine hours).

Booklist, November 1, 2006

THE CRUELLEST MONTH

NOT LONG AGO, AROUND the first of April, I was reading late into the night when it dawned on me that I had wandered into T. S. Eliot's "Waste Land." You remember the opening lines, "April is the cruellest month, breeding / Lilacs out of the dead land, mixing / Memory and desire, stirring dull roots with spring rain." In Chicago, it was spring snow, but you get the picture. The narrator goes on to muse that spring surrounds us with all these images of rebirth ("hyacinth girls," among them), but there you are, unable to get with the program, either too old ("A little life with dried tubers") or too scared ("I will show you fear in a handful of dust"). So what do you do in the face of so much throbbing, burgeoning life: "I read much of the night and go south in the winter."

It's bad enough having to finish the lion's share of a 350-page novel by morning, but when you realize that in the process of doing so you will have become T. S. Eliot's ultimate loser—the symbol of anti-spring, death-in-life, anathema to all hyacinth girls—well, . . . it's a major-league downer. And I didn't even get to go south for the winter.

But wait a minute. Isn't April the traditional month for National Library Week, that special time when the American Library Association celebrates the joys of reading? Something isn't computing for me here. Clearly, ALA should have checked with one of the greatest poets of the twentieth century before authorizing a celebration of dull roots during a season of spring rain. Read, if you must, in the winter, Eliot might have told the Executive Board, but never in the spring—not if you don't want to become "a heap of broken images, where the sun beats," that is. At the very least, ALA should caution its supporters about what they're getting themselves into if they insist on reading in April. How about a poster warning "READ— It's Your Ticket to the Waste Land," or even better, "Fear in a Handful of Dust @ Your Library."

Thank you, Mr. Eliot, for leading me to this epiphany about the dangers of reading. My only problem now is what to do with my life, especially in April. It's still too cold in Chicago to play golf, and I can't seem to find any hyacinth girls hanging around my neighborhood. I went looking for some the other day, but the closest I came was a group of nubile teens playing soccer at a school playground nearby. As I watched the girls cavort, I couldn't help but notice some teachers giving me the fish-eye. As they started walking toward me, I decided to retreat. Clearly, they didn't know their Eliot.

Back at home, I began to have doubts about my new vision. Yes, I was committed to overcoming my fears, closing my books, and experiencing the rebirth that comes with spring, but I wasn't quite sure what to do next. As usual, Eliot was way ahead of me: "What shall I do now? What shall I do? / I shall rush out as I am, and walk the street / With my hair down, so. What shall we do to-morrow? / What shall we ever do?"

So many questions. So few answers. Looking for solace, my eyes landed on the pile of books I had so recently abandoned. There was that wonderful, heartbreaking new novel by Oscar Hijuelos, A *Simple Habana Melody*, about a Cuban composer whose fears keep him from following his dreams into the arms of one particular hyacinth girl and a whole bunch of hyacinth boys. There was Iain Pears' new historical novel, *The Dream of Scipio*, set in Provence, about three couples in three different time periods who faced more tangible obstacles to their love: the Goths, the black plague, and the Nazis, respectively. And there was *Deep in a Dream*, James Gavin's new biography of jazzman Chet Baker, whose once-beautiful face, ravaged by the time he reached middle age, became a testament to the fact that too many hyacinth girls (and too much heroin) are sometimes as deadly as too much reading.

The plain fact was I wanted to finish those books, and I wanted to read a big stack of other ones, too. Damn it, I said to myself—a pale imitation of Huck Finn—I'll turn into a handful of dust anyway, so I'm going to keep right on reading, no matter how cruel April turns out to be.

Booklist, April 15, 2002

PERFECTION

THERE'S ONE ADVANTAGE TO being an aging baby boomer: there are lots of us out there, and quite a few of them are authors, which means that, from time to time, some nostalgia-drenched boomer writes a book that seems like it's about you and your life. (I should say that this is a bit of a mixed blessing: yes, it's always exciting to relive key moments of your life in a book, but it's also maddening to realize that some other person, not you, wrote the book.) When a boomer author inadvertently re-creates some aspect of a boomer reader's life, a chain reaction tends to occur: the reader who is stunned to find himself mirrored in some unknown author's memoir feels compelled either to talk about it, or, if the opportunity avails itself, to write about it—perhaps in a column. So, for all you younger *Booklist* readers, who just can't abide the spectacle of another boomer getting misty eyed over his lost youth, read no further. See you next issue, I hope.

On the surface, there's no reason why Phillip Hoose's *Perfect Once Removed* should connect itself to my life. Granted, Hoose and I were born the same year, 1947; we both were avid baseball fans; we began our less-than-distinguished little-league careers in 1956; and, thanks to our overall timidity and profound lack of upper-body strength, we were regarded, in that lacerating sandlot phrase of the day, as "automatic outs." But Hoose was a new kid in Speedway, Indiana, an outsider as well as an easy out, and I lived 2,000 miles away, in Dallas, Oregon, where I had been comfortably ensconced all my life. The most dramatic difference between us, though, was that Hoose had a famous cousin: Don Larsen, the New York Yankee pitcher who, on October 8, 1956, did something no major-league baseball player has done before or since: pitch a perfect game (27 batters up, 27 batters down) in the World Series. My most famous cousin was known only for his propensity to hole up in garbage cans during games of Hide and Seek.

Hoose contrasts the story of his own baseball summer in 1956 with that of the Yankees, winning the American League and squaring off against the Brooklyn Dodgers in the series. The highlight of his summer was a ground ball to shortstop—the first time in his career that he had hit the ball anywhere, fair or foul; unfortunately, he was so shocked by the phenomenon of wood meeting leather that he forgot to run and was easily doubled up to end the inning. Back in Oregon, I was not rooting for the Yankees; I was a New York Giants fan, and my hero was Willie Mays, not Mickey Mantle. My own season as a rookie second baseman on a little-league team called Nameless Market (I'm not making this up) was progressing along exactly the same lines as Hoose's until, in our next-to-the-last game, I just barely made contact with an outside fastball and sent a dribbler off the end of the bat down the first-base line. It hit the bag and careened into the weeds in short right field, giving me the cheapest stand-up double in Dallas baseball history. But it was a hit. You could look it up—in the *Polk County Itemizer-Observer*.

When the World Series rolled around that October, Hoose and I were no longer rooting for different teams. As a Giants fan, I followed the National League, and when, as usually happened in the mid-1950s, the Brooklyn Dodgers beat the Giants and wound up in the series against the Yankees, I immediately adopted the Yanks as my team—anything was better than rooting for the despised Dodgers. Rooting for your team in the World Series was not an easy thing for a kid to do in the fifties. There were no night games then, so the action took place during the day—

school days, mostly. Radios were not allowed in the classroom, so we were resigned to learning what happened to our heroes after the fact. Hoose, living in Indiana, in the central time zone, had it a little better than I did. He was at least able to ride his bike home for lunch and catch a couple innings before his draconian mother forced him to return to school. Exiled in the hinterlands of Pacific Time, where the series started at 10 a.m., the games were often over by the time I could pedal home for lunch at 12:30.

For me, the most resonant chapter in Hoose's book concerns the deal he negotiated with his mother regarding the lunch-hour routine: she would have his lunch (Campbell's chicken-and-noodle soup with Oscar Mayer liver sausage on saltines) waiting for him on a TV tray when he arrived shortly after noon, and he would watch the game until 12:43, when he would reluctantly ride back to school. Imagine his frustration leaving the perfect game in progress in the fifth inning, with the Yanks and his cousin, Larsen, leading the Dodgers 1–0 on Mantle's home run.

Hoose heard the news that his cousin had completed the perfect game when the school principal came into his classroom and made the announcement. Young Phil's once-distant classmates erupted into applause, and his days as an outsider were over.

My situation was both better and worse. With the probability of the games being over by the time I arrived home at around 12:45, there was no need for my mother to have lunch at the ready, but I demanded of her an even sterner challenge: transcribe the entire play-by-play and recite it to me as I enjoyed my grilled cheese. So, while I didn't see even one pitch of Larsen's perfect game, I did hear it, batter by batter. And, as my mother refused to tell me what happened in advance, I was able to experience the building drama that led up to the 27th Dodger hitter, Dale Mitchell, taking a called strike to end the game. No, I didn't see Yogi Berra leap into Larsen's arms after the last pitch, but I feel like I did, and in my mind's eye, the reception was better than HDTV.

Booklist, September 1, 2006

SHARING SPUTNIK

OCTOBER 4, 1957, WAS my tenth birthday. Long after the festivities, I was in bed, snuggled under my Roy Rogers bedspread and enjoying my best present—a new transistor radio in a snappy leather case. This was a clandestine operation since I had been ordered to go to sleep hours ago. The radio, under the cover of Roy, was playing softly as I scanned the dial. Rather than the rock 'n' roll I sought, what I heard was the excited voice of a newscaster discussing something called Sputnik, a Russian satellite that had just been launched and, judging by the newscaster's agitated tone, should be a cause of great concern to everyone.

At this point, my knowledge of the Russians was a bit sketchy. I knew, of course, that they were the bad guys, responsible for making me practice hiding under my desk to ward off fallout in the event of a nuclear attack. I knew, too, that the Russians were supposed to be very smart and very tough. I knew this because my uncle often chided my cousin and me for our lag-about ways by telling us that someday we were going to have to fight the Russians, and he—a veteran of the European theater in World War II—happened to know that they were "smart, tough sons of bitches." His prediction seemed to be coming true on my tenth birthday. I hadn't expected to be forced to fight the Russians quite so soon, and I certainly hadn't expected to contend with missiles fired from the moon (which the newscaster was saying would be the inevitable next step, after Sputnik). I didn't yet know how to spell Sputnik, but I did know it was big trouble.

In the following days and weeks, I quickly realized that I wasn't the only one worried about the Russians and their satellites, but somehow I never lost the notion that the first Sputnik belonged to me. In some part of my mind, I think I assumed that I was the first private citizen in the U.S. to hear the news. Who else would be up in the middle of the night listening to the radio? (In fact, the launch had occurred some hours before I heard about it, but it was inconceivable to me that anything newsworthy might have taken place during my birthday party.) So even as the decades rolled by, as the word Sputnik first became a part of popular culture and then receded from center stage, I continued to nod quietly to myself every time I heard the name, secure in the belief that, although everyone claimed a knowledge of Sputnik, I had a special, even secret, relationship with it.

About 20 years ago, when I happened to interview Stephen King, I had my first inkling that I might have to share a little bit of Sputnik. It turns out that King was also celebrating his tenth birthday in the fall of 1957 (on September 21, just a few days before the launch) and was also shaken by the idea of the Russians in space—so much so that he contends to this day that Sputnik was a key factor in his becoming a writer of horror fiction. Well, maybe so, but he wasn't born on October 4, and he didn't have a Roy Rogers bedspread.

After reading Paul Dickson's fascinating *Sputnik: The Shock of the Century* (Walker), I'm afraid my illusions are shattered once and for all. Sputnik was a slut, a tramp, and she enjoyed special relationships with virtually the entire population of the U.S. alive on October 4, 1957. Dickson has all the details: the Stephen King story is there, but that's just the beginning. Little Richard was so shocked by the appearance of Sputnik in the sky as he was performing an outdoor concert that he renounced rock 'n' roll (temporarily) and became a preacher. Ross Perot was inspired by Sputnik to create an electronics dynasty. And countless other Americans, great and small, remember the launch of Sputnik as a turning point in their lives. Damn.

As disappointed as I was to read of Sputnik's infidelity, I was also caught up in the scientific and social history surrounding the satellite's creation and its aftermath. Dickson makes the space race come alive in layman's language, and he shows how the shock of the Russians being first at something galvanized this country in all sorts of far-reaching ways. Who would have thought, for example, that Sputnik was responsible for the Summer of Love? Here's how it worked: Sputnik proved the Russians were doing a better job than we were at education, prompting the National Defense Education Act, which stressed science but also advocated creative and independent thought. A generation removed from Sputnik, young people wearied of science but used their NDEA-funded, independent-thinking skills to challenge the establishment on everything from civil rights and Vietnam to long hair and free love. That Sputnik was some satellite—but I've known that for 44 years.

Booklist, September 15, 2001

CHARACTER EDUCATION, THE POSTGRADUATE COURSE

What is honour? A word. What is that word, honour? Air. A trim reckoning! Who hath it? He that died o' Wednesday.

— Falstaff, from Shakespeare's *Henry IV, Part One*

WHEN I SAW MY first "Character Counts!" sign on the window of a store in Highland Park, Illinois, I thought to myself, "Of course it does, far more than plot." Alas, I soon discovered that "character driven" means something very different in the schools of my town than it does in the minds of grown-up fiction readers. It turns out that the No Child Left Behind Act of 2001 spurred interest in what is called character education by providing additional funds to states and districts for training teachers in the fine art of character building. As Susan Dove Lempke points out in her *Booklist* article "Series Nonfiction and Character Education," "Character education has been formally written into many schools' curricula, often with accompanying charts, workshops, Web sites, materials for teachers and students, and lists of virtues." In fact, many of these programs structure their instruction around a "virtue-a-week" or (perhaps for the slower learners) a "virtue-a-month" approach.

On the face of it, I suppose there's nothing very objectionable about the idea of teaching our young to be good people as well as good students. But the programmatic nature of many of the instructional packages has proved disappointing to many teachers and librarians, which is why Susan's essay will be so valuable.

My purpose here, however, is not to provide more insight on character education or on the children's literature that most usefully supports it. No, what I'd like to do is introduce a few fictional characters who skipped school during the weeks when certain key virtues were under discussion. Let's call it the postgraduate course on character education. And our topic is a tough one: Why is it that the most memorable characters in literature, the ones we like to call well rounded, are almost certainly going to be the ones who flunked, or at least settled for an incomplete, in character education?

We have chosen to employ a team-teaching concept in our postgraduate course. Sharing the podium in our discussion of why character counts more than virtue will be the irrepressible Falstaff, whose definitive comments on honor open this column, and Milton's Satan, who, as every English major knows, stole *Paradise Lost* from a hopelessly boring, character-education grad called Adam and even from the more-spirited Eve. It isn't so much that we like Satan, you understand, or that we espouse his beliefs; only that, as we read the poem, we respond to him in ways we can't respond to all-powerful God or to whiny Adam, even though Milton wants us to do just that. But it's Satan to whom he gives lines like "Here at last we shall be free" (Satan on why Hell, while lacking in amenities, may turn out to be a nice play to live), or, in another mood, "All Good to me is lost." We respond to Satan because he sounds like us: he wants the same things we want (freedom, a room of our own), but he has second thoughts, too, just like we do. Adam is the party-line boy; he memorized all the virtues in character ed, and he spouts them by rote, just like that obnoxious nerdy kid in the first row whom the greasers beat up while you silently cheered them on and later felt bad about yourself.

And Falstaff? This is the class he was born to teach. In fact, he does teach it, throughout Shakespeare's Henry IV history plays. If character education can instill a virtue a week, Falstaff can demolish several per day. He polishes off honor in a quick retort, something that it takes anti-war novelists like Remarque or Heller several hundred pages to do. And he is even better when defending such anti-virtues as drunkenness or cowardice. Yes, it's true that Falstaff loses Prince Hal, his protégé, when the young prince opts for responsibility, but if you ask me, the fix was in. The Elizabethan worldview required that princes come to their senses in the third act, but when Hal turns away from his rotund drinking buddy, I'm not buying it for a second. In my book, Hal and Falstaff ride off into the sunset in a '48 Ford, responsibility be damned.

But Falstaff is unquestionably lazy and can't be counted on to get to class every day, so you can expect quite a few guest lecturers. Among them will be Frederick Henry, the hero of Hemingway's *A Farewell to Arms*, who will explain in short, crisp sentences why "abstract words such as glory, honor, courage, or hallow were obscene beside the concrete names of villages, the numbers of roads, the names of rivers, the numbers of regiments and dates." Perhaps Barley Blair, the sax-playing bookseller from John le Carré's *The Russia House*, will drop by to play a little Ellington and explain why betraying your country can be an act of courage. And, if all goes well, we can even expect a visit from Parker, Donald Westlake's thief par excellence, who may want to share the details of the time he held up a Christian Crusade to the tune of a half-million dollars. Maybe he'll even tell us why we like him so much.

About a year ago in this column, I suggested that the best road novels are about unlearning things and finding new ways to stay uncivilized. Who knew I'd come up with the mission statement for postgraduate character education? Don't get me wrong, though: I'm not necessarily against feeding our young one virtue per week. You can't unlearn something if you don't learn it in the first place. And if you don't want your babies to unlearn anything, don't let them grow up to be English majors.

Booklist, October 15, 2005

BIG WHEELS

NOT LONG AGO ON this page, I noted the curious fact that there seem to be more children's books published these days about jazz musicians than about trucks. This phenomenon continues to bother me. Frankly, it's just wrong. Don't misunderstand. I'm much more interested in jazz than I am in trucks, and if I were to write a children's book, I would be much more likely to write about jazz than trucks (in fact, I know very little about trucks). Still, one of the things I remember about my toddlerhood is that, back then, I did like trucks a lot—or, to be more precise, I liked all vehicles with big wheels. Fire engines were my favorite, and legend has it that, when I was about three, I insisted on giving my father a shiny toy fire engine for *his* birthday. Ever since that event, this technique of giving a loved one a gift that you want more than the recipient does has been known in my family as the "old fire-engine trick." I'm afraid that jazz picture books (and biographies about Woody Guthrie) have become the fire engines of the children's book world. Just as I played with my dad's fire engine a lot more than he did, I'm guessing that the dads and moms who give their kids books about Ella, Duke, and Monk spend a lot more time enjoying them than their kids do. Why not give the little rascals a book about trucks now and then?

Fortunately, one publisher agrees with me. There's a great new series book out about all manner of big-wheeled vehicles. Published by Sterling, it's called, very straightforwardly, *Heavy Equipment Up Close*, and it's featured on the cover of this issue of *Booklist*. If I ever have a grandchild who gives me a fire engine for my birthday, I hope it's this book.

Paging through *Heavy Equipment* prompted me to realize how little a role trucks have played in my adult reading. There just aren't that many novels starring truck drivers or celebrating the sheer enormity of big-ass vehicles with wheels "longer than a Kentuckian is tall" (to borrow a phrase that Herman Melville used to describe a sperm whale's penis). It's a shame, really, that truck literature is so paltry, as all of us onetime truck-loving toddlers would appreciate an opportunity now and then to reconnect with that tiny part of ourselves that once felt the romance of big machinery.

If you're looking for novels about trucks, you're probably going to have to settle for pickups, whose tires are—let's face it—not all that big. Still, there are plenty of pickups in the works of James Crumley, C. J. Box, Craig Johnson, and other western crime writers. But the pickups in these books aren't really central to the action. That's not true, though, in "Drinking and Driving," a great essay by William Kittredge (collected in *Owning It All*, 1987). Before all you socially conscious readers start sending me e-mails, let's make clear that Kittredge recognizes the dangers inherent in drinking and driving. But that doesn't change the fact that, in the rural West, if you've ever spent much time in a pickup, either as driver or rider, it's a good bet you had a beer in your hand. Maybe that's why we liked trucks so much as kids. Somewhere, deep in our subconscious, we recognized that load-carrying vehicles were our tickets to ride, our way of breaking free from parental control and doing all those things we weren't supposed to do.

Full disclosure here: Kittredge admits that some of his teenage drinking and driving in eastern Oregon was done in his father's '49 Buick, but I like to think that, later, after he'd moved to Montana, when he and Richard Hugo were driving the country roads and stopping for beverages in sleepy general stores, they were riding in a pickup. Both of them wrote about their booze-fueled rambles: Hugo in verse (see his poem "Silver Star") and Kittredge in prose so close to the bone that it reads like poetry: "We learn it early in the West, drinking and driving, chasing away the ticking stillness of home toward some dim aura glowing over the horizon, call it possibility or excitement."

Drinking and driving on country roads in pickups or '49 Buicks may be as close as many of us come to big-ass trucks, but finally, it's not quite the same. For a great story about a real truck driver, we need to move from books to movies—and not American movies. You might wonder what a Japanese "noodle western" could possibly have to do with trucks, but if you've seen *Tampopo*, you know that the hero, Goro, is a truck-driving Shane who rolls into town just in time to help Tampopo, the widowed owner of a noodle shop, compete against the gangster-run restaurant down the road. Goro can sling ramen as dexterously as Shane can draw a six-gun, and soon enough the evil noodle cooks are washed up, and Tampopo is riding high. That's when Goro, clad in cowboy hat and boots, of course, climbs back into his semi, unleashes the air brake, and sets off down the road. No, Tampopo doesn't scream "Goro-o-o-o-o" as the truck rolls out of sight, but we find ourselves wanting to scream it for her.

I'm convinced that every kid who was ever fascinated by trucks has somehow imagined that his or her own Goro would someday ride into town on a set of big wheels and make everything right. Most of our Goros never showed up, but if we take time to look at a really big truck (or, in my case, a really big fire engine), we can almost convince ourselves that he will be parking at the curb momentarily.

Booklist, April 1, 2008

JAZZ BIOGRAPHY

AS I WAS WORKING my way through the February 1 *Booklist*'s Spotlight on Black History, I noticed Gillian Engberg's starred review of Robert Andrew Parker's *Piano Starts Here*, a new picture-book biography of jazz piano great Art Tatum. After reading the review, I tracked down a copy of the book and could only agree with Gillian's opinion: it's a beautifully illustrated, inspirational rendering of Tatum's early life. But the fact of the book's existence brought to mind again one of the true oddities in contemporary children's publishing: classic jazz, especially from the swing and bebop eras, seems on the verge of displacing trucks and talking animals as the hottest topic in the picture-book world.

Name a jazz star from the 1940s and 1950s, and you can bet there is at least one—and probably several—high-end picture books devoted to that artist's life and work: Duke Ellington (of course); Ella Fitzgerald (more than one); Charlie Parker (natch); Dizzy Gillespie (check); John Coltrane (his "sheets of sound" apparently don't faze the preschool set); Thelonious Monk (your tykes may go to bed at eight, but they're humming "Round Midnight" as their wee heads hit the pillow).

I started paying attention to jazz as a teenager, late by modern standards (that might have been different if the freethinking hero of my favorite picture book, *And to Think That I Saw It on Mulberry Street*, had encountered a jam session on his eventful stroll home). But at least when I began listening to what was then considered modern jazz, it was still thought of as edgy music, something your parents couldn't abide. (My father echoed Louis Armstrong's early assessment of bebop: "sounds like Chinese music.") Nowadays, though, syncopation, blue notes, and flatted fifths are force-fed to kids like strained peas. One can only wonder if the little darlings' taste for Tatum will survive the terrible twos any more successfully than their tolerance for pea pudding.

Still, as a jazz fan, I can't help but applaud the phenomenon of jazz picture books. Anything that gets the word out about some of the most astoundingly creative artists this country has ever produced has to be a good thing. And the wealth of children's books on jazz performers is especially welcome in light of the sad fact that no such phenomenon is anywhere apparent in the adult publishing world. Although most of the other names mentioned above have been the subject of at least one full-length account, such books are rarely published by big-name commercial publishers and almost never receive the kind of attention that a jazz picture book gets routinely. Ben Ratliff's *Coltrane*, published by Farrar in 2007, and Donald L. Maggin's *Dizzy*, published by HarperCollins in 2005, are two notable exceptions, at least in terms of their publisher's stature.

You wouldn't know it to look at children's books, but jazz ceased being this country's popular music at the end of the swing era and has spent the last 50 years or so relegated to the small world of aficionados. Every now and then, something like Ken Burns' Jazz series on PBS gives the music a momentarily higher profile, but even those blips on the screen usually appear in some sort of "educational" context. That works fine in children's books, but it's usually not enough to get you a contract on the other side of the publishing aisle. That's too bad because, unlike most writers, jazz players often live fascinating lives, even apart from their music, lives that deserve more than a 32-page, inevitably bowdlerized treatment.

Da Capo is one smaller publisher who has long done its part to see that children, weaned on jazz picture books, have something to read about once they reach maturity. Among the many fine Da Capo jazz books is Ashley Kahn's *Kind of Blue: The Birth of the Miles Davis Masterpiece* (2000), a surprise hit that helped launch a new kind of jazz literature: the biography an album. Another, much older biography from Da Capo remains my favorite jazz book: *Treat It Gentle*, by legendary clarinetist and soprano sax player Sidney Bechet, who lived much of his life in Europe and brought to both his music and his life an exuberant joie de vivre that is as apparent in his words at it is in his sound. Bechet's story as he tells it definitely isn't for kids, but that's my point: jazz lives are too rich to be the sole province of milk drinkers.

That being said, I have this book project in mind that I think might be just the ticket for a high-profile children's publisher: a 16-volume picture-book series devoted to the lives of every member of Duke Ellington's classic early-1940s band. Clearly, this enterprise would fill a gaping hole in children's literature. Just the other day, I was chatting with a two-year-old Ellington fan who was bemoaning the absolute dearth of picture books on the band's fine clarinetist Barney Bigard.

Booklist, February 1, 2008

TRAIN WEASELS

I'M NOT FOND OF my fellow passengers on the commuter train I ride to work every morning from the Chicago suburbs. They are lawyers, mostly, or so I've gathered from their incessant cell-phone blabbering, although there may be a commodities trader or even a "wealth manager" thrown into the mix. Almost to a one, they read the *Wall Street Journal* — when they're not blabbering, that is. I haven't much liked lawyers ever since I read Dickens' *Bleak House*, and I'm convinced that the *Wall Street Journal* is the single most boring publication ever printed, but, finally, it is not my fellow passengers' choice of either profession or reading material that causes me to dislike them. No, it's the way their conspicuous consuming sullies everything they buy and everywhere they go, ruining for the rest of us some perfectly good products and destinations. That's why I call the lot of them train weasels.

I like to think that the weasels and I share no interests. I've never seen one of them reading a noir novel, for example, but, of course, they have little time for fiction, what with all the getting and spending they're doing. And I'm dead certain their favorite Democratic candidate in the upcoming election isn't Mike Gravel. Ah, but the sad fact is the train weasels and I do like some of the same stuff. I have nothing whatsoever against money ("Comes in pretty handy down here, Bub," as George Bailey said to the angel Clarence in *It's a Wonderful Life*); I would love to eat at Chicago's finest restaurants on a regular basis (if I had the money and if there weren't train weasels sitting at every table); but most of all, I like to play golf. If there is one endeavor that train weasels have polluted more than any other, it is surely golf.

Of course, golf has never had a good image, especially among the literary crowd. A few years ago, I wrote about how John Updike, a committed golfer and author of a fine collection of essays called *Golf Dreams*, had rescued the game from the clutches of the Philistines, but from what I hear out of the mouths of train weasels, the counterattack has begun.

Last week my simmering resentment nearly reached critical mass. A gang of train weasels sitting in front of me on the 5:45 were discussing their trips to Scotland to play the great links courses: what airline they flew (business class, of course), how long in advance they booked their reservations at the best inn in St. Andrews, how they birdied the Road Hole, etc., etc. I admit there was more than a little envy in my violent response—just this side of going postal—but the thought that American train weasels were swarming through Scotland, flashing their gold cards and dragging their $500 titanium drivers behind them, like marauding cavemen brandishing knobby-headed clubs, was more than I could handle.

Then I remembered that I didn't have to go to Scotland to enjoy the links courses. I could read about them, in books that were blessedly train-weasel free. Just as reading about Calvin Trillin eating spectacular street food in Singapore is almost certainly more satisfying than actually doing it—What if, without Trillin at your side, you picked the wrong street vendor?—so is reading Andrew Greig's *Preferred Lies: A Journey into the Heart of Scottish Golf* infinitely more satisfying than topping your tee shot on the first hole at St. Andrews, with half-a-dozen foursomes of low-handicap train weasels sniggering in the background.

I know that many Back Page readers have no more interest in golf than I have in the *Wall Street Journal,* but bear with me for a moment while I demonstrate that golf isn't just about train weasels showing off. Andrew Greig, an outstanding poet and novelist (check out his wonderful novel, *The Clouds Above,* based on a diary kept by his mother during the Battle of Britain), grew up near the heart of Scottish golf and was quite an accomplished player as a young man. He abandoned the game in his 20s, though, and only returned to it recently, when he was recovering from brain surgery. His book recounts his own golfing tour of Scotland, but his itinerary and style of play are very different from those of the train weasels. Drawn to the fairways of his youth, he travels his native country playing courses that have personal significance to him (few of which are on the British Open rota). Mostly, he plays alone, reconnecting to the game and its "inner-directed, individualistic pleasures." Words to soothe my weasel-battered soul.

So I'll forgo Scotland and continue searching for my own inner-directed pleasures on a little nine-hole public course built on top of a landfill in Glenview, Illinois. (There's nothing like a few tons of garbage to keep the train weasels away.) But the point here goes well beyond golf. Whatever your pleasure, whether it's cigars or single malts or a nice bike ride on a Sunday morning, beware: the train weasels are lurking. And before you can say Laphroaig, they will have turned your special thing into yet another symbol of trendy consumption. Stay resolute, I say. Keep smoking, keep drinking, keep riding, keep doing whatever the weasels try to steal, but remember, if it gets too bad, you can always read about it.

Booklist, October 15, 2007

BLAME IT ON MY YOUTH

"IT'S NEVER TOO LATE for a misspent youth."

That wonderful sentence is the last line from Keir Graff's November 3, 2006, posting to his ever-fascinating *Likely Stories* blog, which continues to be one of the most popular features of *Booklist Online.* On the way to his revelatory conclusion, Keir was bemoaning his failure this past November 1 to observe what he calls McGoorty Day, in honor of Danny

McGoorty, an "unapologetic billiard bum" whose story was told in Robert Byrne's *McGoorty*, one of Keir's favorite books. After conceiving of the idea to pay tribute to McGoorty every year on his birthday by "spending the entire day in a poolroom, drinking and playing pool," Keir made two big mistakes. He took a job at *Booklist* and had kids. Still, he remains determined, and for that we should all admire him, because misspending one's youth is one of those long-term goals that sometimes takes a lifetime to achieve.

I've been at it a few decades longer than Keir and have run into many of the same problems, working at *Booklist* perhaps chief among them. In recent years, I have managed to revive my moribund golf game, but, sad to say, golf doesn't really qualify as a means of misspending a long-lost youth. Great game that golf is, you can't really consider yourself appropriately dissolute if you're simply indulging in a form of recreation enjoyed by lawyers and politicians.

When I think back to my own deplorably half-assed attempts to misspend my actual youth, I, too, remember poolrooms, though I was never the accomplished pool player that Keir is today, despite his toil at *Booklist*. I'd never heard of McGoorty when I was in graduate school, but I did waste numerous hours playing pool at a bar called Jilly's East in Seattle—hours that should have been spent preparing for my upcoming master's exams. Like me, my friends Denny and Rob, also preparing for the same English exams, couldn't bear tackling some of the real dogs on the University of Washington's MA reading list. So we hit upon the idea of each of us reading one-third of those unread and uninspiring books on the list and then comparing notes over pool and beer at Jilly's. To this day, I've only read the middle third of William Dean Howells' *A Modern Instance*, and I'm afraid I don't remember a damn thing about either that third or the thirds that Denny and Rob described to me while we were playing pool. I do remember that I won my share of the "cutthroat" eight-ball games we played, and I'll even hazard a guess that I came out on top on the night we were "discussing" Howells.

That brief period of pool-playing may have been my most legitimate attempt to misspend my youth (aside from imbibing or inhaling the popular stimulants of the era, of course). My other attempts at dissolute behavior, I'm afraid, fall into a category that might charitably be called nerdy, as they mostly involved playing baseball board games (accompanied, at least, by plenty of imbibing and inhaling). Before we had graduated to pool at Jilly's, Denny, Rob, and I wasted time as undergraduates playing a children's board game called All-Star Baseball, which involved spinning a dial to determine if Babe Ruth had hit a home run or struck out (a far cry from today's lifelike videogames). We lacked the courage of our convictions, however, and were constantly afraid of being outed as middlebrow nerds who would fiddle with board games when there were important points to be made about the symbolist poets. Thus, we were ever ready—should there be a knock at the door—to stash the game and pull out our copies of *Les fleurs du mal*.

After such lame attempts to misspend my youth, it's no surprise that, as the decades have accumulated, I've been forced to take refuge in reading about the great misspenders in literature. I've celebrated Falstaff many times in this column, so I'll try to contain myself here, mentioning only that Sir John remains the ultimate role model for those of us determined to never let go of our dreams of dissipation. (In addition to Shakespeare, try Robert Nye's 1976 novel *Falstaff*, which does the great man proud.) And speaking of great men—in the misspent post-youth division—how about Mr. Pickwick, who, despite his middle-class-businessman persona, is nothing more than a little kid looking for a good time? Let's not forget that Dickens' *Pickwick Papers* ostensibly chronicles the adventures of the Pickwick Club, founded by Samuel Pickwick and including three of his buddies, Mr. Nathaniel Winkle, Mr. Augustus Snodgrass, and Mr. Tracy Tupman; the club's sole purpose is to give its members excuses for drinking a lot of sack and taking road trips around Victorian England. Forget McGoorty Day; Pickwick was after a McGoorty Life.

Which brings us to Bertie Wooster, who carries on the Pickwick tradition in grand style, devoting himself to capering about England between the wars in search of frivolity in all its forms. Both Bertie and Pickwick, it should be noted, would never have succeeded nearly so well in avoiding all the entrapments of adulthood had they not had at their services those indefatigable ironicists, Sam Weller, Pickwick's footman, and Jeeves, Bertie's butler. One can pick and choose from P. D. Wodehouse's Bertie and Jeeves novels almost at will, but my own personal favorite may be *Right Ho, Jeeves* (1934), which includes this immortal line: "And yet you come bringing me Fink-Nottles. Is this the time for Fink, or any other kind of Nottle?"

So, Keir, there's reason to hope. Even with kids and *Booklist*, it's still possible to misspend one's vanishing or vanished youth vicariously, in the company of such paragons of the art as Falstaff, Pickwick, Bertie, and so many others, from the motley crew in Michael Malone's *Handling Sin*

(1986) to the "chops" in Rick Reilly's *Missing Links* (1996) and *Shanks for Nothing* (2006), who play booze-and-wager-filled golf at the worst course in the country and show by example that lawyers have given the game a bad name.

But even with so many misspent youths to read about, there's no reason not to take time out next November 1 for McGoorty Day. It's on my calendar.

Booklist, November 15, 2006

PANDORA IN BLUE JEANS

IT HAS BEEN NEARLY 50 years since Grace Metalious' *Peyton Place* was published in 1956, and the novel, while still in print, is little read today. Yet the title, like *Catch-22*, remains immediately recognizable to anyone with even the flimsiest hold on American pop culture. The words *Peyton Place* mean two things in today's iconic shorthand: first, they stand for the hypocrisies of a typical American small town in the 1950s, and, second, they evoke the whole world of trashy books and films. It is no surprise that in 1998, during the House Judiciary Committee's hearings concerning the impeachment of President Clinton, a U.S. Representative asked on the floor of the House, "Is this Watergate or Peyton Place?"

To read *Peyton Place* in 2005 and to reflect on its publishing history is to recognize that our inherited assumptions about the novel are both incomplete and largely inaccurate. It is a shock, for example, to realize that the story is set not in the 1950s or early 1960s—as were the movie and television series it spawned—but rather in the late 1930s and 1940s. The rebellious teens in *Peyton Place* don't listen to Elvis Presley but to Glenn Miller. There is no doubt, on the other hand, that the novel was considered trashy by both its early readers and its censors. ("This library does not carry *Peyton Place*. If you want it, go to Salem," read a sign on the front lawn of the public library in Beverly Farms, Massachusetts.) *Peyton Place* may not have been the first guilty pleasure in pop lit, but at least for a while, it was the guiltiest and the most pleasurable. Yet, when read today, it seems far too tame to be trashy, more akin, in fact, to the social commentary of Sinclair Lewis than to the bodice ripping of Nora Roberts.

So if *Peyton Place* the novel has nothing to do with the 1950s and only qualifies as trashy in the most straitlaced of surroundings, what was all the fuss about?

As with most cultural phenomena, timing was crucial to the success of *Peyton Place*. When the novel was published in 1956, the Hays Office—supporting marriage, family, and morality—still controlled Hollywood, and James Joyce's *Ulysses*, D. H. Lawrence's *Lady Chatterley's Lover*, and Henry Miller's *Tropic of Cancer* were still being banned somewhere in the U.S. Best-seller lists tended to be dominated by such middlebrow melodramas as *The Man in the Gray Flannel Suit*. On the other hand, as Ardis Cameron points out in her introduction to Northeastern University Press' 1999 reprint of *Peyton Place*, the audience gap between the hardcover best-seller, province of the middle class, and the paperback pulps, reading matter for the working class, was narrowing in the mid-1950s. Such hardcover novels as *Naked Came the Stranger*, *Mandingo*, and *Kings Row* (the last, a major influence on Metalious) were being read surreptitiously by more and more respectable housewives. (My mother kept a copy of *Naked Came the Stranger* in her underwear drawer.) Middle-class fiction readers were gradually becoming more daring, but it took *Peyton Place* to bring them out of the closet altogether.

But why *Peyton Place*, why did this particular first novel by an unknown, unpublished, and largely self-educated housewife from New Hampshire change the nature of fiction publishing in this country? Yes, it was content—sex, rape, abortion, and domestic abuse, all in the white-picket fence world of small-town New England—but behind every blockbuster there is always good marketing. Kitty Messner, the president of Julian Messner, the small New York firm that published *Peyton Place*, sensed that Metalious' novel could be a "big book," and she set out to sell it like a TV show. By carefully spreading the idea that *Peyton Place* was about to blow the lid off the small New Hampshire town where its author lived, Messner's publicist, who dubbed Metalious "Pandora in Blue Jeans," started the PR snowball rolling downhill. Then came the avalanche. Grace's school-principal husband, George, was fired shortly before the novel was published. Did the growing furor over the book lead to his dismissal? Maybe, maybe not, but it sure kick-started sales. *Peyton Place* was fourth on the best-seller lists one week before it was published.

As fascinating as the history of *Peyton Place* as a publishing and pop-cultural phenomenon can be, it tells us little about the novel itself. Is salacious subject matter—and salacious only for its time, at that—the whole story? Not at all. *Peyton Place* is very much a New England novel. Its power to shock comes not just from its content, but from the juxtaposition of that content against its very specific and well-realized setting. Metalious carefully juxtaposes her vision of Peyton Place against our Hallmark ideals of New England. She begins with Indian summer, postcard beauty at its most sublime, some might say, but Metalious goes a different way: "Indian summer is like a woman. Ripe, hotly passionate, but fickle, she comes and goes as she pleases so that one is never sure whether she will come at all, nor for how long she will stay." That is not the Indian summer of postcards, nor, for that matter, is it the woman of most novels written in 1956.

If *Peyton Place* is still read after another 50 years, though, it won't be because it turned the tables on our sense of life in a New England village, and it won't be because a generation of young readers thrilled to the phrase "her nipples were hard as diamonds." No, it will be because of the novel's stature as a precursor of the feminist movement and as a kind of grandmother to what today we call "women's fiction." Metalious, who died of cirrhosis of the liver in 1964, on the eve of the women's movement, would never have recognized herself as a feminist, but her female characters prepared the way for Erica Jong's Isadora Wing and for all the other sexually assertive, independent women who would appear in the fiction of the 1970s and beyond.

As Emily Toth, author of *Inside Peyton Place*, puts it: "The winners in the novel are independent women like Allison, who pursues her writing, putting an unhappy love affair behind her; Connie who acknowledges her sexuality and keeps her career; and Selena, who transcends desertion, rape, and murder and relies on herself and her female friends." *Peyton Place* was once the top-selling novel in history; it achieved that pinnacle because it managed to connect the middlebrow female reader to the passion of the pulps. Everyone from Helen Fielding to Terry McMillan to Danielle Steel owes the Pandora in Blue Jeans a royalty check or two.

Booklist, March 1, 2005

DANCING TO THE MUSIC
OF ANTHONY POWELL

WHEN TWO ANTHONY POWELL devotees encounter one another and learn of their mutual enthusiasm, something happens that's not unlike members of a secret society exchanging funny handshakes. There is an immediate recognition of having shared a common world, of having lived through the roughly 60 years of human history covered in Powell's multifaceted, majestic 12-novel sequence, *A Dance to the Music of Time*. Written over 25 years (1951–75), encompassing more than 300 characters, and stretching to nearly one million words, these 12 books constitute one of the twentieth century's towering literary achievements. And yet, despite glowing praise from critics on both sides of the Atlantic (the series placed number 43 on Modern Library's best-of-the-century list), Powell, who died on March 28, 2000, at age 94, has never been widely read. Most American readers, in fact, still don't know how to pronounce his name (it rhymes with Lowell not vowel).

Powell, who was a contemporary of George Orwell, Graham Greene, and Evelyn Waugh at Oxford, wrote several charming, small-scale comic novels before embarking on his masterwork in the 1950s. In a sense, all 12 books in the *Dance* sequence make up one extended flashback—the musings of narrator Nicholas Jenkins as he observes a group of workmen on a London street warming themselves by a fire. The first book begins with this image, and the twelfth concludes with it, as neatly as if the two passages had been written on the same day, rather than 25 years apart. In between, there are six decades of modern British history, from World War I through the mid-1970s, spanning the lives of the narrator and the group of mostly upper-class English people he encounters. The result is a vast panorama of human relationships, of connections made and broken.

The pieces of Powell's *Dance* fit together on levels other than technique. As we watch Nick Jenkins grow from schoolboy to university student to young man about London, and then from fledgling writer to soldier to aging man of letters, we listen to his reflections on the follies of the human comedy, and we nod in bemused agreement when he declares that "in the end most things in life—perhaps all things—turn out to be appropriate." On the road to becoming appropriate, however, human affairs tend to be hopelessly muddled, providing bittersweet testimony to what Nick calls "the ultimate futility of all human effort."

Those who fail to appreciate this melancholy truth, and who attempt to make the world conform to their will, manage to cause most of the trouble in Powell's world. Chief among this group is the protean figure of Kenneth Widmerpool, a schoolmate of Jenkins who appears and reappears throughout the novels like a theme in a fugue. Widmerpool—a man with the "knack of treading on the corns of others"—is one of the few characters in *Dance* who speaks in straightforward declarative sentences. Jenkins' sentences, on the other hand, are masterpieces of equivocation; full of subordinate and qualifying clauses, they reflect our inability to know anything for sure. Widmerpool always knows for sure, though at any given moment he may be running for office or chanting Hare Krishna.

The rich panoply of Powell's characters and the tantalizing juxtaposition of the comic and the serious ("melancholy should be taken for granted in any writer with a gift for comedy," Powell says) make *Dance* rewarding reading on a multitude of levels. Even so, many readers have experienced difficulties in first getting into the books. Part of this problem may stem from the fact that Powell undermines many of our commonly held assumptions about what realistic fiction should be. Name another mainstream novel in which the narrator lives mostly offstage. The significant events in Jenkins' life tend to happen between chapters and are summarized in almost cursory fashion, allowing him to get on with what he thinks is the good stuff—the actions of others. "I always enjoy learning the details of other people's lives," Nick observes matter-of-factly.

It shouldn't be assumed, however, that because Nick doesn't talk much about himself, we don't know much about him. On the contrary, the reader of *Dance* develops a most intimate relationship with Nick, but it happens indirectly, by watching him watch others. We come to know Nick the way we come to know people in our own lives—not by listening to them bare their souls in Eugene O'Neill–like monologues but by observing them in the office and hearing them talk to their spouses or friends.

Many critics have called *Dance* a comedy of manners. They're right, to be sure, but they've also missed the point. "It is always difficult," Powell observed, "to know how human beings really live. If you describe it, you often appear to be a humorous writer, even if you have merely reported exactly what happened." In its uniquely backhanded, understated, supremely ironic way, *A Dance to the Music of Time* comes as close as a novel can come to telling us "exactly what happened."

Booklist, May 15, 2000

HEARING AND SEEING THE MUSIC OF TIME

I FREELY ADMIT THAT I'm slow in adapting to new technologies, but don't send me that early-retirement-for-anachronistic-editors package quite yet. I usually come around eventually, as I've finally done with audiobooks. My slowness in strapping on the headphones has nothing to do with a dislike of listening to books being read. Quite the opposite, in fact. I don't drive to work, but when I am behind the wheel, my traveling companion reads aloud. Frankly, I prefer this form of the audio experience.

For the last 10 years, nearly all of my driving time has been spent listening to Anthony Powell's 12-volume *Dance to the Music of Time*. Taking 10 years to listen to one book (well, 12 books) may seem extreme, but it's really the perfect way to experience Powell's meandering story of a British writer's life from World War I through the mid-1970s. The music of time, after all, is no three-minute pop song, so it makes perfect sense to spend a decade hearing a story that itself spans 60 years. Everything about Powell's masterwork demands a slow pace, from the way the tale creeps back and forth across time (in a sense, all 12 books are one extended flashback) to the elaborately constructed sentences themselves. *Dance* unravels itself through the first-person narration of the bemused Nicholas Jenkins, who reflects on his interactions with a group of friends and acquaintances, offering ironic commentary on their various attempts, invariably unsuccessful, to structure their lives around some organizing principle. Unlike many of the people he encounters, Nick never professes to know anything for sure, and his sentences, full of subordinate and qualifying clauses, are masterpieces of equivocation, a perfect grammatical analogy to his tentative worldview.

Reading those sentences aloud is no easy task. Fortunately, I was required only to keep my aging Nissan moving forward on largely straight toll roads, while my companion was forced to negotiate the never-ending S curves of Powell's prose. As longtime Back Page readers may remember, I've been a Powell devotee for years, having read the entire sequence twice before embarking on the listening decade. Hearing the books, though, was an entirely new and surprisingly revelatory experience. Listening to every word over an extended period of time—rather than skimming now and again—drives home the rhythm of the books, forcing the listener to experience them as a protracted waltz in which themes disappear and resurface as the dancers shuffle their way through their lives. Yes, you forget the tune now and then, but it always comes back to you. That's the whole point, really: as Jenkins notes, "in the end, most things in life, perhaps all things, turn out to be appropriate." It's easier to appreciate that deliciously ironic statement if you come to it over time, even if most of that time was spent lumbering across the seemingly interminable Ohio Turnpike.

The last word of the last book in our oral reading of *Dance* was spoken, appropriately, on New Year's Eve 2007. Next up was an entirely different experience: Powell on DVD. Back about the time we were reading volume 1, *Dance to the Music of Time* appeared on BBC's *Masterpiece Theatre*, but the program was never picked up in the U.S. Now, though, a decade after its first release, the DVD is available for sale here. Watching the four-hour drama made the perfect coda to a decade's worth of oral reading. There was much to like in the program (the performance of Simon Russell Beale, in the central role of Kenneth Widmerpool, for example, was absolutely spot-on), but frankly, it was an utterly disconcerting experience, as if you'd been forced to watch an entire movie in fast-forward mode, or listen to a 33-rpm record at 45-rpm speed. "Slow down," I kept screaming at the screen, as the scenes zoomed by. "What happened to *Casanova's Chinese Restaurant?*" I asked incredulously, as volume 5 of the series, my favorite of the lot, was reduced to a passing reference.

And, yet, it wasn't the mere telescoping effect that bothered me the most; that occurs whenever even a one-volume novel is turned into a two-hour movie. No, in this case, it was what happened to the texture of the piece when it was packed into the viewing equivalent of a zip file. That crucial sense of ironic bemusement was largely missing, as there was no opportunity—with the exception of a very few voice-overs—for Jenkins to reflect on the world around him, or for us, as readers, to sense how patterns in human behavior make themselves felt incrementally. And by moving the narration from first person to third, we lose completely the masterful way Powell builds character indirectly; Nick's wife, Isabel, for example, rarely appears in the books, yet we have a vivid sense of their strong marriage, built through several carefully nuanced moments, stretched over several novels. In the DVD, Isabel is a full-fledged character, nicely portrayed, but by seeing so much more of her, we know her less well, or at least more conventionally.

So what do I conclude from my reading, listening, and viewing of *Dance to the Music of Time*? It's very simple, really. A good story can be told in multiple ways, using all variety of media and all forms of available technology. But it's told best when there is the least interference with the author's words. You'll never be able to learn Powell's dance if you don't know all the steps, and to learn the steps, you have to hear the words. All of them.

Listening will never replace reading, but I now realize that it can bring another level of understanding and enjoyment to a much-loved story. As long as my personal reader's voice holds out, I'll stick with her. But maybe I should get myself some new headphones, just in case she gets a sore throat before we finish our latest project: A. N. Wilson's Lampitt novels (they're much like Powell's, only with shorter sentences).

Booklist, April 15, 2008

EXTOLLING IMPURITY

Brown as impurity.

I write of a color that is not a singular color, not a strict recipe, not an expected result, but a color produced by careless desire, even by accident; by two or several. I write of blood that is blended. I write of brown as complete freedom of substance and narrative. I extol impurity.

I eulogize a literature that is suffused with brown, with allusion, irony, paradox — ha! — pleasure.

I write about race in America in hopes of undermining the notion of race in America.

— Richard Rodriguez, from *Brown: The Last Discovery of America*
(Viking, 2002)

IF YOU WOULD LIKE to publish a straightforward sociological analysis of Hispanics in America, the kind of book that supports mainstream thinking on a controversial topic, you probably aren't going to want Richard Rodriguez to write it. But if you want a book that begins with an observable fact of American public life and uses it as a jumping-off point for a reflection on how the mixing of different races, religions, styles of dress, kinds of food, and expressions of sexuality has produced a glorious impurity, and how the color brown is the perfect symbol of that impurity, then you surely would want Rodriguez as your author. After all, as a self-described "Queer Catholic Indian Spaniard at home in a temperate Chinese city in a fading blond state in a post-Protestant nation," he knows a little something about what he calls "the cement between leaves of paradox."

I met Rodriguez in 1982, shortly after *Hunger of Memory*, the first volume of his now three-volume autobiography, had been published by David Godine. The controversy that has followed Rodriguez's career over the last 20 years was just beginning to heat up. How could it not? Here was a genuine American success story, a Mexican American who had earned a Ph.D. in English and made his way into the white-collar world only to renounce the system that had helped get him there. With his stands against affirmative action and bilingualism in the classroom, Rodriguez made himself a target for the liberal establishment and for minority activists of every kind. But the soft-spoken man I interviewed in a Chicago coffee shop wasn't much interested in talking about the pros and cons of affirmative action. As I remember it, we talked mostly about Wordsworth—especially about the scene in "The Prelude" where a young boy rows his boat toward a mountain and, noticing that the mountain appears to grow larger the closer to it he gets, becomes both terrified and furious. Dealing with that first glimpse of the ominous public world outside the self—and outside the security of family—was the real subject of *Hunger of Memory*, and the ongoing conflict between public and private selves remains at the heart of all Rodriguez's work.

In Days of Obligation (1992), subtitled *An Argument with My Father*, Rodriguez sees the war between public and private selves manifested as the split in his multicultural soul between his American faith in the future (the Protestant heritage) and his Mexican (and Catholic) sense of the tragic past. Now, as he sets out to contemplate the meaning of brown in America, and his own brownness, he once again confronts the split between his different selves. But this time, instead of bouncing from one self to another, he seeks and finds reconciliation in the very impurity of being brown, the "ability of bodies to experience two or several things at once." Race, he says, is not such a terrible word. Although many take it for "a tragic noun, a synonym for conflict and isolation," he sees it more optimistically: "Maybe because my nature is already mixed. The word race encourages me to remember the influence of eroticism on history. For that is what race memorializes. Within any discussion of race, there lurks the possibility of romance."

But the romance doesn't come easily. Rodriguez's optimism for the future of a brown America is truncated by all the forces at large in the world that won't tolerate impurity. September 11, Rodriguez notes in his preface, reminds us of the "combustible dangers of brown," of the fact that the terrorist dreams "of purity and of the straight line." But puritans come dressed as liberals, too, as in the book critic who will only assign another gay Latin American to review one of Rodriguez's books or those who feel that Rodriguez is disloyal to one of the many groups he has come to represent. Gays have accused him of not writing enough about his sexuality, while some Latinos charge that he hates his race. To such attacks, Rodriguez responds, "Yes, as a child, I dragged a razor blade against the skin of my forearm to see if I could get the brown out. I couldn't. A clandestine experiment. Just checking. Did I hate my brown skin? No. Would I rather have been white? I would rather have been Jeff Chandler. Jeff Chandler would rather have been Lauren Bacall, according to Esther Williams' autobiography."

Reviewing *Days of Obligation* 10 years ago, I said that "Rodriguez's spiritual autobiography is to the late twentieth century what John Stuart Mill's autobiography was to the Victorian era." A decade later, with a new chapter in Rodriguez's life story in front of me, I remain even more convinced that my comparison was an apt one. Mill, too, knew something about the conflict between public and private selves. Committed to social reform and the teachings of Jeremy Bentham, he found himself in a deep spiritual crisis that no amount of good works could heal. Poetry, scorned by his fellow activists as trivial, was his salvation, reconnecting Mill the rationalist to his emotions and to the world of passion. Like Rodriguez, Mill could not live with the purists' straight lines. Poetry was his color brown. Mill's conversion to poetry was attacked by his fellow radicals, just as Rodriguez surely will be attacked for his thoroughly unconventional take on the browning of America. Yet this challenging, eloquent, witty, searingly beautiful book will long outlive its detractors. Time, after all, is always on the side of impurity.

Booklist, March 1, 2002

A FAILURE TO COMMUNICATE

USUALLY, AS THE END of the year approaches, I can be counted upon to clutter the Back Page with a burst of Grinchy grousing about the mandatory gaiety of the Christmas holidays. This year, 1999, Christmas is small potatoes; I have a whole millennium to grouse about. Until recently, my stance on the millennium has been simple: ignore it. Unfortunately, the recent Thanksgiving weekend acted as an unwanted wake-up call, forcing me to do what I'd vowed not to do: millennial musing. What happened was I caught a cold—a bad one that knocked me out of Thanksgiving dinner and most of the weekend as well. Sitting at home with no turkey and no conviviality (except for my longtime pal, Jack Daniels), I vowed to take a serious run at the impressive pile of books I'd been meaning to read for weeks. Perhaps it was the low-grade fever or the frequent injections of Dristan nasal spray (not good when mixed with Jack Daniels), but I found myself drifting from book to book, often ignoring entirely the pile of "need to read" titles. Oddly, the two volumes I spent most of my time with were Thomas L. Friedman's *The Lexus and the Olive Tree*, a penetrating analysis of globalization and all that lofty term implies, and T. S. Eliot's *The Waste Land and Other Poems*. Blame the fever, but eventually I saw myself as a timid J. Alfred Prufrock facing the globalized twenty-first century.

It began with Friedman's paradigm of the Lexus and the olive tree. The Lexus—luxury car for the new century, produced in Japan, largely by robots, for conspicuous consumers everywhere—is Friedman's symbol for the new international economic system of globalization: "The Lexus represents all the burgeoning global markets, financial institutions and computer technologies with which we pursue higher living standards today." The olive tree, with its thousand-year-old roots digging deep into the earth, represents "everything that anchors us, identifies us and locates us in this world." Olive trees give us "the warmth of family, the joy of individuality, the depth of private relationships." They also give us communities that are based on the exclusion of others and can lead, at their worst, to war and genocide. Friedman sees the challenge of the new century to be making globalization work on both ends of the scale: marketing the Lexus and nurturing the olive tree. He predicts a tough job ahead of us, but he's confident that the best minds of a new generation are up to the challenge.

It's a lucid, accessible, brilliantly analytical book, but it left me feeling exhausted, overwhelmed, and utterly unable to take the great leap forward. Here's where Prufrock comes in: "I have heard the Webmasters singing, each to each. / I do not think that they will sing to me." Suddenly it was clear, with that special clarity that only a fever and a little whiskey can bring: as the world joins hands, buys and sells goods electronically, and forms new global identities, I will grow old and, maybe, if I can summon the nerve, wear the bottoms of my trousers rolled.

Part of me, however, feels defiant rather than defeated, resolved rather than reticent. From my narrow individualistic perspective, Friedman's new global world translates to too many cell phones and too much e-mail. My title for this millennial rant comes, of course, from the signature line spoken by an evil prison guard to a rebellious Cool Hand Luke: "What we *have* here is a failure to communicate." The line became a catch-phrase because it turned a universal piety, communication, into an expression of evil. For most of the twentieth century, failures to communicate caused the lion's share of our international and interpersonal problems; in the next century, I would argue, our troubles, especially in terms of quality of life, will come from too much communication. Unlike at the Tower of Babel, we will all speak the same global language, but we won't be able to hear what anyone is saying because we'll all be jabbering on our cell phones at the same time. In this brave new world, the idea of Prufrock paralyzed because he fears misunderstanding becomes inconceivable, even charmingly anachronistic. If you bear your soul in an e-mail, and your correspondent answers, "That is not it at all, / That is not what I meant, at all," you don't fret about eating a peach. You simply click on reply and fire away again, churning out another few hundred words of lowercase, unpunctuated babble. What we *need* here is a failure to communicate.

Or maybe it's just me. Friedman devotes a whole chapter to the backlash against globalization, showing how hysterical reactions from the frightened few could threaten the new world. No doubt he's right. I'll be quiet. Eliot has me pegged in "Gerontion": "An old man in a draughty house / Under a windy knob."

Have a Merry Millennium.

Booklist, December 15, 1999

HIGHER NUMBERS

THERE ARE FOUR GUYS in a bar when Bill Gates walks in. The four recognize the new arrival and start whooping, exchanging high fives, and ordering another round. "Why the fuss?" Bill asks. One of the four answers enthusiastically, "Don't you realize what you've just done to our average income?"

That joke appears in a swell little book to be published in January called *The Numbers Game: A Commonsense Guide to Understanding Numbers in the News, in Politics, and in Life*, by Michael Blastland and Andrew Dilnot (Gotham, 2009). It's hard to get away from numbers in daily life, especially during an election season, and these days the numbers with which we're confronted tend to be extremely depressing. One strategy, commonly used by those of us on better terms with words than numbers, is to ignore the world of digits altogether. A better approach, though, is to overcome one's natural tendency to be intimidated by numbers and their assumed inviolability. Don't get me wrong. I'm not advocating buying a copy of *Math for Dummies* or, God forbid, taking a class to hone your Excel skills. No, all you need to do is give this book a quick browse, and you'll realize that, while numbers are unambiguous enough when left alone, they are every bit as subjective as a reviewer's string of flowery adjectives once they've been interpreted by human beings.

Take averages. Just as those four guys in the bar would be wise not to switch from beer to single-malt scotch because of their newfound average wealth, so we shouldn't put too much significance in the startling fact that the average number of feet possessed by human beings is less than two. Yes, that's right: if you look down and find two shoes supporting your two feet, you are an above-average person, foot-wise. Do the math, as the saying goes. If nine (or nine million) people have two feet and one has only one, the average will dip, however microscopically, under two. The only way to get it back up is to find a three-footed human.

It's easy enough to get the point about average feet, but it's something else again when politicians start talking about how much the "average American" will save from a tax cut. (Blastland and Dilnot are British, but they use plenty of meaty examples from this side of the pond.) When George Bush told us that 116 million Americans would see their taxes rise by an average of $1,800 if his tax cuts were allowed to expire, he was not exactly lying. If you add up the total amount of additional taxes that would be paid if the Bush tax cuts expired and divided that figure by the number of tax-paying Americans, you would indeed get a figure very close to $1,800. But what Mr. Bush wasn't telling us was that most of the 116 million taxpayers would be paying far less than $1,800, his "average" figure having been skewed way upward by the incomes of the very rich. As Blastland and Dilnot put it, "So rich are the richest Americans that you can dilute them with millions of middle and low incomes and the resulting blend is still, well, rich." Bill Gates is back in the bar.

Even more interesting to me than the matter of distorted averages is what numbers—and especially percentages—do to our sense of risk. We've all seen the scary headlines: the American Cancer Institute says don't eat bacon—period—because an extra ounce a day increases the risk of colorectal cancer by 21 percent! Some of us may react to this sort of thing with immediate obedience, others with determined defiance, but very few of us look behind the numbers the way Blastland and Dilnot do. The thing about risk factors tied to percentage increases, they remind us, is that you don't know anything until you know what the risk was in the first place: "Double a risk of one in a million (risk up 100 percent!), and it becomes two in a million; put an extra bullet in the revolver, and the risk of Russian Roulette also doubles." As to bacon eating, when you look behind that 21 percent increase, here's what you find: "About five men in a hundred typically get colorectal cancer in a lifetime. If they all ate an extra slice of bacon every single day, about six would."

When I was an undergraduate, I foolishly took a math class. Naturally, I was trying to fulfill a requirement, but no one told me I could also do it by taking Geologic History of Life. I promptly dropped math after one angst-filled semester and transferred into "rocks for jocks," but I've always bragged to my oldest friends, English majors all, that, unlike them, I was a veteran of "college math." I took one thing away from that class: once you leave the placid waters of addition and subtraction, weird things happen with numbers, and all hell breaks loose when parentheses come into play. "Don't trust the higher numbers," I've always counseled my literary pals, speaking as one who had ventured into the dark woods and returned to tell the tale.

Now, though, thanks to the obliging authors of *The Numbers Game*, I realize that what people do to numbers is far scarier than the numbers themselves. I still don't trust parentheses in math, but I've developed a new strategy for whenever I encounter a troubling average or a potentially lethal percentage: order a double scotch with a side of bacon. But if Bill Gates is in the bar, he can buy his own.

Booklist, October 15, 2008

INADMISSIBLE EVIDENCE

WHEN D. H. LAWRENCE admonished readers to "trust the tale not the teller," he was warning us of the unfortunate tendency of many novelists to load the dice by injecting their own moral views into their work, usually in the form of authorial commentary on what the characters are doing or saying. Lawrence believed that such tactics never work; the novel will not be shanghaied, even by its creator.

In his wonderful essay "The Novel," Lawrence uses *Anna Karenina* as an example: "Vronsky sinned, did he? But the sinning was a consummation devoutly to be wished. The novel makes that obvious: in spite of old Leo Tolstoy." Novels, Lawrence believes, won't let their authors get away with telling didactic lies. The living passion between Vronsky and Anna is the heart of the book, not Tolstoy's moralizing about that passion. Lawrence sums it up this way: "The novel itself gives Vronsky a kick in the pants [pushing him into Anna's arms], and knocks old Leo's teeth out."

So if we trust the tale not the teller, we're protected against the tendency of novelists to put their thumbs on the scales. But what happens when there is no tale to trust? When the writer presumes to tell us about the lives of his or her characters outside of the novels in which they live? I refer, of course, to the recent case of J. K. Rowling and her character Dumbledore. While speaking at Carnegie Hall on October 19, Rowling was asked by a young fan whether Dumbledore finds true love. Rowling replied that Dumbledore was gay and had fallen in love as a young man with his eventual foe, the dark wizard Grindewald. She went on to offer several other, less-sensational revelations about the supporting cast in the Harry Potter series, such as the fact that Neville Longbottom, Harry's meek classmate, married another classmate, Hannah Abbott.

Naturally, it was the Dumbledore announcement that caused a firestorm of response, mostly from right-wing commentators who deplored what they viewed as Rowling's attempt to foist a social agenda on tender minds and hearts. The response of the Bill O'Reilly crowd is really too ridiculously pitiful to merit much comment. Poor Bill-O, as Keith Olbermann calls O'Reilly: it's getting harder and harder for even an indefatigable right-wing bloviator to keep the world safe from real life. Huff and puff all you want, Bill-O, but you've already lost this one. Even without Dumbledore on the team, gay characters have been an important part of our literature for quite some time and will remain so as long as there are stories to tell.

Still, for any fiction reader or anyone who writes about fiction, there is a troubling aspect to Rowling's comments and the manner in which they were reported. *Newsweek*, for example, subtitled its story on Rowling and Dumbledore with the line, "Harry Potter author breaks big news in New York." No, she didn't, not really. Newsflash, *Newsweek*: Harry Potter, Dumbledore, and the rest of the cast of the seven-novel series do not have lives outside the books. Rowling didn't walk through a magic wardrobe into the world of Hogwarts and then report on her findings, and she can't walk back through that wardrobe whenever she pleases to bring us "news" on what's up with Neville Longbottom.

That's not to say, however, that Rowling shouldn't be perfectly free to comment on what she *imagines* Neville's life after the books to be, or what Dumbledore's life might have been like before the books began. But it's only that—her imaginings—because she chose not to explore those topics in any detail in the only world open to her characters, the world of the books. On the other hand, anyone—Rowling, you, or me—is free to offer interpretations of those lives based on what we know from the books. That's called literary criticism, and it's open to all. Arguing the thesis that Dumbledore is gay based on what we know of his character and his relationship with Grindewald is a perfectly legitimate essay topic, and if written by a talented author—with a somewhat broader focus than simply pinpointing one fictional character's sexuality—it could be quite fascinating. Look what Leslie Fiedler did in his classic essay "C'mon Back to the Raft, Huck Honey," about the homoerotic element in *Huckleberry Finn*.

But the main point here isn't whether Dumbledore is gay; it's that J. K. Rowling doesn't have the authority to say he is just because he's her character. Twain, no doubt, wouldn't have agreed with Fiedler, but that doesn't make Fiedler wrong—anymore than it makes Rowling right when she offers an interpretation of her characters' lives outside the books in which she wrote about them. Fiedler, at least, tried to make his case; Rowling just broke the news. If Rowling thinks Dumbledore's sexuality is an idea worth exploring, she might consider writing a love story starring Dumbledore and Grindewald as young men. That could make a fine book, and she wouldn't be the first writer to do a prequel.

But, in the meantime, she should realize that she does not have omnipotent power over her characters. Many years ago, I had the opportunity to interview the late British novelist Anthony Powell, author of the 12-novel sequence *A Dance to the Music of Time*, a series that never amassed even a fraction of Harry Potter's audience but that, among its devotees, is held in equal esteem. I had labored over a long question involving my interpretation of the novels and its central character—the question I hoped would establish my bona fides and elicit a detailed response—but when I asked it, Powell replied simply, "Oh, I never think about the meaning of my books. That's for you readers to decide." Remember that, Ms. Rowling. Unless you write more books about Harry and friends, the ball is now in our court.

Booklist, November 15, 2007

OUTSIDE IN AND INSIDE OUT

I LIKED GEOGRAPHY FINE until I learned the disconcerting fact that it's possible to go so far west you're east. Similarly, my disenchantment with politics may have begun with the realization that left and right can be equally confusing; thus, you can be so far to the left, you're really on the right, as in the sixties-generation defender of personal freedom who woke up 30 years later to discover he'd become a libertarian. Recently I experienced this odd brand of cultural vertigo in a new form. As I was watching a perfectly good little movie called *Ghost World*, about two teenage misfits who find each other, it dawned on me that there are so many outsiders in literature and movies that, strictly speaking, outsiders now find themselves on the inside. To be an outsider in a novel, especially a YA novel, guarantees that you wear the white hat. I really fear for the psychological stability of these millions of young outsiders, so proud of their otherness, when they finally realize that they are trapped on the inside, and the student body president is the new outsider. How could such a thing happen?

A lot of the blame must fall on a smart-mouthed preppy in a red hunting hat. It was, after all, Holden Caulfield who turned outsiders into cult figures. At the time, we loved Holden because he wasn't afraid to accuse the standard bearers of the mainstream world—teachers and parents, mainly—of being phonies. That seemed gutsy then, something you just didn't do unless, of course, you were an outsider. The teens in *Ghost World* are also very good at spotting the phonies around them, but frankly, as I watched the movie, I was shocked to discover that I was feeling a little sorry for the phonies. At first, I attributed this unlikely response to age. I must admit to being in an age bracket that harbors some of the world's biggest phonies, so perhaps I was just sympathizing with my own kind. But, no, it was more than that. I was feeling sorry for the phonies because I realized that, at least in literature and film, they had become the underdogs. A card-carrying phony insider simply can't survive the third reel of a movie these days; there are just too many outsiders, children of Holden, out there, and they aren't taking any prisoners. The plain fact is that rooting for outsiders today is like rooting for the Yankees.

So what to do? You wound up in the east when you wanted to go west, and you've learned to love outsiders only to discover that they aren't outside anymore. If there were only a few more books or movies about likable insiders, perhaps the odds would start to even out again, and maybe even someday the outsiders we know and love would finally be able to break free of the inner circle. To start the ball rolling, let's pay tribute to a few notable insiders.

Insiders aren't always phonies, just as outsiders don't necessarily look like James Dean. Take Mr. Pickwick, the affable and utterly genuine hero of Dickens' first novel. Unlike Groucho Marx, Mr. Pickwick never met a group he wouldn't be proud to join. He is literature's ultimate hail-fellow-well-met, and as such, he just naturally gravitates to the inside. He would be pleased to share a grog with James Dean, but he certainly wouldn't understand why the young fellow seemed so mopey. Mr. Pickwick is an insider, yes, but he isn't Babbitt. If we can like Pickwick, we're on the road to treating insiders with the same humanity we regularly afford outsiders.

For a different kind of insider, how about poor Stradlater, Holden's roommate? I've always felt Stradlater got a raw deal. Yes, he's not particularly sensitive, and, no, he doesn't much care who's a phony and who isn't, but all in all, he's not a bad guy. I know that, in today's world, the fact that you like sports and have a lot of friends is never going to win you a starring role in a YA novel, but that doesn't mean we can't still feel a little sorry for Stradlater. He was playing by the rules and doing just fine when a little runt in a funny hat who couldn't even hack it as the manager of the fencing team somehow turned the world upside down. Isn't it about time somebody writes *Pitcher in the Rye*, the story from Stradlater's point of view?

The real problem at the heart of this inside-out mess is that, thanks to literature and film, we all see ourselves as outsiders. Every successful politician, no matter how different, spins himself as an outsider and his opponent as an insider. No one willingly admits these days to being an "inside-the-Beltway" person. We can thank everyone from Holden to James Dean to Woody Allen for the popularity of the outsider, but unfortunately, they've all done their job too well. When being outside becomes fashionable, the committed outsider faces a crisis of conscience. Look at Woody Allen: he saw himself, the outsider as schlemiel, dangerously close to becoming an insider, and, in a desperate move to get back on the outside, he was forced to fall in love with his stepdaughter. Woody's strategy may be distasteful, but it's going to take his kind of courage if outsiders are ever going to get back outside where they belong. Maybe then it will be time to tackle the east-west thing.

Booklist, September 1, 2001

THE IRONY IN IRONY

WHEN I WAS A callow undergraduate, I took a class on Victorian poetry. It was the professor who piqued my interest. He had long hair, wore paisley ties, and gave standing-room-only lectures on the meaning of the Beatles' lyrics. The class began not with "Penny Lane," as I'd hoped, but with lectures on paisley-tie-guy's own personal literary theory. Imagine my surprise when, after having scrupulously avoided any form of mathematics involving parentheses, I found my class notes covered with what looked like algebraic formulas. The hip professor, it turned out, used formulas to help define his four categories of literature—tragedy, comedy, romance, and irony. Tragedy ($1/0=0/1$) covered stories in which the hero's life started out good and ended up bad (I'm oversimplifying here, at a distance of 40 years); comedy was the opposite ($0/1=1/0$), with the hero starting out bad and ending up good. In romance, the arc of the hero's life started out good and ended up good ($1/0=1/0$), while the ironic life started out bad and finished bad ($0/1=0/1$).

We worked our way through the Victorians, puzzling over which of the formulas fit the poem at hand. My scores were hardly better than they were when I was fumbling through eighth-grade algebra. I had the most trouble with irony. The whole $0/1=0/1$ business had me completely baffled. This was a bitter blow because, like most wannabe intellectuals, I considered myself a connoisseur of irony. Don't we all? Just as no one will admit to not having a sense of humor, few will admit to not appreciating irony. I think the most important thing I learned in that class (other than discovering Matthew Arnold's "Dover Beach," an ironic poem, I think) was that understanding irony was no easy trick, with or without formulas.

Is it ironic that most of the time when you hear someone say, "That was so ironic," you think to yourself, "No, it wasn't"? What we all need is a book that defines once and for all what irony is and isn't. I'm happy to say there is such a book, and I'm even happier to say that my former professor didn't write it. It's a very little book called *The Big Book of Irony*, by Jon Winokur (yup, that title is ironic, even if the arc of the author's life didn't start out bad).

Winokur, who is a very witty writer, gets right to the heart of the matter, defining what irony isn't. It isn't contradiction. "Irony," he tells us, "involves the incongruity between what is expected and what actually happens; coincidence merely denotes spatial or temporal proximity." Got it? If not, here's an example: "It is ironic that Beethoven was deaf, but merely coincidental that while two members of ZZ Top, Billy F. Gibbons and Dusty Hill, have beards, the third member, Frank Beard, is clean shaven."

Irony also isn't the same as hypocrisy. It isn't ironic, Winokur explains, that William Bennett, author of *The Book of Virtues*, had a secret gambling habit. It merely proves that Bennett is a hypocrite. Irony isn't sarcasm, either. Irony is subtle, sarcasm blunt. Nor is irony the same thing as cynicism ("irony discriminates; cynicism does not"). And nor is it euphemism. "Euphemism conceals, irony reveals, albeit by stating the opposite." Political correctness, Winokur points out, is euphemism, but it often generates irony.

OK, that's what irony isn't, but we still don't exactly know what it is. When dealing with definitions, it's always a good idea to start with Samuel Johnson. As usual, the Great Lexicographer gets straight to the heart of the matter, defining irony as "a mode of speech in which the meaning is clearly contrary to the words." That's on the mark, to be sure, but it only covers verbal irony, which Winokur reminds us is only one of many forms this "protean phenomenon" can assume. Perhaps the most interesting part of his book is the chapter "Forms of Irony." There are too many of them to list here—and, frankly, some of them are a bit dull (take philosophical irony, "which seeks to triangulate the truth by assuming a variety of mutually exclusive points of view"). Can't you just see a gang of philosophers sitting around on a Saturday night, pounding some Budweiser and triangulating a little truth? (That was sarcasm, by the way, not irony.) But enough of philosophers. Here are my Top Four Little Known Forms of Irony:

> *Ambient Irony (aka cosmic irony).* Irony, many of us feel, is part of the human condition. Winokur calls it the difference between what we want and what we get. Of course, if you believe in Rhonda Byrne's *The Secret,* you believe in the Law of Attraction, which says that the universe gives you exactly what you attract. Watch out, though: if there is such a thing as ambient irony out there, you Law of Attraction types might as well be wearing scarlet I's on your breasts.

> *Ironic Consumption.* "Acquisition of pop-culture artifacts from bygone eras not for their intrinsic worth but for their very lameness, for example, lava lamps and velvet Elvises." The big problem here is the slippery slope from ironic consumer to genuine nerd.

> *Meta-irony.* "Irony that refers to the ironies associated with irony. For example, to offer as an instance of irony the fact that Lou Gehrig died of Lou Gehrig's disease is to practice meta-irony, or to be incredibly obtuse."

> *Morissettian Irony.* "Irony based on a misapprehension of irony, that is, no irony at all. Named for pop singer Alanis Morissette, whose hit single 'Ironic' mislabels coincidence and inconvenience as irony." "It's a traffic jam when you're late," Alanis croons. No, Alanis, that's not irony. But isn't an unironic song called "Irony" a perfect example of meta-irony?

Our little irony seminar is now over, and I hope we've all learned something, thanks to Mr. Winokur. But I still don't know if Robert Browning's "Fra Lippo Lippi" rates an 0/1=0/1.

Booklist, April 1, 2007

EIGHTEEN STRAIGHT WHISKEYS

I'VE BEEN TOYING FOR years with writing a Back Page column about famous last words, but I've never quite managed to finish the job. Now, with the help of two excellent sources, I'm ready to give it a go. The first source is a handy new book, *Famous Last Words: The Ultimate Collection of Finales and Farewells*, by Laura Ward. The second is an essay in the online magazine *Knot* called "Famous Last Words: An Introductory Guide to Entering the Pantheon," by *Booklist*'s own John Green. I have a serious problem with John's essay, one that I'm forced to acknowledge up front: it's a lot funnier than this column has any chance to be. For someone shockingly young, John has done a lot of thinking about last words, and he offers those of us who haven't plenty of advice on how to prepare for the end. Avoid the pretentious, he wisely counsels, as in Dreiser's "Shakespeare, I come." Asserting faith in God (Anne Boleyn's "Oh, God, have pity on my soul") may be wise in terms of firming up your afterlife plans, but, as John rightly points out, it just doesn't work as pleasure reading. Banal declarations of love are also to be avoided (Kurt Cobain's tepid "I love you, I love you"), unless you add something a little extra to the basic message, as W. C. Fields did when he opined, "God damn the whole friggin' world and everyone in it but you, Carlotta." Thanks, John, for pointing out that Fields' wife was named Hattie.

There is really only one absolute rule about last words, and it applies, interestingly, every bit as well to first words and all those words in between: try not to be boring. You're dead, OK, but the rest of us aren't, and we still need to be entertained. After reading John's essay and the 250 pages of last words in Ward's book, I have a few observations of my own on what sort of final remarks the dead people of tomorrow should utter if they hope to entertain the living.

BE IRONIC

Webster defines irony as "the incongruity between the actual result of a sequence of events and the normal or expected result." Death has a tendency to make ironists of us all. Take Dylan Thomas. "I've had 18 straight whiskeys," Thomas announced to his fellow drinkers at the White Horse Tavern in Greenwich Village. "I think that's the record." He then walked back to the Chelsea Hotel, where he dropped dead.

Many years ago, I learned a trickier definition of irony from a cantankerously philosophical English professor who had his own theory of literary genres. He believed that a work of literature was tragedy if the protagonist expects everything and gets nothing; it's romance if the protagonist expects everything and gets everything; it's comedy if he or she expects nothing and gets everything; and it's irony if the hero expects nothing and gets nothing. Death is the quintessentially ironic experience when it confirms our expectation of nothing with nothing. Victor Hugo must have understood irony in this way when he uttered his last words: "I see the black light!" I like to think that Victor was poking a little fun at those who were expecting a different kind of light—like Goethe, whose famous last words were "More light! More light!" Of course, we'll never know for sure whether the romantic view or the ironic view is accurate until we check out the color of light for ourselves. In the meantime, we can sit on the fence with Rabelais, whose last words were, "I go to seek the great Perhaps."

BE MUNDANE

If you're worried about coming up with suitably ironic last words, one good strategy is to stick with mundane observations. Usually, the juxtaposition of death and the mundane delivers all the irony you'll need. D. H. Lawrence was no ironist; he believed in the senses, above all, and despised the trickery of words. And, yet, even Lawrence couldn't avoid irony in the end, when he made this thoroughly practical final utterance: "I think it's time for the morphine." The similarly mundane last words of French writer Paul Claudel just might be my personal favorites: "Do you think it could have been the sausage?"

BE APPROPRIATE

In his exquisitely ironic 12-novel sequence *A Dance to the Music of Time*, Anthony Powell observed that "in the end, everything turns out to be appropriate." Is that ironic? Damned if I know, but it sure can be funny, especially in the case of last words. There's Conrad Hilton, who cautioned us to "leave the shower curtain on the inside of the tub." Or Marshal Foch, who made this observation before his demise at the second battle of the Marne in World War I: "My center collapses, my right recedes, situation excellent. I attack!" But perhaps it was James Joyce who uttered the most appropriate last words of all. "Does anybody understand?" Joyce asked. We don't know exactly what he was talking about, of course, but then, we never did. Now that's appropriate.

Booklist, May 15, 2004

THE SEABISCUIT SWEEPSTAKES

PICKING WINNERS AT THE racetrack is a lot like picking which books, of the 60,000 titles published every year, will reach the best-seller lists. Just as handicappers rely on a horse's past performances to judge who is likely to win a race, so publishers look for trends to determine what kind of books have the best chance to capture the fancy of the book-buying public. If it worked once, publishers convince themselves, why shouldn't it work again? Unfortunately, past-performance charts aren't foolproof for picking horses, and subject matter doesn't guarantee repeated trips to bookstores' cash registers or libraries' circulation desks.

The unpredictability of best-sellers is most evident in the area of what we call narrative nonfiction, factual accounts of historical phenomena that use fictionlike techniques to tell their stories. You can't blame publishers for trying, but sometimes they just miss the point. Dava Sobel's *Galileo's Daughter* was a wonderful book, but what made it a breakthrough best-seller in 1999 wasn't the apostrophe in the title or even the fact that it was about Galileo; it was Sobel's ability to turn Galileo's trial before the Inquisition into a compelling human drama told from the point of view of his daughter, a Clarisse nun who died at age 33. But look what *Galileo's*

Daughter spawned: *Galileo's Treasure Box, Galileo's Finger, Galileo's Pendulum,* and *Galileo's Mistake,* all published in the wake of Sobel's book. It would seem obvious that one word followed by an apostrophe doesn't make a best-seller, but the power of past performances sometimes blots out all common sense, even in the shrewdest editors. (It's just not true, by the way, that certain parties, in late 1999, entertained the idea of changing the name of *Booklist* to *Galileo's Reviews.*)

The most imitated narrative nonfiction best-seller of recent years, surpassing even Galileo and his apostrophe, may have been Laura Hillenbrand's *Seabiscuit.* Talk about transcending your genre! Who would have thought it possible for a sports book—and a horseracing one at that—to become a book-club favorite, discussed and adored by the wine-sipping, Jodi Picoult crowd. So, what accounts for this remarkable success story? We'll assume it wasn't the horses themselves, or even the Nathan Detroit types hanging around the backstretch. So was it the underdog angle? Or the heartwarming look at Depression-era America (*Annie Goes to the Races*)? Or the multiple protagonists—horse, jockey, and trainer—each a rich, fully developed, novelistic character, complete with plenty of backstory? Or was it simply Hillenbrand's storytelling ability?

Publishers have tried everything to recapture the *Seabiscuit* magic, from a long string of horse biographies (Man o' War, Native Dancer, Funny Cide, and Barbaro all have their own books) to an even longer line of historical rags-to-riches sagas starring all manner of athletes (golfers, bicycle racers, swimmers, boxers). Most of these entries in the Seabiscuit Sweepstakes have been perfectly good books, but so far, none of them has captured nearly as wide a range of readers as the "nondescript little bay horse" who dominated the sport of kings in the 1930s.

Frankly, whenever a new galley arrives on my desk with the words "For every reader who loved *Seabiscuit*" plastered on the promo copy, I feel sorry for the unlucky author. There's nothing worse than being called "the next Michael Jordan," "the next Tiger Woods," or "the next Seabiscuit." In the case of Seabiscuit, it's almost an oxymoron. Both horse and book came from nowhere, free of media hype, and it was that obscurity— the very unlikeliness of the horse's victories and the book's appeal—that made the subsequent success stories so remarkable. Therefore, as soon as someone mumbles "the next Seabiscuit" about a new book, it is immediately impossible for that poor book to become anything like Hillenbrand's phenomenon.

But that doesn't mean the faux *Seabiscuits* deserve anonymity. So, as a way of offering mea culpas for those occasions when *Booklist* has joined the chorus and heralded a new book by comparing it to *Seabiscuit*, I'd like to mention a few books that deserve to be read by narrative nonfiction lovers for the stories they tell and the way they tell them—not for any similarities to you know who:

> *Major: A Black Athlete, a White Era, and the Fight to Be the World's Fastest Human Being,* by Todd Balf (Crown, 2008). Marshall "Major" Taylor, an African American bicycle racer in the early twentieth century, when the sport was just emerging, became the world's least likely celebrity, "the fastest man on two wheels." Balf tells the parallel stories of Taylor's triumphs and the transition of bicycling from leisurely pastime to spectator sport with a cinematic eye, combining strong visual descriptions and sharp characterizations.

> *The Great Swim,* by Gavin Mortimer (Walker, 2008). In 1926, four Americans competed to become the first woman to swim the English Channel. Tabloids promoted their favorites, and the public was enthralled, much as we are today with the contestants on, say, *Dancing with the Stars.* The swimming story is absorbing in itself, but what really works here is the exploration of our timeless fascination with celebrity.

> *Twelve Mighty Orphans,* by Jim Dent (St. Martin's, 2007). No, it's not *Annie in Shoulder Pads,* but it is about orphans in the Depression, and the orphans do overcome great odds, and they are definitely lovable—thankfully, nobody sings "Tomorrow." Instead, the orphans at the Masonic Home outside Fort Worth play football and play it very well, despite being severely undersized and ill-equipped. Yes, we've heard it all before, from *The Bad News Bears* to *Rocky* to *The Karate Kid,* but when a writer combines sports, inspiration, and popular history with the proper eye for realistic detail and the ability to keep his foot off the smarm pedal, it's hard to resist.

And if these books sound good, have I got a horse for you . . .

Booklist, May 15, 2008

TRYING TO READ STENDHAL

His Lordship's servants appeared, carrying a magnificent dais; M. Chelan took one of the poles, but actually it was Julien who bore it. The Bishop took his place beneath it. He had really succeeded in giving himself the air of an old man; our hero's admiration knew no bounds. "What cannot one do if one is clever!" he thought.

—from *The Red and the Black*, by Stendhal (1830)

His room was on the south side of the hotel. I went over and looked out. It was still foggy, gray. But you could see south to the squat, monstrous Merchandise Mart Building, and between the Wacker and it the ugly west near-north side. Mostly ugly old brick buildings hiding ugly lives.

—from *The Fabulous Clipjoint*, by Fredric Brown (1947)

LAST AUGUST, I BEGAN a four-month sabbatical leave from *Booklist*. I had many lofty goals (write a book, clean the basement, find my golf game), all of which remain unachieved. In fact, I don't think I truly believed I would accomplish any of those projects (especially cleaning the basement), but I had another, more realistic goal, and I was absolutely determined to achieve it. I would, finally, read Stendhal's *The Red and the Black*, thus ending 35 years of frustration. I failed.

What happened? You would think that a book review editor with four months of time on his hands could manage to read one book, even a big one. The short answer is, after a mere 154 pages of Stendhal, I wandered into a fabulous clipjoint operated by pulp novelist Fredric Brown, and I never came out. But how could a relatively unheralded paperback writer of the 1940s and '50s, a man whose books are now almost all out of print, steal my attention from *The Red and the Black*, often considered the father of the modern novel?

Questions of why fiction readers like what they like are much on the minds these days of an enterprising group of academics doing research in the burgeoning field of reader's-advisory studies. It turns out that a reader's motivations can be every bit as psychologically rich as those of a fictional character, say, Julien Sorel, the hero of *The Red and the Black*. Many critics believe Sorel paved the way for a long line of twentieth-century characters (think Proust and Joyce, especially) distinguished not so much by their actions as by the complexity of their thoughts. (I can't tell you all that much about Sorel's thoughts, having sampled so few of them, except to say that he's an ambitious poor kid trying to make it with the provincial big shots, but he's weighed down by an enormous chip on his shoulder and a tendency to mope—sort of a nineteenth-century version of Faulkner's Flem Snopes, albeit neither as smart nor as focused.) According to the scholars, however, Sorel's thoughts, whatever they may be, are no more important than my own! Now we're getting somewhere: my reasons for not reading the story of Julien Sorel are as psychologically tasty (in that Proustian kind of way) as Sorel's own motivations for his actions, which are commonly thought to be the main reason to read about him.

Unfortunately, I must leave it to the academics to decide if I really am as interesting a character as Julien Sorel. Clearly, I'm prejudiced on the matter. I only made it through 154 pages of Sorel's story, but I remain consumed by even the smallest details of my own. And, yet, I continue to view my failure to read *The Red and the Black* as a stain on my character. It hardly seems fair. Why shouldn't I be drawn away from Restoration France, Stendhal's setting, by a snappy, hard-boiled tale that takes place right in my own backyard? Fredric Brown, you see, spent much of his life in Chicago, and *The Fabulous Clipjoint*, the first in his series of Ed and Am Hunter novels, is set just a few blocks from my office. In the quote above, narrator Ed Hunter is describing the view from the Wacker Hotel, which still stands three blocks down Huron Street from ALA Headquarters. I used to live in an apartment not far from there, and I shared the view Brown describes of "the squat, monstrous Merchandise Mart."

I don't claim, of course, that a familiar setting carries much weight as a reason for reading fiction. Clearly, it's not on the same scale as getting a handle on the father of the modern novel. Fredric Brown is no Stendhal, that's for sure, but in his defense, there are a few more reasons to read him than having lived in his neighborhood. Brown is something of an anomaly among so-called noir novelists. His work is not nearly as dark and perverse as that of, say, Jim Thompson, and his style is far more polished. His streets are mean, but his characters are amiable, and the prose is almost jaunty. If Stendhal gave birth to the psychologically ripe hero, Brown anticipated the hordes of contemporary detective writers who combine grit with wit.

Ah, but let's face it. It's a fool's errand to try to justify reading Brown over Stendhal on literary critical terms. I know readers' advisors are taught not to make value judgments about what they call "appeal factors," but what if the reader himself—that would be me, he of the fascinating thoughts—feels guilty about his own reading choices?

Perhaps the best way out of my Stendhal quandary is to blame my parents. If they hadn't fed me all that stuff about growing up in the Depression, and how you had to work hard because disaster could strike at any second, maybe then I could just read what I wanted to read when I wanted to read it. I'm starting to feel better about my sabbatical already. Frederic Brown is no longer the lowbrow who seduced me away from a mind-expanding literary experience with the cotton candy of familiar pleasures. On the contrary, thanks to Brown, I am released from the chains of guilt, free to enjoy my literary moments however I choose. Now there's some real grist for the reader's-advisory mill.

But what of poor Stendhal, reduced from the father of the modern novel to a symbol of outmoded, Depression-era thinking? Well, there's always my next sabbatical.

Booklist, February 1, 2003

SHORT LISTS, APPLES, AND ORANGES

WHEN YOU WORK AT a magazine published as often as *Booklist*, it's not hard to grasp what Einstein was getting at with that whole relativity thing. Time is a very elastic concept around here. As I'm writing this column for the December 15, 2008, issue, I'm also editing material for our January 1 and 15, 2009, issue and writing reviews that will appear in February. So it seems perfectly natural to begin this column with a quote from Joyce Saricks that won't be published until next month. If that bothers you, consult Einstein.

But back to Joyce. She opens her January "At Leisure" column with a rhetorical question: "Who among book lovers doesn't love this season, when everyone lists their top books of the previous year?" Well, Joyce, I know you think the answer to that question is no one, but there is one group of book lovers who might have some ambivalent feelings about the book-award season. I'm referring, of course, to the people who select the awards.

We've just finished compiling our 2008 *Booklist* Editors' Choice and Top of the List winners. Along with Adult Books Editor Brad Hooper and his staff, I take part in choosing the Top of the List books in adult fiction and nonfiction. It's never an easy job, but this year, in the fiction category, it was particularly agonizing—so much so that when I read Joyce's question about book awards, I immediately thought, I don't, that's who.

Yes, we all like to read best-book lists and be reminded of what we've missed or, contrarily, revel in righteous indignation when we believe the wrong book won and the right book was overlooked. That's the point of lists, after all, so the worst thing a book-award selector can do is to take him- or herself too seriously. Yes, yes, I understand all that, but when you're faced with choosing one novel as the best of a short list of three, and when all three are brilliant books and utterly different from one another, well, that's just too damn hard.

I'm not going to reveal our 2008 Top of the List winner for adult fiction—barring any Einsteinian abilities to bend time, you'll have to wait until January for that—but I am going to talk about the short list of books from which we chose our winner. One of those three was Dennis Lehane's *The Given Day*. Lehane usually writes crime thrillers that jump between past and present, but this time he has produced his first full-scale historical epic, a detail-rich exploration of America at the end of World War I that takes as its centerpiece the Boston Police Strike of 1919. Like William Kennedy's Albany novels, *The Given Day* looks closely at the conundrum of the American family and its power to simultaneously imprison and sustain us, and like E. L. Doctorow in *Ragtime*, Lehane captures the sense of a country's turbulent coming-of-age. *The Given Day* would make a superb Top of the List novel.

But so would Richard Price's very different *Lush Life*. Where Lehane's novel is broad-canvas historical fiction, Price's has a narrow scope—the events surrounding one robbery-murder on New York's Lower East Side. Lehane embraces the past, while Price locks into the present moment. The streets of the Lower East Side are rich in immigrant history, of course, but Price's characters—the young professionals who are gentrifying the neighborhood, the kids with guns who hover on its edges, the cops who clean up the messes—are all consumed by the nowness of life. But that nowness is a fragile commodity, and Price shows us the fear and desperation behind the swagger of the moment, whether it's the café owner wondering how long his place will stay hip, or the waiter-writer trying not to admit that he's really just a waiter, or the aging detective who sees all of life with cop eyes—"the compulsion to imagine the overlay of the dead wherever he goes." Price's experience as a writer on *The Wire* is evident here in the seamless way he combines social drama with a penetrating portrayal of the inner life of city streets, where a bullet remains the quickest way to change now into then.

If Lehane rolls on the wave of history and Price stands firm in the present, Aleksandar Hemon, in *The Lazarus Project*, the third novel on our Top of the List short list, manages to keep one foot in each camp. Vladimir Brik is a contemporary Bosnian writer living in Chicago who returns to Eastern Europe to research a novel he is writing about Lazarus Averbuch, a Jewish immigrant in the early twentieth century who attempted to visit Chicago's chief of police and was shot to death before he could state his business. Weaving between the Lazarus story, his own experience as an immigrant in Chicago, and his travels in Bosnia and Moldova, Brik proves a mesmerizing narrator, part Nabokovian tragic hero and part new immigrant scam artist. Past and present blend into a bloody superhighway across time in this bravura road novel, the pogroms of one era morphing into the genocide of another.

Stylistically, Hemon is a dizzying mix of baroque and postmodern, while Lehane, at least in *The Given Day*, is mainstream Dickensian; Price, on the other hand, combines the muscular prose of Jim Harrison with the poetry of Daniel Woodrell. Three radically opposed styles, then, but each employed brilliantly to tell three equally moving stories. So how do you say which one is the best? You don't, not really. Yes, you pick a winner in the end but always recognizing that apples and oranges have their own appeal. If everyone who reads this column reads all three of these books, then my belief in book awards will be reaffirmed. Joyce, I guess you were right all along.

Booklist, December 15, 2008

FIGHTING THE GOOD FIGHT

NOT LONG AGO I received an e-mail from a Back Page reader who said, "Why are you always bringing up D. H. Lawrence? Don't you know nobody reads him anymore?" Yes, yes, I thought to myself, of course I know that Lawrence is out of favor, but I don't give a damn. He's not out of favor with me, and it's my column. But, later, after yet another management meeting at which the ever-scintillating topic of "changing demographics" was bandied about, I started worrying. Maybe I was losing touch with my audience. Should I join the twenty-first century and start writing columns about Web 2.0?

Then a book with a simple black-and-white cover arrived on my desk called *Resisting Our Culture of Conformity: In the Hills of Southern Ohio and in the Groves of Academe*, by Wayne Burns. Further investigation found a personal note inside, confirming that this was the same Wayne Burns with whom I'd studied at the University of Washington some 36 years ago. I had come to know Wayne a little at that time, after taking his graduate course on European fiction, a class that would forever change the way I read books. I had abandoned my graduate studies in English by then and was slogging my way through library school, determined to get a degree that would make me employable but trying to do so while taking as few library-science courses as humanly possible.

My goal in sneaking back to the English department as often as I could was merely to earn some credits while reading books I wanted to read. I got that in Wayne's class, but I also got a lot more. Wayne believed in letting his students know how he approached literature, and as he explained the literary theory he called the Panzaic Principle, I felt a kind of resonance that I had rarely experienced through my years as an English major. The theory amounts to a relatively simple notion: in the finest novels, the real will always undercut the ideal, the way Sancho Panza's belly gives the lie to Don Quixote's idealistic posturings. This was only the starting point, of course; there was much talk of Lawrentian phalluses and Cézanne's apples, and how they, too, exhibited the Panzaic Principle, and how systems of belief, any belief, stood firmly in the way of an individual's ability to experience life fully. It was exciting stuff, whether or not you agreed, but beyond the theory itself, what really distinguished Wayne's teaching was the way he insisted on making connections between literature and life, your life and my life.

I had lost touch with Wayne over the decades, though I had heard that he was running into more and more trouble in his classes at Washington. The late 1960s and early 1970s were not a good time to suggest that ideals—any ideals—were potentially deadly. The radicals of my generation loved the idea of undercutting the ideals of the Establishment, but they didn't take kindly to the notion that their own ideals were fair game, too. When Wayne responded to a student's irate question by saying that, yes, he would put his own life before any cause, the battle lines were drawn. After fighting McCarthyism in the 1950s, he would now face what he called the McCarthyism of the student Left.

I knew a little of all of this—it had begun in my era—but I knew virtually nothing of Wayne's earlier life, which is detailed in his new book, published last year as its author turned 90. This autobiographical sketch tells the remarkable story of how one man managed to live through most of the twentieth century and into the twenty-first as a no-holds-barred nonconformist. Such a life, utterly inconceivable today, probably wouldn't have been possible then, either, had not Burns experienced an almost Huck Finn–like early childhood on a farm in southern Ohio, virtually free of societal interference and protected by a doting mother and two eccentric uncles. Society got its licks in eventually, though, in the form of a tyrannical scoutmaster, disapproving parents of various girlfriends and wives, the FBI (who were convinced that his application to be a "non-religious conscientious objector" during World War II meant he was a Communist), and eventually, English departments across the country, from Harvard to Berkeley, who objected to Wayne's manner of engaging his students in discussion and his refusal to become what he calls a "scholar-clubman."

Wayne finally found a home at Washington, where his theories and classroom techniques were no more popular with his colleagues than before, but where he at last enjoyed the kind of academic freedom that allowed him to teach the way he wanted to teach and write what he wanted to write. Until the 1970s, that is, when students decided they would only listen to what they wanted to hear.

Much of his book is literary theory, but amazingly, it rarely reads that way. When Wayne talks of how Lawrence's critical writings and those of Ortega y Gasset crystallized his own ideas into what became the Panzaic Principle, it doesn't sound like a professor spouting theory but like a man passionately describing a watershed moment in his emotional and intellectual life. The tone is no different, really, than when Wayne describes his marriages and relationships and how they have affected his life or when he recounts the horrific ordeal he endured in the process of applying for and eventually receiving his conscientious-objector status.

Wayne finds little hope in today's world, a world in which he believes individual human beings are more under the thumb of tyrannical scoutmasters than ever before. But he does believe that the intransigent few, those who still covet Falstaff's "self-sufficient careless individuality," can find ways to be happy, bobbing and weaving in the belly of the organizational beast. I think so, too, and that's why, even in the face of changing demographics, D. H. Lawrence still has a home on this Back Page.

Booklist, December 1, 2007

Genre Fiction

DETECTIVE OF THE HEART

You might come here Sunday on a whim.
Say your life broke down. The last good kiss
you had was years ago. You walk these streets
laid out by the insane, past hotels
that didn't last, bars that did, the tortured try
of local drivers to accelerate their lives.
Only churches are kept up. The jail
turned 70 this year. The only prisoner
is always in, not knowing what he's done.

— From "Degrees of Gray in Philipsburg," by Richard Hugo

IT WAS RICHARD HUGO'S "Degrees of Gray in Philipsburg" that gave James Crumley the title to what many consider the best American hard-boiled mystery ever written: *The Last Good Kiss*. Crumley and Hugo were friends—they both taught creative writing at the University of Montana in Missoula—so it's hardly surprising that the novelist dedicated his book to the poet who supplied the title. But the dedication itself—"for Dick Hugo, grand old detective of the heart"—suggests more. Yes, Richard Hugo's poems display an uncommon understanding of the human heart, the kind of understanding that requires a detective's ability to look beyond the surface of things. But, more than that, many of Hugo's poems are hard-boiled novels waiting to happen. Noir means black in French, of course, but the unremitting bleakness we associate with the noir novel lives in degrees of gray, Hugo's lonely men sitting in lonely bars, nursing their drinks as they recite their grievances against an unforgiving world.

Hugo, who died suddenly in 1982, wrote about the noir world with both a poet's precision and a detective's heart. It was as if every burst of eloquence that ever found its way into a hard-boiled novel, sneaking in through the side door past all the whodunit detritus, had somehow been expressed—sharper, deeper, more resonant—in Hugo's poetry. In his early work, he found in the Seattle of his youth, along the forlorn streets that lined the lower reaches of the Duwamish River ("Some places are forever afternoon," he said in "West Marginal Way"), echoes of the same desolation that he would later locate in the bars and along the roadsides of rural Montana. Is it merely a coincidence that, today, hard-boiled fiction

61

thrives not only in the Northwest in general but in Seattle and Montana in particular?

The connection between Hugo and crime fiction extends well beyond the imagery in his poetry. Hugo wrote one mystery, the now criminally out-of-print *Death and the Good Life*. It was published in 1981 to considerable acclaim, but Hugo died only a year later, denying his readers a full-fledged series starring the inimitable Al "Mush Heart" Barnes, deputy sheriff of Plains, Montana. Barnes earned his nickname in Seattle, where he was regarded as the city's softest cop, too sentimental even to give a parking ticket. Relocated to Plains, Mush Heart has little to occupy his working hours, but he finds plenty to enjoy off the job: fishing, drinking, sleeping with Arlene, the owner of his favorite bar. Then an ax murderer comes to town, and Mush Heart must go back to being a detective. And, not surprisingly, he is very much a detective of the heart: "People tell me things, and I don't why. For some reason, people trust me. I must look sympathetic and understanding."

A first novelist, Hugo fumbled a bit with plotting and procedural detail, but you could tell from the start, he was a natural. *Death and the Good Life* may be the only hard-boiled novel in the genre with a soft-boiled hero, but it works perfectly. Mush Heart is the kind of guy who cries when he drinks. He's seen a lot of people whose lives broke down, and he knows that, one day, his might, too. But all that pain doesn't make him tough or stoic; it makes him want to have a drink and maybe a good cry. There's nobody quite like Mush Heart in the crime-fiction world. Sure, there are plenty of softies, but they don't live in hard worlds, and, sure, there are plenty of tough guys standing up to the toughness around them. But Mush Heart—soldiering on amid degrees of gray, fretting about the sadness he sees and feels, drinking it away sometimes, finding someone in whose arms he can try to love it away—is probably a lot more like you and me.

It would have made a great series, and we know he planned to write more. In an interview with fellow Montana writer William Kittredge, published in *The Real West Marginal Way*, a wonderful collection of Hugo's autobiographical essays, he talks about what would have been the second Mush Heart novel. It was going to start in Plains and perhaps end up in Seattle. But death got in the way. We're left with the poems, but if we look closely at them, we can find dozens of crime novels that might have been. In "The Lady in Kicking Horse Reservoir," for example, Hugo imagines the dead body of a former lover submerged and forgotten in the reservoir: "Not my hands but green across you now, / Green tons hold you down, and ten bass curve / teasing in your hair. Summer slime will pile deep on your breast." Think about Mush Heart investigating that murder, sympathizing with the jilted lover, wanting him to be innocent, spilling a tear over his pain. Or find the backstory from "Death of the Kapowsin Tavern," about a favorite bar on the Washington coast, destroyed by fire: "I can't ridge it back again from char. / Not one board left." But every bar holds dozens of stories, and any of those stories could make a crime novel: "Nothing dies as slowly as a scene. / The dusty jukebox cracking through the cackle of a beered-up crone — / wagered wine — sudden need to dance — / these remain in the black debris."

Richard Hugo didn't have time to write all the noir novels hiding in his poems, but his detective's heart still beats loudly in the Northwest, not only in the work of Crumley but in dozens of others, writers who taste their first drink of the evening and think immediately of Hugo's line from a poem called "Port Townsend": "A novel fakes a start in every bar."

Booklist, May 1, 2005

MICHAEL CONNELLY'S LOS ANGELES

A SENSE OF PLACE is one of those terms, like noir or character-driven, that reviewers bandy about when they are having trouble getting at the heart of the matter. Hiding behind a phalanx of recognizable critical catch-phrases allows us to move forward without ever really making sense of such questions as why, in the works of certain writers, the landscape of the story seems to acquire a level of meaning far beyond geography. Sure, readers of crime fiction recognize that Raymond Chandler's Los Angeles is a special place, intimately connected to the birth of the hard-boiled novel, and that, more recently, Michael Connelly's Los Angeles is special, too, a kind of redrawn version of Chandler's map, but what is it precisely that makes those places special? To say that Chandler's or Connelly's novels possess a "great sense of place" is hopelessly vague, like directing a Chicagoan to Los Angeles by telling him to go south and then turn right.

What we need to help us understand landscape in fiction is a different kind of map, one that recognizes the intersection of metaphor and meaning the way a topographical map shows varying kinds of terrain. Readers who are quick to buy Connelly's superb new novel, *The Narrows*, will receive something like that metaphorical map in the form of a limited-edition DVD, *Blue Neon Night: Michael Connelly's Los Angeles*. Combining excerpts from Connelly's 14 books (read by William Petersen, star of *To Live and Die in L.A.*) with the author's musings on why he finds the city such a fertile setting for crime fiction, the DVD sets Connelly's words against expertly photographed footage of the places he discusses. (Interestingly, the DVD is directed by filmmaker Terrill Lee Lankford, whose first novel, *Earthquake Weather*, is a moody crime tale set in Los Angeles.)

But the DVD is no simple travelogue. Lankford wisely has Connelly do much of his talking while driving the streets of the city, thus capturing the single most significant aspect of landscape in Connelly's novels: motion. Harry Bosch, Connelly's hero, sees the city, usually at night, through the windshield of his car, and he describes it to us from that vantage point. Occasionally, he comments on the vista from the porch of his stilt house in the Hollywood Hills, but even then, motion is implied, both by the "carpet of lights" he sees on the freeway below him and by the ever-present possibility of an earthquake, which would "send his house down the hill like a sled."

Motion is significant in Connelly's world because it suggests constant change, which in turn creates an all-pervasive sense of randomness: If the victim had taken the Santa Monica Freeway instead of Wilshire Boulevard, he might not have stopped for a drink at that particular bar and met that particular woman. . . . Life can seem random anywhere, of course, even in relatively stationary landscapes, but it is exaggerated when we are so often in motion and when the distance between safety and danger is never a fixed point.

Raymond Chandler knew about motion, too. The "carpet of lights" wasn't quite as long when he was writing, but it was growing steadily. Chandler saw the birth of Connelly's L.A., and he hated it. When his hero, Philip Marlowe, was driving the streets, his eyes never quite left the rear-view mirror, looking back to a different city, a more innocent place, a more static place, a place not quite so prone to random violence. Chandler gave us our first detailed map of Los Angeles as a nightmare landscape, our first glimpse of where the wild things are. Nobody (except Nathanael West) had seen Los Angeles that way before Chandler, but now it's become second nature, the way we see urban life in general, the reason Connelly named his hero, known as Harry to his friends, after the master of surrealistic nightmare, painter Hieronymous Bosch.

The difference between Chandler's landscape and Connelly's is the way Chandler fights it. He wants to be somewhere else—the England of his childhood, perhaps, where the white cliffs of Dover don't move in the night. Marlowe dreams bitterly of a house in the country; Bosch knows he could never live anywhere except L.A.: "He loved the city most at night. . . . It was in the dark slipstream that he believed he moved most freely, behind the cover of shadows, like a rider in a limo. There was a random feel to the dark, the quirkiness of chance played out in the blue neon night. So many ways to live, and to die."

Toward the end of the DVD, Connelly makes a curious remark: "In their own way, I want my books to be love letters to Los Angeles." Chandler never wrote love letters to his city, or if he did, it was only to the city the way it used to be. Connelly finds and treasures emblems of lost innocence, or at least lost beauty, in the past of Los Angeles, too, in the Bradbury Building, for example, which Bosch celebrates in *Angels Flight* (1999). But the difference is that, for Connelly, the nightmare side of Los Angeles today is a source of energy as well as pain, of grace under pressure as well as random bursts of senselessness, and he sees that duality every day through his windshield. You won't find that concept on a map, though, not even a metaphorical one, but it's not so hard to visualize as Bosch steers his way down Sunset Boulevard, "from the barrios to the beaches," or as he gazes at the city from his deck, admiring the sunset even as he remembers that it's the smog that makes the colors so beautiful. Maybe, in fact, if we can start to understand how the blue neon nights of a character named Hieronymous Bosch are the stuff of both nightmares and love letters, we'll begin to know what it means to say that Michael Connelly's novels have a great sense of place.

Booklist, May 1, 2004

WASHINGTON, D.C., THROUGH PELECANOS' EYES

WASHINGTON, D.C., IS HOSTING the American Library Association's Annual Conference this month, prompting the idea that I should write something about the city for the Back Page. But then I remembered that I'm uniquely unqualified to do that. Although I've spent a fair amount of time in Washington over the years, it's been mainly as a tourist or a conventioneer—probably the two least-respected kinds of visitors to any city. I was invited to the White House once, for a school library conference organized by Laura Bush, but I wrote about my ambivalent responses to that experience some years ago ("Bill's Excellent Adventure—at the White House"). And my well-documented aversion to politics of every stripe—and, especially, to political commentary—certainly rules out any musings I might come up with on the latest spate of books by and about today's crop of aspiring politicians. "A plague on both your houses" hardly fills up a whole column, even if I did add a paragraph or two about my new favorite crackpot, Mike ("These candidates scare me!") Gravel. Is it too early to hope that he might be the Admiral James Stockdale of the twenty-first century?

But, then, after ruling out Washington politics as a subject, it occurred to me that I do know something about the city. It's secondhand knowledge, of course, acquired reading novels rather than walking streets, but if you're going to learn about a place through books, you could do worse than picking George Pelecanos as your guide. In novels like *Down by the River Where the Dead Men Go* (1995), Pelecanos' graphic, hard-boiled style and noir sensibility quickly established him as something special, but it wasn't until a few books later that the full scope of his vision became clear, and readers began to realize that he was fashioning a multifaceted fictional universe united by a common landscape—the streets of Washington, D.C.—and featuring an interlocking set of characters that eventually would span several generations. The characters in Pelecanos' world fall into distinct groups—Nick Stefanos, Marcus Clay, and Derek Strange all have what amounts to their own series—but the people from one group intermingle with those of another in Faulknerian fashion, and individual novels go back and forth in time, allowing Pelecanos to evoke the same streets and neighborhoods during different decades, from the 1940s through the present, and build context both in terms of character development and landscape.

The streets of Pelecanos' Washington aren't just places—14th and S, where Nick's diner sits during World War II, in *The Big Blowdown*; or Connecticut Avenue, where Marcus Clay's Real Right Records is located in *King Suckerman*—but sounds, too. I can't think of another writer who uses popular culture as well as Pelecanos to evoke not just an era but also subtle differences in character. It's commonplace, of course, to clutter the scenery in a period novel with brand names, but Pelecanos goes further, using music, cars, and clothes as effective entrées into the troubled hearts and minds of his characters. *King Suckerman*, for example, starts off as an homage to the blaxploitation films of the '70s, but it sucker punches you with its humanity, revealing the desperation and even the naked fear that lurk behind the strut. The novel's cinematic, ultraviolent climax takes place in the shadow of the Washington Monument, during the July 4, 1976, Bicentennial Celebration, but it's not about patriotism or honor. It's about two men, one black and one white, craving the solace of an ordinary life but being forced to fight for it.

A tour of Pelecanos' streets starts with *The Big Blowdown*, his second novel, which takes place from the 1930s through the 1950s. The featured players are the first generation of Pelecanos' people: Pete Karras, father of Dimitri, who takes part in that confrontation at the end of *King Suckerman*, and Nick Stefanos, grandfather of the Nick Stefanos who stars on his own in the earlier noirs and makes supporting appearances in the later Derek Strange novels. Grandfather Nick owns a diner in the city, and Karras is his cook. The novel is awash in the sights and sounds of wartime D.C. and its aftermath; we see the postwar growth of the city and the beginnings of the racial conflict that would eventually tear it apart, but we also see a Greek immigrant walking the streets, listening to the blues:

> *Karras walked up to U, headed east. He took his time, stopped to put fire to a smoke, watched the stylishly dressed Negroes arm-in-arm with their women on the street. Karras listened to the blues singers' voices coming from the clubs, the strange jazz further along U, the occasional horn blast from taxis and cars, the hiss of tire on asphalt, the gentle, southern rise and fall in the inflection of these people's voices, their laughter, all of it comforting somehow, this warming, familiar symphony.*

The voices on Pelecanos' streets aren't always comforting. As the novels move through the decades, the sounds of conflict tend to dominate. In the foreground of the novels set from the 1980s to the present (*Hell to Pay* or *Soul Circus*, for example), there is typically a train wreck waiting to happen—often drug deals soon to go bad—but Pelecanos focuses our attention on the people destined to cross the railroad tracks at the wrong time: doomed criminals, equally doomed cops, soul-suffering mothers and fathers. We hear their voices, we listen to them talk movies and music, and we watch them die.

But people live on Pelecanos' streets, too. His real subject isn't crime; it's the nature of daily life in an American inner city—the potent mixture of resolve, weakness, love, and, yes, violence that percolates in Washington, D.C.'s roughest neighborhoods, where obstacles far outnumber opportunities. That's a subject that few of Washington's politicians know much of anything about.

Booklist, June 1, 2007

HARD-BOILED CHICAGO JUST AROUND THE CORNER

THE CHICAGO NEIGHBORHOOD WHERE my office is located began its decline when the Woolworth's was torn down and replaced by an Omni hotel. It was a classic Woolworth's, with rows of serendipitously displayed "novelties" and one of those horseshoe-shaped lunch counters, the kind where you could get a grilled-cheese sandwich on plain white bread for about $2. The Omni, of course, is a horse of an entirely different color, and soon it was followed by more of the same breed, including an upscale mall called Chicago Place, where the usual suspects—Talbots, Ann Taylor, et al.—have been rounded up yet again.

Tourists pouring into a mall and embarking on the great American pastime—shopping—certainly sound like the antithesis of hard-boiled. Yes, but not always. As I was working my way through the books discussed in the "Hard-Boiled Gazetteer to Chicago," I realized that my neighborhood's glorious past goes well beyond grilled-cheese sandwiches. There are plenty of bodies—fictional and otherwise—buried in the blocks around ALA, and on a chilly Tuesday afternoon not long ago, I set out to find them.

Slipping out the 50 E. Huron entrance to ALA Headquarters undetected by our security guards, who recently reported me for failing to wear my identity badge 70 percent of the time during 2002, I strolled east on Huron Street in the midst of the lunch-hour crowd. Looking nostalgically at the corner where Woolworth's once sat, I turned north on Rush and proceeded past Chicago Place to the corner of Rush and Chicago Avenue, where I was nearly trampled by a gaggle of prepubescent girls swinging American Girl bags. I avoided being beaned by a Molly doll, but I couldn't escape a full frontal assault of irony. On this same corner, now shared by American Girl and Comp USA, once sat a liquor store run by novelist Barry Gifford's gangster father in the 1940s and early '50s. Described in Gifford's wonderful memoir, *A Good Man to Know*, the store was a "drop joint for stolen goods, dope, whatever somebody wanted to stash for a while." Gifford used to see his dad giving friends "penicillin shots" in the basement, just a few feet below where young girls now take tea with their dolls.

Just south on Rush from Gifford's liquor store was the Club Alabam, where Gifford watched the showgirls rehearse on Saturday mornings and where the bookies in Steve Monroe's *'57 Chicago* listened to jazz after a hard night laying off bets. The oh-so-chic Peninsula Hotel now sits about where the Club Alabam was, but when I first worked at *Booklist*, the original building was still there, complete with the remains of a neon sign on the roof. In those days, in the early '80s, the club had morphed into Joe Pierce's Deli, renowned for its Italian beef sandwiches (an excellent alternative to Woolworth's).

Proceeding west on the north side of Chicago Avenue, one undergoes culture shock in reverse. For some reason, this block has resisted the American Girl influence. A check-cashing store, a tavern, and a down-market McDonald's all help to keep the tourists away. Perhaps that's why Eugene Izzi picked a dead-end alley on this block to dump the body in *The Criminalist*. A couple of blocks further down Chicago Avenue used to be the location of the Twenty-Eighth District police station, home to the cops in many of Izzi's and Barbara D'Amato's novels. Now there's an empty lot on the spot, apparently awaiting condos.

A couple more stops before it's time to go back to work. If we turn south from Chicago Avenue on Franklin Street and follow the El tracks a few blocks, we come to an alley where the body of Ed Hunter's father was found in *The Fabulous Clipjoint*. Now called River North, this trendy art-gallery district was considered a slum in the '40s, when the novel was written. Today, at the corner of Huron and Franklin, there is an art gallery called Arms Akimbo. I suppose it's too much to hope that the gallery owner named his space after the position of a fictional body that landed nearby about 60 years ago.

It's a five-minute walk down Huron back to the office, so we have plenty of time to pause at the Wacker Hotel on the corner of Clark and Huron. The Wacker was home to Am Hunter, Ed's uncle, who helped his nephew solve the murder of Ed's father. Remarkably, the hotel itself hasn't changed much since Am lived there. Brown describes the view south from Am's twelfth-floor room as "mostly ugly brick buildings hiding ugly lives." Ugly takes on a new meaning for anyone looking out Am's window today. The brick buildings are largely gone, but in their place, at the intersection of Clark and Ontario, sits this stunning display of ersatz gaudiness: a Hard Rock Café, a Rainforest Café, and a supersized McDonald's. On any given Friday night, thousands of tourists stand at the intersection pondering their chain-dining alternatives.

Speaking of food, my lunch hour is over, and I'm hungry. The Italian deli on the ground floor of the ALA building does a perfectly serviceable three-cheese tostino, but no, on second thought, I'll pass. It would just remind me of Woolworth's.

Booklist, May 1, 2003

IT BEGAN WITH BECK

Sexual intercourse began
In nineteen sixty-three
(which was rather late for me)—
Between the end of the Chatterley ban
And the Beatles first LP.

—from "Annus Mirabilis," by Philip Larkin

THE TROUBLE WITH BIG pictures is that they're always too big. When we generalize about eras in anything—literary history, sports, even sex— we always strive to find precise demarcation points ("between the end of the Chatterley ban . . ."), but in fact, none exist. And yet, those demarcation points usually do make a kind of sense, if only in that wobbly sort of way that everything makes sense after the fourth drink. Philip Larkin gets it exactly right, ridiculing the whole idea of generational time lines but still feeling a bit perturbed about being too old to get the most out of the sixties.

These musings are prompted by having spent the better part of the last month reading and rereading Scandinavian crime novels and looking, perhaps foolishly, for big pictures. I found a few—it's an easy enough trick, really, a little like setting your printer on "landscape"—and I report my findings in "A Hard-Boiled Gazetteer to Scandinavia." But, like all big pictures, my vision gets a little out of focus when you turn the zoom lens on. Yes, it's certainly true that Swedish author Henning Mankell led an onslaught of Scandinavian crime novelists to international popularity beginning in the late 1990s, but Mankell wasn't the first writer to see trouble brewing beneath the placid surface of Scandinavian society.

The husband-and-wife team of Maj Sjöwall and Per Wahlöö were on the case 30 years before Mankell, and the hero of their groundbreaking 10-novel police procedural series, Detective Inspector Martin Beck, is unquestionably godfather to Mankell's Kurt Wallander and all the other twenty-first-century Scandinavian sleuths. Both committed to radical politics, Sjöwall and Wahlöö set out "to use the crime novel as a scalpel cutting open the belly of an ideologically pauperized and morally debatable so-called welfare state of the bourgeois type." The 10-novel sequence began in 1965 with *Roseanna* and continued through 1975, when the finale, *The Terrorists*, was published shortly after Wahlöö's death. Unlike most European crime fiction of the time, the series was immediately translated into English and met with widespread critical acclaim in the U.S.—surprising given the political emphasis (the last word in the series is, symbolically, "Marx").

I first read the Martin Beck books in the late 1970s and found them unlike any other crime fiction of the time, with the exception of Ed Mc-Bain's 87th Precinct series, to which the Beck novels, also in the "station house" tradition and portraying the lives and careers of a squad of homicide detectives, are clearly indebted. But Sjöwall and Wahlöö are more interested in the inner lives of their characters than McBain, and Beck is a far more vulnerable figure than McBain's Steve Carella or any of the other hard-boiled heroes of that era. And, of course, the overtly left-wing point of view set the Beck series apart while giving it something in common with the similarly inclined younger readers of the sixties generation.

But how does Martin Beck hold up today, when vulnerability has become a common character trait among European detectives and when the idea of communism as a solution to society's ills seems naive at best? I decided to find out and reread three Beck novels, *The Laughing Police-man*, *The Fire Engine That Disappeared*, and *The Terrorists*. Not only do they hold up just fine, they also seem remarkably contemporary. In *The Laughing Policeman*, about the seemingly motiveless mass murder of the riders on a Stockholm bus, one of Beck's detectives exclaims, "Are there no limits?" The same scene is replayed throughout Mankell's *Face-less Killers*, after the murder of an elderly farm couple in remote Ystad unleashes an ugly wave of racist hate. The contemporary Scandinavian crime novel is defined by this sense that the old rules no longer apply, and while good cops might "solve" an individual crime, they are power-less to stop the slide of society into hate-fueled chaos. These are familiar ideas today, of course, and have worked their way into popular culture in the form of movies like *Traffic*. But the theme has even greater resonance in Scandinavian fiction because it plays against our image of the region as somehow beyond all that—neutral in war, liberal in sex, tolerant in society. Henning Mankell burst that bubble once and for all in 1997, but Sjöwall and Wahlöö were posting Danger! signs before many of today's Mankell fans even knew how to read.

But what of the politics? Shouldn't a pair of committed socialists rail-ing against capitalist injustice seem, well . . . quaint today? Sjöwall and Wahlöö might seem exactly that if they were sitting in your living room and espousing power to the people. But in their Martin Beck novels, they show rather than tell, and what they show seems like everyday life to today's reader. We might not draw the conclusions the authors drew about how to fix the problems of society, but we certainly recognize those problems in all their prickly detail. Bureaucracy run amok, for example. It hardly sounds like Communist propaganda to describe a world where most institutions are mired in their own rule-making and incompetence and where government leaders are, well . . . shall we just say not very bright. The world we live in today is simply Martin Beck's world writ large.

It's no wonder that when Mankell's *Faceless Killers* appeared in 1997, it came with a blurb from Maj Sjöwall.

Booklist, May 1, 2007

HIMES COMES TO HARLEM

MANY READERS OF TODAY'S crime fiction will recognize the name Chester Himes. They may know that he was among the first black writers to use the mystery genre to explore life in the inner city. They may even know that one of Himes' crime novels, *Cotton Comes to Harlem*, was made into a film in the 1970s starring Godfrey Cambridge as Grave Digger Jones and Raymond St. Jacques as Coffin Ed Johnson. But even if they do know these few facts, there's still a pretty good chance that they haven't read any of Himes' books. That is a great shame because anyone who cares about the hard-boiled crime novel needs to read Himes, if only because his influence is apparent behind every one of today's big names: Pelecanos, Mosley, Hiaasen, and on and on.

Himes is more than a mere influence on James Sallis, author of the innovative Lew Griffin detective novels. Not only does Himes make an appearance in one of the Griffin novels, Sallis is also the author of *Chester Himes: A Life* (Walker, 2000), a book that languished far too long on my bedside table. Finally reading this moving story of a writer who never received the recognition he so richly deserved sent me scurrying back to the books—not just the Harlem cycle of crime stories but also the largely ignored literary novels. Few literary biographies manage to bring together their subjects' lives and works into a living, breathing whole, but that's exactly what Sallis does for Himes. Looking behind what he calls "the pillars and lean-to porches of his work," Sallis finds an angry, brilliant writer and a difficult man: "Offering up little comfort or safe ground to the ideologue, he stood, sometimes by choice, always by inclination, at a hard right angle to the world."

Himes (1909–84) began writing in the Ohio State Penitentiary, where he served seven years for robbery. His early stories were published in *Esquire* in the 1940s, alongside Hemingway, Lardner, and other luminaries of the day. Yet this auspicious start soon gave way to a vicious cycle of rejection and racist treatment. Himes' first novel, an angry coming-of-age tale called *If He Hollers, Let Him Go*, received its share of good reviews, but it also ignited controversy from all sides. Pigeonholed as a "protest novel," the book was criticized by both white liberals and some black civil-rights leaders, who found Himes' vision of race relations and left-wing politics too negative. Himes put it another way: "Reactionaries hate the truth and the world's leaders fear it; but it embarrasses the liberals because they can't do anything about it."

Himes went on to write several more literary novels, all of which slipped quickly into obscurity, none faster than *The Primitive* (1955), which Sallis believes is "one of America's great novels" but whose subject matter—Himes' no-holds-barred take on the black man's fascination with white women and his own rage at being rejected as a writer—doomed it from the start. (After numerous rejections, the novel was published as a paperback original, complete with a lurid cover that played up the interracial theme.) Reading *The Primitive* today, one is struck by the book's incredible intensity and by the terrible injustice of its reception. Yet, it is one of those novels whose very power and frankness might well offend the pieties of any age, including our own.

In a life and career filled with the bitterest of ironies, it should not be surprising that Himes decided to write mysteries only as a last-ditch effort to make money. And yet, as Sallis notes, when Himes began working on the first of the Harlem mysteries, something happened: "The supposed lightness of what he was writing relieved him of what had become burdens—protest, high seriousness, autobiography—and offered him instead a new freedom of imagination." Himes made the most of it. The 10 mysteries in the Harlem cycle combine elements of surrealism, myth, and black folklore with a looseness of form that allowed him to capture the "fervid, feverish activity" of the inner city as no writer had ever done before.

Echoes of Himes are everywhere in contemporary crime writing, from George Pelecanos' uncompromising evocation of racial tension on the violence-riddled streets of Washington, D.C., to Carl Hiaasen's use of black humor to suggest approaching Armageddon. (Hiaasen's psycho with a weed whacker attached to the stump of his arm is just another version of Himes' blind man with a pistol.) And Himes' sense, so evident in the later Harlem novels, that the world was running amok, making even the good guys powerless, anticipates a whole movement of European hard-boiled writers, from Britain's John Harvey to Sweden's Henning Mankell, whose world-weary cops crumble under a new wave of hate-filled crime just as Grave Digger Jones and Coffin Ed Johnson watch Harlem slip away from them at the end of *Blind Man with a Pistol.*

Yes, Chester Himes came to Harlem to make a quick buck, but he made literary history instead. Sallis believes he is "America's central black writer." Others may disagree with this claim, but there can be no doubt that, compared with James Baldwin or Ralph Ellison or Toni Morrison, he is far too little known and far too undervalued. Most of his Harlem novels and some of his literary fiction are currently in print. Start reading; you won't regret it.

Booklist, February 15, 2002

007 TURNS 100

"BOND STARED AT HIS dark reflection in the window, listened to the sweet ting of the grade-crossing bells and the howl of the windhorn clearing their way, and shredded his nerves with doubts, questions, reproaches."

Doubts, questions, reproaches? Who is this Bond fellow? Surely not "Bond . . . James Bond," the invincible 007 of Her Majesty's Secret Service. And, yet, it is, at least as he appears in print rather than on screen. Those words come from *Goldfinger,* the seventh of Ian Fleming's 14 Bond books—and arguably the most well known, thanks largely to the movie version and the Shirley Bassey title song. In fact, if superspy James Bond is one of the most widely known fictional characters ever created, it's largely due to his movie career. How many human beings are there between the ages of, say, 8 and 80 who have not seen at least one James Bond movie or, at the very least, read a billboard advertising a James Bond movie? The answer, I'm guessing, would be very, very few, but if you rephrased the question to ask how many people have read at least one James Bond book, I'm certain you would get a very different answer.

I began pondering Bond's iconic stature a couple of weeks ago when I learned that 007's creator would be celebrating his centenary on May 28. Then, after a set of the 14 Bond books, newly reissued from Penguin in eye-catching, retro-hip covers, arrived on my desk, I decided it was time to reacquaint myself with the world's most famous fictional spy. Frankly, I've never been a big fan. Sure, I liked the early movies well enough—they came out in my teen years, though, and I would have paid to watch Ursula Andress read the Bible. But later, when I started reading espionage fiction, Bond had become synonymous in my mind with silly, shown up as a cartoon character by le Carré and other "serious" spy novelists. I've referred to Bond dozens of times in my reviews over the years but always in sentences like "Unfortunately, the sense of moral complexity dissipates in a James Bondish finale." Like most people, though, I was basing my point of view on the Bond movies, not the books. Would my position change if I read the novels?

I haven't made it through all 14 yet, but I've read enough to learn that the James Bond who appears on Ian Fleming's pages is a very different chap from the one on the silver screen, whether he's being portrayed by Sean Connery, Roger Moore, Daniel Craig, or any of the other 007 impersonators. Bond, even on paper, is no George Smiley, but, yes, he does feel the occasional doubt. The Bond of the novels is a male fantasy figure, to be sure, but he is much less the comic-book superhero he became in the movies and much more in the pulp tradition of John D. MacDonald's Travis McGee, or, later, Lee Child's Jack Reacher.

Like McGee and Reacher, Bond encapsulates a male generation's idea of cool (which, interestingly, has evolved from tux-wearing sophistication to beach-bum hedonism to off-the-grid self-sufficiency), overlaid, of course, with phenomenal strength and hand-combat skill, razor-sharp intelligence, and overwhelming sexual magnetism. If you're going to write to a formula, you might as well make it an irresistible one.

The Bond, McGee, and Reacher novels are also linked by their authors' ability to ground their supercool heroes in largely realistic, carefully detailed worlds—maybe not the ground on which you and I tread every day but recognizable ground nonetheless. I can hear your shouts of surprise already. What's recognizable, you ask, about Bond's gimmicky world, where cigarette holders perform all manner of lethal tasks, and our hero is outfitted with a trick device for every possible situation? This is probably the biggest difference between Bond on screen and in print. Yes, even in the books, Q Section does provide James with gadgets, but nowhere near as many or as outlandishly sophisticated as in the movies. By and large, the Bond of the novels gets by on strength, courage, and cunning, just like McGee and Reacher.

Fleming died in 1964, only having seen two Bond movies (*Dr. No* and *From Russia with Love*, perhaps the least tricked up of the lot). Soon enough, the movies came to rely more and more on gimmicks, special effects, and cartoony premises, leaving far behind Fleming's original concept: a portrayal of cold-war espionage, drawn from his World War II experience in naval intelligence, and based, at least in broad terms, on fact (Bond's recurring adversary, SMERSH, the subset of Russia's secret service charged with assassinating foreign spies, was a real-life organization).

But Fleming was interested in more than just tradecraft. He wanted to write high-concept entertainment, too, and for that you need really bad guys, not faceless, gray Russians. So he pitted Bond against a series of megalomaniacal evil geniuses who were somehow tied to SMERSH but whose grand scams stretched far beyond the party line (Goldfinger being the most memorable). Similarly, McGee and Reacher achieve archetypal stature by battling bad guys who are nearly as larger-than-life as Bond's foes.

Just as the Travis McGee books and (so far) the Jack Reachers have never made it as movies (too much detail, too much scene setting), so, too, might the Bond books not have translated nearly as well (nor had so long a life) had not the moviemakers seen the potential there for kicking it up a few notches and, in effect, turning Bond into Batman and his adversaries into the Joker.

Nothing wrong with spiders bounding between buildings to subdue jokers, of course, if you like that sort of thing, but the appeal is distinctly different from Fleming's idea of a supercool (if occasionally self-doubting) spy besting superbad foes on a more-or-less realistic battlefield. If that's your drink of choice, try a dry 007, written not filmed.

Booklist, May 1, 2008

VIOLENT NOVELS IN
A VIOLENT WORLD

RECENTLY, THE *NEW YORKER* celebrated the late Pauline Kael's career by presenting excerpts from some of her more memorable movie reviews. Discussing *Bonnie and Clyde*, Kael said, "[The movie] needs violence; violence is its meaning." She goes on to defend not only the rights of artists like Arthur Penn to use violence in their work but also "the legal rights of those filmmakers who use violence only to sell tickets, for it is not the province of the law to decide that one man is an artist and another is a no-talent."

Kael's words were on my mind as I set out to review James W. Hall's latest literary thriller, *Blackwater Sound* (St. Martin's/Minotaur). Hall is by no means a no-talent; in fact, he is one of the very best thriller writers alive. He has taken the popular subgenre of Florida noir further into the heart of darkness than have any of his contemporaries. His vision of a kind of art deco armageddon in South Florida employs flourishes of Carl Hiaasen–like surrealism but without the tempering effect of Hiaasen's absurdist comedy. We face the horror straight on in Hall's world—whether it's the human havoc wreaked by sociopaths or the environmental disasters perpetuated by profit-hungry corporations. And yet, alongside the explosive violence in Hall's novels, there is great lyricism, too. His descriptions of Florida's marine world capture with a Hemingway-like precision both the poetry of the sea and its awesome power, and his grasp of the tenderness of individual human relationships is all the more moving for its juxtaposition against bursts of horrible violence. That, ultimately, is the point: the fragility of both human and marine life in the face of potential destruction.

These themes are at the forefront in Hall's new novel, which brings together two of his recurring characters—the would-be hermit Thorn, in desperate retreat from the evils of the modern world, and crime photographer Alexandra Rafferty, whose father, Lawton Collins, is kidnapped by members of one of literature's most profoundly dysfunctional families. What brings the issue of violence in Hall's work to center stage this time is the unfortunate timing of its publication in the wake of the appalling terrorist attacks on the World Trade Center and the Pentagon. The novel's plot hinges on the development of a high-tech weapon capable of dismantling electrical systems in an instant—almost like a ray gun. In the story's opening set piece, the weapon is used to bring down an airliner, causing a Gulf Coast crash that kills more than 100 people. The crash is described in vivid detail, and the awful, random suddenness of the horror is shocking even without the chilling parallels to the events of September 11. With those parallels utterly unavoidable, it begs the question of whether artists must censor their imaginations. Are the horrors of the moment off limits to artistic interpretation?

Realistically, it must depend on how one defines "the moment." It is impossible to quibble with decisions to postpone the release of an Arnold Schwarzenegger movie dealing with terrorist themes, but should our necessary desire to protect the feelings of the grieving lead to a wholesale campaign to do what Pauline Kael counseled against more than 30 years ago? Because Americans have been the victims of terrorist outrage, should terrorism cease to be a fair subject for fiction writers, moviemakers, poets, and visual artists?

These are difficult questions, fraught with powerful emotions, and now is perhaps the worst moment to debate them in their larger contexts. With the Hall novel in front of me, however, I was forced to ask myself what to do with this one book at this one moment. Certainly, we must respect the feelings of any reader who, in the wake of our national tragedy, can't stomach reading about violence or air crashes or terrorism. (Assessing a reader's mood, after all, is at the heart of good readers'-advisory work.) Because the Hall novel will not reach stores until January, perhaps its content will not be offensive to as many people as the Schwarzenegger movie might have been had it been released as planned. But Hall's story is sure to offend some.

The fact remains, however, that it is an excellent novel, a sensitive if graphic exploration of how random, senseless violence affects the fabric of our lives. Thorn remains perhaps the most complex hero in Florida crime fiction. His conflicting desires to retreat from the madness of the modern world and to fix it single-handedly, drawing on "the white knot of gristle at his stubborn core," just may mirror many of our own responses to the real-life madness that surrounds us. Thorn is part archetypal hero, sallying forth to slay the dragon (the image our newscasters struggle to project on our national leaders), but he is also a scared individual trying to come to grips with the fact that it may no longer be possible to hide from the world's horrors.

Hall's novel should not be ignored, despite the unfortunate timing of its publication. It may not be a book that even dedicated crime-fiction readers will choose to tackle right now, but it is a book that, however upsetting, should be available to those willing to read it. If Pauline Kael were here today, I'm confident she would agree that it may be our novelists, poets, painters, and filmmakers—rather than our politicians—who are best equipped to help us live in an increasingly alien world.

Booklist, October 1, 2001

REMEMBERING GEORGE HIGGINS

WHEN THE ADVANCE GALLEYS of George V. Higgins' novel *At End of Day* were going to press, Higgins died suddenly, ending a remarkable career that spanned 30 books and nearly 30 years. *The Friends of Eddie Coyle*, his superb first novel, appeared in 1971 and was an immediate hit with reviewers, nearly all of whom recognized that a special talent had arrived on the crime-fiction scene. In the opening paragraph of that debut novel, a gun dealer named Jackie Brown says the words, "I can get your pieces probably by tomorrow night." That sentence, unremarkable on the surface, deserves a place in literary history as the first line of dialogue in the first novel of a man who would become one of the finest creators of dialogue in the twentieth century.

As his crime novels rolled by over the years, Higgins' ability to write dialogue became celebrated almost to the point of cliché. But if praising Higgins' knack for putting talk on the page became a knee-jerk reaction, the talk itself never lost its vitality. Nor did it lose its uniqueness. Other masters of dialogue (Elmore Leonard comes to mind) excel at repartee—snappy, staccato exchanges between characters engaged in dramatic action. Higgins, on the other hand, typically wrote not so much dialogue as a series of monologues, characters rambling on discursively, revealing as much about themselves as about the events they describe. His books move in sweeping, slowly inclining curves, like a highway gradually winding its way up a mountain, moving in one direction without ever seeming to point there. Gleaning information from Higgins' speakers—whether it's the criminal lowlifes in *Eddie Coyle,* the small-time lawyers in the Jerry Kennedy novels, or the Boston politicians in *A Change of Gravity* (1997)—is like gleaning information in life: you piece it together slowly, often learning more from the tangents a speaker follows than from any direct answers he or she might give.

Unlike other crime-fiction innovators, Higgins did not transform the genre. Why? Because no one else has ever been able to do what he did: tell a story not through action in the present but almost entirely through backstory, characters commenting on what happened in the past. Higgins is one of the few successful crime novelists who rarely describes a crime as it is occurring, although (as if to show he could do it if he wanted to) his last novel includes a vivid, chillingly precise description of a real-time killing. Usually, however, we hear only postmortem discussion, reminding us again and again that events are less important than how we react to them.

Attempting to copy this technique is a surefire method for accumulating publishers' rejection slips. Among mystery writers, only Higgins could make it work consistently, and it's satisfying to discover that he did it as well in his last novel as in his first. In *At End of Day,* he returns to the Boston criminal underworld that has served him so well throughout his career. The novel tells the story of the undoing of a Boston mobster, Arthur McKeon, but much of what we learn about McKeon and his top henchman, Nick Cistaro, we hear at dinner parties—gatherings at which the two underworld figures break bread with two FBI agents. This unholy alliance is at the heart of Higgins' tale: Is it corruption to attempt to contain the Mafia by protecting their rivals or is it creative policing? Higgins doesn't give us an answer, of course, but he makes the question a human one by showing us how mobsters and FBI agents think and how similar they are to one another.

Higgins has always been a writer who respected work well done—a low-rent lawyer digging into a case, a car thief plying his trade shrewdly, a mobster outthinking his rivals. There is a moral dimension to his work, too, but it grows out of the details and the interactions between people, and it is never a conventional view. At the end of his too-few days, Higgins should be remembered not only for talking his special talk but also for the way he used that talk to create context—rich, ambiguous, full-bodied context.

Booklist, February 15, 2000

MICHAEL DIBDIN

WITH THE DEATH OF Michael Dibdin on March 30, 2007, crime fiction lost one of its most distinctive voices. It's entirely fair to say that Dibdin's Inspector Aurelio Zen series, which debuted in 1988 with *Ratking*, launched what eventually would become the still-flourishing renaissance of the Italian crime novel. Obviously, there were Italian mysteries before Zen, written by Italians, of course, but also by expats—the formidable Magdalen Nabb jumps quickly to mind—but with Zen came the distinctive world-weariness that eventually would define the new European procedural, not only in Italy but also in Scandinavia. Zen's weariness comes as much from within the justice system as without; he is adept at battling bureaucrats but is always on the verge of being overwhelmed by the complex web of deceit and corruption that surrounds him. But unlike the American hard-boiled hero—even the most cynical of whom tend to be squishy idealists at the core—Zen is perfectly OK with a corrupt world. A typical Zen novel finds the inspector doing his level best to play the system—rubber-stamping cases with the convenient solution, double-dipping if possible, taking long lunches. Alas, this approach never quite works. Although he believes utterly in the maxim that a policeman must never "think you have any hope of ever achieving anything," Zen cannot resist the lure of an undiscovered fact. And it is from those facts, once discovered, that Dibdin's Zen novels grow.

Appropriately, the path of Zen's career moves ever downward. The more he fails to sweep his undiscovered facts under the rug, the more alienated he becomes from the politicos who run the Italian police system, and the more they, in turn, attempt to sweep Zen under the rug, sending him on one apparently dead-end assignment after another to far-flung outposts around Italy, well away from his nominal home base in Rome. As this pattern becomes established, a funny thing happens to the series: the tone changes dramatically, from the hard-edged neo-noir of the early novels—*Ratking*, *Vendetta*, *Cabal*, and *Dead Lagoon* (which returns him to his Venice home)—to a peculiar black comedy, which often merges into a kind of dark farce.

This daring shift in tone is announced in *Cosi Fan Tutti*, which finds Zen, typically in the dog house, assigned to the backwaters of Naples, where he lands in the middle of a comic opera. Complete with chapter titles lifted from those in the libretto to Mozart's *Cosi*, the plot of this absurdist farce hinges, like the opera, on lovers testing the fidelity of their mates. And, yet, just as we wonder if Dibdin hasn't lost it all together, throwing his neo-noir hero into *opera buffa*, we recognize all the signature elements of Zen's world: an enormous muddle encompassing bureaucrats, criminals, friends, and lovers. Patching together quotes from two philosophers, Zen observes in the novel's last pages that in life "everything happens twice . . . the first time as tragedy, the second as farce." The remainder of the series quite effectively show us how this view of life plays itself out, as Zen moves from tragedy, in the brilliant *Blood Rain*, perhaps the series' high point, through more black comedy in *A Long Finish*, *And Then You Die*, and *Back to Bologna*.

All of which brings us to Dibdin's final novel, published last month and called, prophetically, *End Games*. (This macabre juxtaposition of a writer's sudden death against the unfortunately appropriate title of his last book links Dibdin to the great George V. Higgins, whose swan song, published only months after his unexpected death in 2000, was called *At End of Day*.) On the surface, *End Games* follows in the tradition of the later Zen novels: the inspector has been exiled once again, marking time as the replacement chief of police in the remote Calabrian village of Cosenza. Once again, Zen is the outsider in an insular world, but here, remarkably, he has found a place in Italy where even the food is bad (Zen's tirades against the horrors of tomato sauce are the inspired rants of a man who has reached his nadir). The murder of an American front man for a movie company planning to film in Calabria changes everything, however, and soon enough Zen is plowing through a fertile field of undiscovered facts, most of which point to a morass of family rivalries overlaid with the absurd quest of a whacked-out software tycoon determined to find the elusive Tomb of Alaric, the fifth-century barbarian who sacked Rome and then died in Calabria, where his treasures were purportedly buried with him.

The mix of tragedy and farce is as delicious here as it ever has been in the later Dibdin novels, but there is something else, too: the melancholy that has been hanging from Zen's shoulders throughout the series has deepened, the sense of futility that was once accepted with a cynical shrug now having seeped into his pores and caused a chemical reaction in his soul. At one point, early in the book, when Zen is interviewing a colleague of the dead man, Dibdin describes his hero like this: "Zen's face was as expressionless as the frescoed image of some minor saint who was being martyred in some unspeakable way but, thanks to his steadfast faith, remained at peace with himself." That's a feeling most of us have had while sitting in an interminable staff meeting—in my case, without the illusion of being at peace with myself—but usually the sensation passes; one senses with Zen that it has become more or less permanent. Though he can still follow the trail of a new round of undiscovered facts, there is a listlessness now, a sure sign that the end games are at hand.

Late in the book, an old woman in the community, who has latched on to Zen as the man who can resolve the town's still-lingering feuds, exhorts him to act: "You know what you must do." "I'm just a lone hawk, signora," Zen replies. "Here in Calabria, it seems that the crows always win."

And so they do.

Booklist, September 1, 2007

MAGDALEN NABB

IT'S BEEN A ROUGH couple of years for fans of the international crime novel. First, Israeli writer Batya Gur, author of the groundbreaking Michael Ohayon series, starring the brooding Jerusalem police detective, died of cancer at only 58 in 2005; then Michael Dibdin, author of another landmark series starring a brooding detective, Italian investigator Aurelio Zen, died in March of last year, a few days after his sixtieth birthday. And more recently, on August 18, Magdalen Nabb, also author of a superb Italian crime series, died in Florence, again at 60. (On a personal note, I had another reason to be dismayed by the death of three of my favorite crime writers: like all of them, I was born in 1947.)

Nabb came to crime writing fairly late in life. After a divorce, she left her native England and moved to Florence with a young son in tow. A trained artist, she was working as a potter at a studio near Florence when she noticed the carabinieri officer, tears streaming from his eyes, apparently the result of an allergy, who would become the model for her fictional creation, Marshal Salvatore Guarnaccia. The first Guarnaccia novel, *Death of an Englishman,* appeared in 1981 and was followed at regular intervals by 13 more, most of which were based on real crimes committed in Florence. The last of the series, *Vita Nuova,* to be published posthumously in June, will be reviewed in our March 1, 2008, issue. In addition to crime fiction, Nabb wrote numerous children's books, including 11 novels in the popular Josie Smith series.

Nabb's mysteries were never as popular in the U.S. as Gur's and Dibdin's, probably because those authors' world-weary protagonists helped signal an essential shift in the nature of the international crime story, away from the Georges Simenon model and toward a global updating of the American hard-boiled hero. But if Nabb's Guarnaccia novels remained in the Simenon style (Simenon, in fact, was a big fan of Nabb's), they still prepared the soil for Dibdin and Donna Leon, whose Guido Brunetti novels, along with Dibdin's Zen series, are often credited with launching what many have called the renaissance of Italian crime fiction.

Though he shares Aurelio Zen's melancholy and Guido Brunetti's love of family, Nabb's Guarnaccia is very different from either of those heroes. He is not nearly as sophisticated as they are and is far less cynical, much more of an ordinary man. And, above all, he is not a detective, not renowned for his investigative abilities. No, Guarnaccia is essentially a street cop; even with the rank of marshal in the carabinieri, he is a relatively minor cog in the massive bureaucracy that is Italy's law-enforcement system. The carabinieri, an arm of the military, provide the kind of day-to-day policing that Americans associate with uniformed beat cops, while serious investigatory work is usually the province of the *Polizia di Stato* (state police), or what we would call plainclothes detectives. Typically, the heroes of Italian crime series are members of the *Polizia di Stato*, and the carabinieri, when they appear in novels at all, are usually inefficient, corrupt, or both—institutional roadblocks around which freewheeling mavericks such as Aurelio Zen or Guido Brunetti must steer.

The idea of a crime series starring a carabinieri marshal, therefore, is in itself a bit of a shock. If Guarnaccia has an antecedent, it would be Columbo, but even he was a detective. Like Columbo, Guarnaccia is uninspiring at first glance, utterly self-effacing, and, as a Sicilian stationed in Florence, an outsider, seen by most of his superiors and many of those he encounters as a slow, even dim-witted southerner (Columbo, of course, is viewed in much the same manner by the Los Angeles elite with whom he often spars). Usually in uniform, Guarnaccia lacks Columbo's rumpled raincoat as a symbol of his apparent inadequacy, but he makes up for it with his own personal quirk, the same allergy to sunlight that Nabb noticed on the officer that became her model. With his eyes likely to tear up at any moment, Guarnaccia is constantly putting on dark glasses, even indoors (a weeping cop hardly inspires confidence).

Over the 14 Guarnaccia novels, Nabb developed her hero into a working-man's Maigret, a bit of a plodder, yes, but hypersensitive to human nuance and to the sometimes overwhelming sadness that lurks beneath the surface of daily life (Guarnaccia's tears aren't always caused by his allergies). Handled less subtly, the marshal might have become a sentimental figure, but Nabb places him in an utterly unsentimental world, a place where his sensitivity typically leads to his own heartbreak rather than others' salvation. If you love Italian mysteries, but you have avoided Nabb, thinking she was either too cozy or too Old World, you've made a big mistake, but one that's easy to remedy. Presuming there are no other Nabb novels to be published posthumously, her oeuvre has reached a sadly premature ending point, but there are still 14 Guarnaccias in print and waiting for new readers. Here's hoping they find them.

Booklist, February 15, 2008

REAL POLITIK, ROSS THOMAS–STYLE

AS I WRITE THIS, the 2000 presidential election is only a couple of weeks away, and frankly, I'm a little disappointed. A few months ago, it looked like we were in for a real treat: what with Bush's bumbling and Gore's pontificating, it seemed as if the election season would produce one belly laugh after another. I'm sorry to report that neither candidate has lived up to his early-season promise. Bush started fast ("There are three great religions in this country: Christianity, Judaism, and Muslimism"), but in the end, he proved he was no Sam Goldwyn. Gore spent less time pontificating than he did apologizing ("I exaggerated, and I'm truly sorry"). What fun is that, Al? There were some choice moments, of course, when the facades almost crumbled: Gore's lockbox rap evoked Captain Queeg's strawberries, and Bush's sinister grin reminded me of a kid I knew in junior high with a reputation for torturing cats. Still, as happens so often these days, the artificiality of the real world sent me scurrying back to fiction in search of reality.

If you want real politik, forget the six o'clock news; read Ross Thomas instead. Thomas, who died in 1996, was perhaps the most intelligent author of political thrillers in the history of the genre. His most popular books were those featuring two groups of recurring characters: the cold-war stories starring saloon keepers (and reluctant spies) McCorkle and Padillo, and the delightfully labyrinthine caper novels showcasing the hysterically funny con men Artie Wu and Quincy Durant. Earlier in his career, though, in the 1960s and 1970s, Thomas wrote several stand-alone thrillers that were more directly about politics. Today a political thriller inevitably means some high-concept extravaganza in which terrorists hijack a new superweapon, blow up a couple of countries, and kidnap the president before our hero (soon to be played by Harrison Ford) puts it all right. Thomas' political novels took place in the backroom. He showed us how the hired guns get their candidates elected (*The Porkchoppers*, 1972, about the election of a union president); how it's possible to corrupt an entire city (*The Fools in Town Are on Our Side*, 1970); and how American political savvy can rig an election in an emerging African nation (*The Seersucker Whipsaw*, 1967).

There is usually a murder somewhere in the plot of one of Thomas' political novels, or at least enough rough stuff to sell the book as a crime novel, but the emphasis is always on nuts and bolts: how the smart guys engineer the scam and what happens to the money. The protagonist of these novels is typically a battle-scarred veteran of the political wars, cynical down to his bone marrow, who is lured out of retirement by the possibility of making an easy score and returning to his farm or his books or his wife. Inevitably, though, the bad guys smell a little worse than even the cynical hero remembers, and he can't resist the temptation to twist the knife in ways that weren't part of the official plan. Thomas' heroes are never idealists, but they aren't scoundrels, either. That you could find such rough-and-tumble individualists on the edges of the beltway may be the novels' only element of fantasy, but what the hell, you have to believe in something.

Perhaps my favorite of Thomas' political novels is *If You Can't Be Good* (1973), about a weak-spined senator who resigns after a bribery scandal. A Washington columnist smells more dirt behind the scenes and hires Deek Lucas to sniff it out. Lucas is the quintessential Thomas hero: a history student lured into politics by the Kennedy mystique, he winds up working as a kind of ombudsman on the New Frontier. His job is to ferret out corruption before it hits the papers (too bad Bill Clinton wasn't up on the Thomas oeuvre). The problem is, his work is too good (example: a 129-page report called "Where the Wheat Went; or, How Many 9mm Rounds in a Bushel"); invariably, his bosses sweep his findings under the rug. Deek finds the dirt on the senator all right, but what he does with it is driven by his own idiosyncratic sense of fair play (tempered by a healthy dose of self-interest). Thomas cuts to the heart of the matter not by portraying his spinmeisters twirling away on Sunday morning talk shows, but by showing us what they were talking about among themselves on Saturday night. Most remarkably, Thomas makes political people interesting, something real life just can't seem to manage.

For the last several years of Thomas' life, you could pretty much count on him to publish a new book every spring. Often I would come away from the annual American Booksellers Association convention in May with the new Thomas galley in my briefcase. A couple of years before his death, at one of those ABA conventions, I had the opportunity to interview him. Listening to him talk about his own experiences in politics—as a p.r. flack and as a campaign mastermind—I found myself admiring him in much the same way I admire his heroes: that special combination of cynicism and expertise that enables a certain kind of person to see the world clearly, react shrewdly, and never take any of it seriously. Name one real-life politician you can say that about. Forget Gore and Bush; Ross Thomas gets my vote.

Booklist, November 1, 2000

SMILEY'S BEGINNINGS

MY FAVORITE MOMENT IN all of espionage fiction continues to be the final scene in John le Carré's *Smiley's People*, when George Smiley watches his longtime nemesis, the Soviet superspy Karla, trudge across a bridge separating East and West Berlin, on his way to defect to the British. Peter Guillam, Smiley's longtime associate, noting the typically melancholic look on his mentor's face, even in his moment of triumph, remarks, "George, you won." Smiley looks up, distractedly, and replies, "Yes. Yes, well, I suppose I did." Thelonious Monk couldn't have written a more exquisitely dissonant final chord, the perfect dying fall with which to end a series of spy novels that changed the genre forever, introducing a new level of ambiguity and moral complexity to a world that only recently had been defined by the cartoonish simplicity of James Bond.

To understand the full force of that sublimely tentative statement—"Yes, well, I suppose I did"—we need to be familiar with not only the three major Smiley novels (*Tinker, Tailor, Soldier, Spy* and *The Honourable*

Schoolboy preceded *Smiley's People*), but also with le Carré's first two books, published in the U.S. in 1962 and 1963, in which the author introduced his "breathtakingly ordinary" hero. *Call for the Dead*, le Carré's debut, written while he was employed by the British Secret Service, and its successor, *A Murder of Quality*, have been long out of print in the U.S. Neither book was a runaway commercial success; it wasn't until *The Spy Who Came in from the Cold* (1964) that le Carré's name began to appear on best-seller lists. Smiley made only a cameo appearance in *The Spy Who* and was out of the picture completely in le Carré's next three books, leaving more than a decade between the character's little-noticed first two starring roles and his real coming-out party, in *Tinker, Tailor*. That gap may account for the fact that many le Carré fans aren't even aware of the early Smiley novels. They have a treat in store for them, thanks to the republication this month of both *Call for the Dead* and *A Murder of Quality*. Walker & Company, the original publisher of the two novels, has thoughtfully returned them to print in hardcover, complete with introductions by le Carré and forewords by P. D. James in *Call for the Dead* and Otto Penzler in *Murder of Quality*.

Although both novels hold up just fine, *Call for the Dead* will be of most interest to Smiley devotees. *A Murder of Quality* takes Smiley out of the espionage world and turns him into an amateur sleuth, solving a murder at an archetypal British public school. Le Carré's signature sensitivity to character is in evidence here, but Smiley, in effect, is on holiday, so we see a very different side of him. *Call for the Dead*, however, makes an ideal introduction to the mature Smiley of the later books. From the description on page one of this most unassuming of heroes—"Short, fat, and of a quiet disposition, he appeared to spend a lot of money on really bad clothes, which hung about his squat frame like skin on a shrunken toad"—we know we've said good-bye to 007. Early on, too, we see the sources of Smiley's world-weary melancholy—the fundamental aspect of his character. "Everything he admired or loved had been the product of intense individualism," le Carré tells us, explaining Smiley's commitment to wartime intelligence work and his aversion to communism. Even at this early point in his career, though, we see the beginnings of his gradual disenchantment with his own profession. The bureaucrats—men "who could reduce any color to gray"—have begun their long march to power, and George is starting to realize that intense individualism stands to be undermined as much in the corridors of Whitehall as in the backrooms of the Kremlin. This is le Carré's most resonant theme—individual human beings versus the gray men—and its evolution through his entire oeuvre, from *Call for the Dead* to last year's *Absolute Friends*, is a topic of enduring fascination. The gray men have been winning for a long time now, in le Carré novels and in life, making Smiley's early uneasiness seem all the more prescient.

There's also the equally melancholy matter of George's on-again, off-again marriage to Lady Ann Sercomb, a situation that, in the later books, bears directly on national security. Ann is usually offstage, a symbol of the enduring sadness in George's life, but in *Call for the Dead*, she appears briefly, albeit in flashbacks, since shortly before the novel's opening she has run away with a Cuban race-car driver. (Ann's unquenchable spirit and endemic lack of fidelity are reminiscent of another British aristocrat, Lady Brett Ashley in Hemingway's *The Sun Also Rises*; Smiley, of course, is always there to bail Ann out of an affair gone wrong, just as Jake Barnes is for Brett.) Readers of *Tinker, Tailor* or *Smiley's People* don't necessarily need to know *Call for the Dead* to understand that sense of inevitable disappointment that haunts George Smiley, but to do so is to heighten the sadness and to make the inevitability seem all the more crushing, especially where Lady Ann is concerned.

Le Carré readers will enjoy *Call for the Dead* most for the context it gives to what they already know about George Smiley, but the book works equally well on its own terms. The plot is vintage le Carré, though in miniature form. A Foreign Office employee kills himself, leaving a note saying that his career had been ruined by charges that he was disloyal. To Smiley, who had interviewed the dead man and cleared him of any culpability, this makes no sense; it makes even less when he learns that the man apparently left himself a wake-up call the night he took his own life. Battling his superiors, who are determined to sweep the matter under any available rug, Smiley lumbers on toward the truth. Le Carré's plots twist back upon themselves not to display their creator's cleverness but to suggest the infinite complexity of human affairs. George follows the tangled trail and learns the truth—but then must live with what he learns, one more source of sadness to furrow his brow. Does he win? Yes, well, I suppose he does.

Booklist, October 15, 2004

ZEN AND THE ART OF
SERIES MAINTENANCE

THERE IS AN OBVIOUS difference between the way we read a mystery series and the way we read a stand-alone novel. The series novel is really a new chapter in an ongoing story, and if we admire a series, we read each installment with the same sort of anticipation that Dickens' original readers brought to each new chapter of one of his serialized novels. It would never have occurred to nineteenth-century Dickens fans to evaluate each chapter on its own rather than as part of the whole, but that's exactly how we usually review mysteries. "It doesn't stand on its own," we say of the latest novel in an ongoing series, but at the same time, we prefer that mystery series evolve over time. And yet, if we insist that each novel in a series tell a completely independent story in which the hero engages us as if it were our first meeting, we inhibit growth by forcing series authors to repeat themselves.

What brought these issues to mind was my recent reading of Michael Dibdin's *And Then You Die*, the latest installment in his Aurelio Zen series. Zen, who takes the world-weary European cop to a new level of no-holds-barred cynicism, is one of my favorite characters in mystery fiction. For anyone who has ever contended with the absurdities of organizational life, or has been trapped in a bureaucratic quagmire from which there is no escape, Zen's daily struggles with Italian officialdom will strike a deep and resonant chord. Unlike most American anti-establishment heroes, who are really just idealists in contrarian drag, Zen is perfectly comfortable with corruption. He believes firmly that a policeman must never "think you have any hope of ever achieving anything," but at the same time, he can't resist the lure of an undiscovered fact. He is the perfect existential hero for a world run by petty bureaucrats on both sides of the law.

Given my attachment to Zen (and, yes, I'll admit it, my identification with him), you can imagine how shattered I was at the end of the previous installment, *Blood Rain*, when it appeared that the much-beleaguered cynic's luck had finally run out. The critic in me, however, recognized that Dibdin had picked the ideal moment to kill off his hero. *Blood Rain* finds Zen in Sicily, caught in a lethal crossfire of power-hungry politicians and crime bosses. As the bodies pile up, Zen is forced to recognize that his obsession with finding the truth is only making matters worse. In a final stroke of bitter irony, he utters the words, "At least we're alive" just before being blown up and, presumably, killed—the perfect exit line for a cynical detective who wasn't quite cynical enough to survive.

But he did survive, we discover in the opening pages of the even more ironically titled *And Then You Die*. Zen is hiding out in Tuscany, waiting to testify against the Mafia chiefs who tried to kill him in Sicily. He meets a woman and is attracted to her just as the bodies start dropping again. Is the Mob on his trail? It takes a while to sort it all out, but remarkably, the story ends on a happy note, with love in the air rather than exploding flesh.

A slight entry in the series, I find myself thinking, a small story with little real punch of its own. And, yet, I loved reading it, first because I was thrilled that Zen survived and then because, damn it, the guy deserves a nice meal and some great sex in the arms of a fascinating woman. Whoa! I'm supposed to be a reviewer here, not a soap-opera addict rooting for my TV friends. But if we read the Zen stories as parts of a serial novel rather than as succeeding stand-alones, my response becomes more legitimate. Like Dickens, Dibdin is telling a complex, multifaceted story, thematically coherent but full of emotional highs and lows. *And Then You Die* works superbly in the context of what went before; like a perfectly placed small course in an elaborate degustation, it accents the heartier fare that preceded it while preparing us for what is to come.

Authors manage series in different ways. Some, like John D. MacDonald and Robert B. Parker, serve the same entree over and over again. Each book stands alone just fine because each repeats the same formula in the same way. There is nothing wrong with this approach; the pleasures of formula require repetition. But MacDonald and Parker don't write serial novels in the Dickensian sense that Dibdin does. First-time readers of the Zen series shouldn't start with *And Then You Die,* just as first-time Dickens readers shouldn't start with the death of Little Nell. As reviewers, we need to recognize that the way an author manages a series dictates much about the kind of books he or she writes. Don't criticize Parker because Spenser is the same smart-ass he was 30 years ago, and don't criticize Dibdin because it takes more than a single book to hear the sound of one of Zen's hands clapping.

Booklist, May 1, 2002

NOIR IS WHERE YOU FIND IT

AND THESE DAYS, YOU can find it almost everywhere. The devaluing of the term noir may have begun with book publicists, who like to throw the word into jacket blurbs for every kind of crime novel that doesn't take place in a Cotswold village or include recipes for blueberry muffins. When a perfume called Noir turned up on the market not long ago ("sexy, with a hint of danger"), you could almost hear Robert Mitchum spitting obscenities from the grave. But if the term itself teeters on the edge of cliché, yet another victim of Madison Avenue, the genre seems to be thriving—if we could ever decide exactly what it is.

Don't expect a definitive answer in this column. Even the experts can't manage that, or so I concluded after attending a panel discussion on the topic at Bouchercon 36, an annual gathering of mystery writers, critics, publishers, booksellers, and fans held in honor of former *New York Times* mystery reviewer Anthony Boucher. The panel, called Twenty-First Century Noir, was chaired by Charles Ardai, the publisher of the exciting new noir imprint Hard Case Crime, and included unquestionably noir writers Ken Bruen, Jason Starr, Simon Kernick, and Sean Doolittle. The wide-ranging and often wildly humorous discussion came to no conclusions: Ardai and Doolittle took a traditionalist point of view, limiting noir fiction to stories in which flawed heroes find themselves trapped in a malign world where ideas of justice or honor are snares and delusions. Kernick, whose British cop novels are as dark as any in the genre, opted for a more inclusive definition, suggesting that noir was just another name for blinkers-off realism. Bruen and Starr, who have coauthored a Hard Case noir called *Bust*, mostly sparred with one another, trading jabs about whose works are the most depraved. (Bruen, who is Irish, argued that at least his characters often go to mass after performing heinous acts.) In the end, no one quite agreed about anything, except that, yes, noir was damned dark.

But is there a difference between the hard-boiled mystery and the noir novel? No clear consensus emerged on the panel, but I'd say yes, there is a difference. Chandler is noir, we all agree, but is Robert B. Parker? I'd say no, just as I'd say yes to Ross Macdonald and no to John D. MacDonald. The difference isn't in body count or style but in worldview. I agree with Ardai that in film noir and noir fiction, the universe is an inevitably alien place: the individual is always an outsider, always trapped or on the verge of being trapped. All it takes is the wrong woman, the wrong gin joint, the wrong raised eyebrow. Sometimes private detectives in noir novels are able to determine who raised which eyebrow, but they can't change the nature of the world, and they are powerless to keep the eyebrows of the universe orbiting peacefully ("It's Chinatown, Jake").

Perhaps the most interesting portion of the Bouchercon panel involved a discussion of noir's antecedents (we may not know what it is, but we know where it came from). Ardai noted that King Lear was perhaps the first noir hero and that Thomas Hardy was a quintessential noir novelist. He's on to something here, and I think it says much about the various shades of noir and possibly even about the difference between a hard-boiled world and a noir world. There's no doubt that *Lear* is a dark play, and that Lear raging on the heath may be the ultimate case of the alienated individual imploring the universe to give him its best shot. But, in Shakespeare's view at least, the Elizabethan world is an ordered place; the Shakespearean tragedies concern temporary fissures in that structure, fissures that are rejoined in the last scene when the cavalry arrives and sets about rebuilding. I'd argue that Parker, John D. MacDonald, and a host of other hard-boiled writers fall into this same camp. Their worlds get severely out of joint on a regular basis, and the hero is charged with setting it right, at least temporarily. Unlike in the noir world, where darkness is all, in the hard-boiled world, there are states of order in between bouts of evil.

Shakespeare may not quite be a noir writer, then, but Thomas Hardy definitely is one. I'd argue that Jude the Obscure posits a universe as unremittingly alien as anything in Jim Thompson. Jude Fawley, an uneducated stonemason, dreams of attending Oxford and ruins his life trying to get there, hooking up along the way with a stone-cold bitch called Sue Bridehead, perhaps the only femme fatale in literature with no sex appeal. From the love of learning comes unmitigated poverty and misery, culminating with the death of Jude's young son, who kills himself so Jude's other children can have more to eat. His suicide note does Jim Thompson proud: "Done because we were too menny."

You don't need postwar city streets or venetian blinds or a Veronica Lake look-alike to produce noir. It's not about stage setting or lighting or unfiltered cigarettes. It's not even about crime. It is about poor saps, sometimes deeply flawed saps, going one-on-one against a world holding all the aces. Noir is where you find it, and you can find it in classics just as well as pulps: Theodore Dreiser, Frank Norris, and the other nineteenth-century naturalists were the godfathers of American noir, just as Hardy stands behind Bruen, Kernick, and Ian Rankin, and Dostoevsky looms behind the entire genre.

Whether you're reading a twenty-first-century Ken Bruen novel, or watching a 1940s film, or rereading an 1895 Thomas Hardy novel, there's finally only one surefire test to determine if that book or movie qualifies as noir: it shouldn't smell like perfume.

Booklist, September 15, 2005

STRANGERS IN THE NIGHT

BOOKLIST CONTRIBUTING EDITOR HAZEL Rochman has written plenty in these pages about strangers coming to town. Recently, after I had occasion to reread Stephen King's 1975 horror classic *'Salem's Lot*, I found myself thinking about literary strangers and just what happens when they come to town. In coming-of-age novels, Hazel's bailiwick, the stranger is usually an agent of change or growth, allowing the hero to come alive. In many horror novels, however, the stranger—fortified by blood, his beverage of choice—drains the life from those he encounters.

Our universal fear of outsiders is what gives frisson to the stranger archetype, and nowhere is that fear more recognizable than in our traditional image of the New England small town, where insularity itself becomes a defense against incursion by strangers. The stereotypical Yankee, befuddling outsiders with a series of cryptic yups and nopes, may be a comic character from folklore, but he is also a soldier defending his Maginot Line against potential blitzkrieg. And behind the crotchety Yankee's seeming impregnability, there is the constant fear that one day a stranger will come to town who won't take nope for an answer.

That stranger comes to Jerusalem's Lot, Maine. Many critics have dismissed King's novel as just another vampire story, but if that were so, what explains the book's enduring hold over so many readers? The answer may lie not with the vampire but with the town he decimated. King's critics are right about the chief villain in *'Salem's Lot*. Mr. Barlow, our lead vampire, is no Dracula. He doesn't even appear until the story is nearly half over, and he is perhaps the most one-dimensional figure in the book. Jerusalem's Lot itself is the novel's central character. King got the idea of writing about a vampire coming to rural Maine from his wife, Tabitha. It just might work, he thought, "if I could create a fictional town with enough prosaic reality about it to offset the comic-book menace of a bunch of vampires."

That juxtaposition of prosaic reality against outlandish terror has always been central to King's technique for scaring his readers. In 'Salem's Lot, he does it by looking beneath the surface of idyllic New England. We see the pastoral beauty, the close-knit community, and the unpretentious lifestyle, complete with hot dogs on the barbecue and badminton on the lawn. Yet from the beginning, we also see the harbinger of something else, something other. The novel begins with a stranger, not Barlow but a writer, Ben Mears, returning to the Lot, where he'd lived briefly as a boy. Mears has come home again not to reclaim his innocence but to expunge his demons—the memory of the body of a man dead for decades, still hanging in the closet of the Marsten House. Mears believes that he hallucinated this horrible scene, but he wants to explore why it happened, why this house could have prompted him to imagine evil.

What Mears finds when he returns to the Lot is that the Marsten House is now occupied by another stranger, our Mr. Barlow. King wouldn't fully explore the haunted-house theme until The Shining; here, the Marsten House takes a supporting role, alerting us to the fact that something is rotten in Jerusalem's Lot. In Peyton Place, Grace Metalious exposes the hypocrisy and callousness that lurk beneath another postcard-perfect New England town. King does the same thing, but he goes one step further. He suggests that insularity breeds not only contempt, as in Peyton Place, but evil.

"Terror," King once observed, "often arises from a pervasive sense of disestablishment; that things are in the unmaking." That sense of the known giving way to the unknown is intensified in the novel by the fact that so few of the town's citizens recognize what is happening. Part of the problem is modernity itself—we no longer believe in things that go bump in the night—and part of the problem is the small-town insistence on maintaining the illusion of tranquility. If 'Salem's Lot were just another vampire novel, it would portray a straightforward struggle between good (people) and bad (vampires). It would not portray the arrival of vampires in the Lot as a kind of supernatural manifestation of the town's distorted sense of itself.

Like Metalious, King feels both affection for and anger toward his small town. A part of him wants to see 'Salem's Lot get its comeuppance, and this part gives the novel something most vampire stories lack. And, yet, in the end, the vampires don't win. Not exactly, at least. King believes that "writers have found it so much easier in the years since World War II (and especially in the years since Vietnam) to imagine characters who grow smaller as a result of their trials rather than bigger. Ben Mears, I discovered, wanted to be big. Wanted, in fact, to be a hero. I let him be what he wanted to be. I have never been sorry."

But how does Ben Mears become big? Not by pounding a wooden stake into the heart of Barlow. He does that, of course, but it isn't enough. The evil continues to thrive. No, Ben Mears becomes big by burning down 'Salem's Lot. Writers of every kind—from Nathaniel Hawthorne to Grace Metalious to John Updike to John Casey to Annie Proulx to Carolyn Chute to Howard Frank Mosher—have wrestled with their mixed feelings about the small towns of New England. But it took Stephen King to burn one down.

Booklist, April 1, 2005

JIM THOMPSON UNDER THE TUSCAN SUN

I BLAME FRANCES MAYES of *Under the Tuscan Sun* fame for putting me off my feed—at least as far as foodie lit is concerned. Don't get me wrong; I wolfed down *Tuscan Sun* like every other wannabe globetrotting gourmand, drooling all the while, but somewhere into Mayes' second book, I had one perfect fava bean too many. Maybe it was just envy on my part, but suddenly the whole genre of lucky people describing their wonderful lives in exotic places, complete with even more wonderful meals, seemed about as appetizing as Cheez Whiz on Wonder Bread. Leave Mayes and Peter Mayle and the rest of the food memoirists to their olive groves, their sunsets, and their tables under the trees. May their vinaigrette fail to emulsify, just once.

Unfortunately, the smarmy, self-congratulatory aftertaste of *Tuscan Sun* and its ilk has also put me off the recent spate of fiction in which food plays a central role. With a clean palate, I might relish the sentimentality at the core of novels like *Chocolat,* but as I'm sampling Joanne Harris' bonbons, I'm tasting Mayes' vegetables (harvested just seconds before they landed on her plate). I like reading about the sensual glories of a good meal, but why must every dish belong to the warm-fuzzy food group?

Before my recent aversion to food in literature had quite taken hold, I brought home a novel called *The Debt to Pleasure,* by John Lancaster. At the time, I thought the title sounded promising, and the paperback cover, featuring a shapely, succulent peach reminiscent of one of Cézanne's apples, was certainly enticing. I picked up the book again the other day, drawn by the peach, and noticed that one of the blurb writers compared Lancaster to Nabokov. That seemed sufficiently far from *Under the Tuscan Sun,* so I gave it a try. What a treat! A novel celebrating the sensual pleasures of food but narrated by a fiendishly witty misanthrope with a very dark secret—foodie fiction for the incorrigibly hard-boiled.

It's an odd, almost unclassifiable book. The *New Yorker* described it accurately as a "novel masquerading as an essay masquerading as a cookbook." The narrator, one Tarquin Winot, lives in Provence, but he's never met Peter Mayle. Imagine the George Sanders character in *All about Eve* dripping venom as he dispenses outrageous but incisive opinions on everything from the Roman definition of a barbarian ("someone who wore trousers, had a beard, and ate butter") to the idea of cheese as "the corpse of milk." But there is an even darker side to Winot that becomes apparent gradually as we salivate our way through his story. I won't reveal the secret, except to say that you can imagine my delight when I discovered that my search for a food novel that wasn't warm and fuzzy had led me to a gourmet version of one of Jim Thompson's twisted heroes.

Winot may be twisted, but he still loves food and talks about it with incredible flair. I love the fact that he really doesn't have any interest in helping the reader cook; the travails of ordinary folk in their ordinary kitchens never reach his radar screen. Here's the beginning of his recipe for bouillabaisse: "Take two pounds of rockfish, ideally bought somewhere on the Mediterranean in a quayside negotiation with a leathery grandfather and grandson team who have spent the long day hauling nets aboard in steep baking coves, their tangible desire for the day's first pastis in no way accelerating the speed or diminishing the complexity of the bargaining process."

If Mayes had said that, I'd want to throw the book across the room because her tone would suggest—in a caring, Oprah-esque way—that she empathizes with our sad inability to be present on the quay with her and the leathery grandfather. Lancaster gloats in the fact that he's there and we're not. His pleasure is more genuine than Mayes' empathy and, thus, more real, more like Cézanne's apple. Taste is a mysterious thing, as any chef or any readers' advisor would be happy to tell you. The idea of mixing Mayle's *A Year in Provence* with Thompson's *Killer inside Me* would surely strike most readers as a poor marriage of ingredients, but for me, it was just the dish to rekindle my appetite for food on the page.

Booklist, October 15, 2001

Life at *Booklist*

BEST AMERICAN FICTION
FROM THE LAST 25 YEARS

LAST MAY, THE NEW York Times Book Review asked 100 prominent writers and editors a loaded question: What is the best work of American fiction published in the last 25 years? Naturally, such high-caliber respondents had numerous issues: What is fiction? What is American? What does best mean? And, yes, even, What is 25 years? (It's probably a good thing that none of these elite writers works for Booklist. When I tell a reviewer that his or her review is due in two weeks, I don't expect to be asked for a definition of two weeks.) Eventually, the NYTBR's posse of pundits fought its way through the ambiguity-laden question and turned to the answer. As Times critic A. O. Scott reported on May 21, the responses featured a hailstorm of equivocation, with many experts throwing up their hands at the prospect of choosing one "best" book, fearing that the idea of such a list would "distract from the serious business of literature" and, worse, "subject it to damaging trivialization." Scott noted also that "one famous novelist, unwilling to vote for his own books and reluctant to consider anyone else's, asked us to 'assume you never heard from me.'"

And, yet, after all the hand-wringing, the prominent 100 finally settled down to the business of serious trivializing. As has been widely reported, the winner of the poll was Toni Morrison's Beloved (although one respondent, anticipating Morrison's victory, elected not to vote for anything but instead to explain why Beloved didn't deserve the crown). Runners-up included, in order, Don DeLillo's Underworld, Cormac McCarthy's Blood Meridian, John Updike's four Rabbit novels (bound jointly in 1995), and Philip Roth's American Pastoral.

Well, OK. Certainly the winning writers are all prominent figures, though it could be argued that Roth, Updike, and Morrison wrote their best books longer ago than 25 years (and even including the Rabbit books as a joint entry seems iffy). Scott gets it right when he says that the prominent 100 tended to choose not personal favorites but books that "successfully assume a burden of cultural importance," books in which "America is not only the setting but also the subject." Yes, but couldn't you also say that picking books that wear their cultural burdens on their sleeves is the equivalent of playing it safe, ordering the surf-and-turf rather taking a chance on the daily specials?

The more I thought about the *Times* list, the more convinced I became that *Booklist* could do it better. For one thing, we make lists all the time, so we're perfectly comfortable with trivializing just about anything. Moreover, *Booklist* editors and reviewers tend not to be shy about supporting the books we really like, whether or not those books assume any cultural burdens, and whether or not their authors have earned academia's stamp of approval. Very few surf-and-turfers around here.

So, with all that in mind, I asked our staff editors, columnists, and freelance contributors to pick their favorite work of American fiction from the past 25 years. Nobody questioned the meaning of American, and nobody looked for the subtext in 25 years. (Our only prevaricator was Will Manley, who nominated *The Scarlet Letter* on the grounds that no great fiction has been published in America in the last 25 years, and if you wanted to read something great, you might as well read Hawthorne.) Those who did respond, however, came up with choices quite different from those on the *Times* list, although every one of the *Times* winners received at least one vote, including the questionably eligible Rabbit novels. Our winner? Michael Chabon's *The Amazing Adventures of Kavalier and Clay*, which was also our *Booklist* Top of the List winner for the year 2000. In her *Booklist* review, Donna Seaman called the book a "funny and profound tale of exile, love, and magic." It's that for sure, but it's also a rip-roaring story about comic-book creators, a subset of the literary world whose members, until recently, were not considered eligible to assume cultural burdens of any kind. Our runners-up were, in order, William Kennedy's *Ironweed*, Louise Erdrich's *Love Medicine*, John Kennedy Toole's *Confederacy of Dunces*, Mark Helprin's *Winter's Tale*, and Barbara Kingsolver's *Animal Dreams*. (See below for a list of all books receiving votes.)

Comparing our list to the *Times*, a few obvious differences emerge. Their gang packs more clout, but the authors are also a lot older. The five *Times* winners were all born in the 1930s, and their average age is a mature 73 years (clearly this group orders their surf-and-turf at the early-bird special). The *Booklist* team represents multiple generations, with birthdates from the 1920s (Kennedy, in 1928) through the 1960s (Chabon, the youngest of all, in 1963). Our average age is a comparatively rambunctious 58, and we include two female writers in their early 50s, while the *Times* list has only one woman, Morrison, who is 75. The age of an author, finally, is neither here nor there in determining the greatness of an individual book, but on a list like this one, it does say something about the overall tendency of the selectors to use the impact of a full career as a key criterion. And, hey, the next time I'm suffering my way through a management seminar in which some wet-behind-the-ears consultant is trumpeting the importance of "addressing the needs of a younger demographic," I can proudly say that *Booklist*'s favorite writers are 15 years younger than those of the *New York Times*. On the other hand, most consultants don't read novels, so maybe I could help myself more by just dying my beard black.

BEST AMERICAN FICTION FROM THE LAST 25 YEARS

—selected by Booklist's *editors, columnists, and reviewers*

Titles receiving two votes or more, in order:

The Amazing Adventures of Kavalier and Clay,
   by Michael Chabon

Ironweed, by William Kennedy

Love Medicine, by Louise Erdrich

A Confederacy of Dunces, by John Kennedy Toole

Winter's Tale, by Mark Helprin

Animal Dreams, by Barbara Kingsolver

Underworld, by Don DeLillo

Infinite Jest, by David Foster Wallace

Beloved, by Toni Morrison

American Pastoral, by Philip Roth

Gold Bug Variations, by Richard Powers

Titles receiving one vote:

The Brothers K, by David James Duncan

Caramelo, by Sandra Cisneros

The Dean's December, by Saul Bellow

Gilead, by Marilynne Robinson

Housekeeping, by Marilynne Robinson

Jayber Crow, by Wendell Berry

John Henry Days, by Colson Whitehead

Lincoln, by Gore Vidal

Maus, by Art Spiegelman

Mickelsson's Ghosts, by John Gardner

Outlander, by Diana Gabaldon

The Rabbit Novels, by John Updike

A Prayer for Owen Meany, by John Irving

The Plot against America, by Philip Roth

The Sportswriter, by Richard Ford

A Thousand Acres, by Jane Smiley

Booklist, August 2006

BLOOD ON THE TRACKS

PERHAPS NO OTHER *BOOKLIST* editorial project has engendered as much staff buzz as The Booklist Century: 100 Books, 100 Years. The idea of celebrating our 100th anniversary by compiling a list of 100 books, one for each year, came late in the production cycle of this issue, causing a lot of scurrying about on our part. First there was the premise: the single book published during a given year that had the most impact over time. Then there was the selection process: lots of talk, lots of lobbying, lots of date checking, lots of agonizing. We even violated our rule of never discussing books at our morning coffee break. This column, though, isn't about the final list; no, my topic here isn't the winning books; it's the losers, the titles that were voted off along the way.

When Modern Library issued its list of the best novels of the twentieth century, it was done with a certain hauteur: we know these are the best books because our scholars say so. We're taking a different tack here at *Booklist*. Our list is made up of the books we think had the greatest societal impact of anything published in each of the years during the century. We could be wrong—we were in a hurry, after all, editors on deadline, not scholars in repose—and we hope you'll tell us if you think we missed the mark. And we're going to make it easier for you to do just that by exposing our weak points—the tough years, the close calls, the blood on the tracks. At least you won't be able to accuse us of hauteur. Here are some of our most fiercely debated decisions:

ADOLF, MAO, AND SOME BOATS BEATING AGAINST THE CURRENT

Here's the problem: in 1922, *The Great Gatsby* was published, a book that many regard, along with *Huckleberry Finn*, as edging ever so close to being the Great American Novel. So you have to have Gatsby on the list, right? Yeah, except that little Austrian paperhanger with the funny mustache also happened to publish his memoir, *Mein Kampf*, in 1922. So which had more impact? The quintessential Jazz Age novel or the ravings of a madman who started a war and caused a Holocaust?

Then you have the matter of Mao's *Little Red Book*: required reading on a certain Long March. Publication date is a little tricky with Mao's opus—Do first editions from Chinese vanity presses count?—but various sources cite 1966 as the official year. (The long marchers must have had bound galleys.) But, if it's 1966, what about *In Cold Blood*, the book that gave us the "nonfiction novel"?

Tough choices, to be sure, but we went against Hitler and Mao. It's books we're talking about here, not political careers, and finally we decided that Hitler's and Mao's impact came not so much from their books as from the post-publication marketing campaigns.

SAUL BELLOW VS. FRANKLIN W. DIXON

OK, this one sounds easy: a Nobel winner, the standard bearer among the great mid-century American Jewish novelists, versus the pseudonymous author of series fiction for children? But whose adventures touched more lives: Augie March's or Frank and Joe Hardy's? Another problem: How do you choose just one Hardy Boys novel from the, well, somewhat similar oeuvre, written by various hands? One might lean toward the debut, *The Tower Treasure*, but frankly, Mr. Dixon hadn't quite hit his stride with that one, and besides, it was published in 1927, the year of Virginia Woolf's *To the Lighthouse*. No, the fact remains that the jewel in the Hardy crown is *The Yellow Feather Mystery*, published in 1953, the year that Augie March announced himself to be "an American, Chicago born."

I must admit I leaned toward *Yellow Feather* on this one, as did my oldest friend, Rob, an English teacher in Salem, Oregon. No doubt our sentiments were influenced by memories of singing *Yellow Feather*'s praises in about 1956, during one of the regular meetings of our two-person Hardy Boys book club. Still, in the end, Bellow triumphs, though only barely. I should also point out that Rob won the day on the D. H. Lawrence question, convincing me to include his favorite novel, *Women in Love*, over mine, *The Rainbow*.

AND COMING UP ON THE OUTSIDE, IT'S YOU, MARGARET

Perhaps the most overcrowded year of all was 1970, in which these very different contenders headed for the finish line in a tightly bunched group: Maya Angelou's *I Know Why the Caged Bird Sings*, Toni Morrison's *The Bluest Eye*, Judy Blume's *Are You There God? It's Me, Margaret*, and the landmark nonfiction work *Our Bodies, Ourselves*. It was a photo finish, but *Our Bodies* seemed to be the winner and, in fact, appeared on the first draft of the final list. Then Books for Youth editors Gillian Engberg and Jennifer Mattson showed up in my office to plead on Margaret's behalf. Yes, *Bodies* was important, they argued, but *Margaret* brought puberty to children's books, changing everything. Are you there God? It's me, Bill. Don't forget I changed my mind.

WHERE THE WILD THINGS AREN'T

On this list, that's where. When *Booklist* contributing editor Hazel Rochman learned that Maurice Sendak's masterpiece had not made our list, her jaw dropped, and she shrieked, "Oh, no!" *Booklist* staffers know that horrified look well: Hazel saves it for those moments of unspeakable pain when an atrocious act of bad literary judgment has been exercised upon a book she loves. It helped—but only a little—when I explained that Betty Friedan's *The Feminine Mystique* was also published in 1963, and we couldn't possibly overlook the book that launched the feminist movement.

MEA CULPA, PART TWO

Last September, I used this column to apologize to E. B. White for the tepid review *Booklist* gave *Charlotte's Web* back in 1952. Now I must apologize again, for failing to include *Charlotte* in our Booklist Century. I would have thought *Charlotte* was a lock to make the list, but that was before I realized White's novel was published the same year as Ralph Ellison's *Invisible Man*. My guilt over mistreating everyone's favorite spider yet again is assuaged a bit by the fact that Hazel, despite feeling Charlotte's pain acutely, agreed with me that Ellison must come first.

Booklist, June 1, 2005

MEA CULPA

I HAVE SPENT MOST of the past summer, when I should have been playing golf, writing discussion guides for Storylines New England, a radio reading series sponsored by ALA's Public Programs Office. The upside of such an endeavor is that it offers a chance both to reacquaint yourself with old friends (Robert Frost and Edith Wharton, for example) and to get to know some writers you had always been meaning to read more of (John Casey, Annie Proulx). For me, though, the most interesting part of the project has been rereading *Charlotte's Web*. Not just for the novel itself but also for a startling discovery I made while nosing around in books about E. B. White, who has long been one of my favorite writers. It turns out that when *Charlotte's Web* was published in 1952, it received dozens of rave reviews, including one in the *New York Times* by Eudora Welty, who called the book "just about perfect." On the negative side, Charlotte garnered only two bad reviews. One of those, by the then-prominent children's librarian at New York Public Library, Anne Carroll Moore, appeared in the *Horn Book*. The other negative review was published in *Booklist*. Definitely not one of the better moments in literary history for librarians and the library review media.

My discovery of what Peter F. Neumeyer, in *The Annotated Charlotte's Web*, called "the gaffe by *Booklist*" turned out to be quite timely, in an ironic way. We are beginning a yearlong celebration of *Booklist's* 100th anniversary, and as part of that celebration, we will be reprinting notable reviews and articles that have appeared in our pages over the past century. Naturally, most of these backward glances will focus on times when we got it right. On the other hand, it's impossible to hang around on this planet for 100 years without committing a few grievous errors, and in the spirit of humility, why not acknowledge those, too, if only to keep the self-congratulation from turning smarmy? So in that context, I offer, in its entirety, our review of *Charlotte's Web*, as it appeared in the September 1, 1952, *Booklist*:

> *Like* Stuart Little, *this fable will have an ostensible appeal for children by virtue of its simple style, nature lore, and realistic juvenile characters; the younger readers, however, are likely to lose interest as the story moves on, leaving it*

> *to adults who enjoy the author's symbolic and philosophic*
> *implications. The story tells of the friendship between*
> *Wilbur, the runty pig, and Charlotte, a comradely spider*
> *who applies spider psychology so that Wilbur may end up*
> *in a prize-winner's stall instead of the pork barrel.*

I suppose we can be glad that our reviews were shorter then because our anonymous reviewer was forced to hold her opinions to a minimum. And when I say anonymous, I mean both in the magazine and in history. Our reviews were unsigned until 1980, but, in the *Booklist* offices, we have a glorious old card catalog that contains—theoretically—information on every book we have ever reviewed, including the reviewer's name. Curiously, there is no card in the file for *Charlotte's Web*, suggesting that, when the extent of our "gaffe" became clear, a red-faced reviewer may have destroyed the evidence. That reviewer should have known that cover-ups never work. The time has come for mea culpas, first to Charlotte and Wilbur, for the absurd contention that younger children would lose interest in their story, and second, to White himself, for our horrendous misreading of a book that is anything but "symbolic."

I know that mentioning *Charlotte*'s "symbolic and philosophic implications" must have rankled White because he despised symbol hunters. Writing to a screenwriter who hoped to develop a film version of the novel, White addressed this issue directly: "I just want to add," he wrote, "that there is no symbolism in *Charlotte's Web*. And there is no political meaning in the story. It is a straight report from the barn cellar, which I dearly love, having spent so many fine hours there, winter and summer, spring and fall, good times and bad times, with the garrulous geese, the passage of swallows, the nearness of rats, and the sameness of sheep."

The worst part of our review is that we ignore the barn altogether. White once wrote that his novel "was a paean to life, a hymn to the barn, an acceptance of dung." Unfortunately, *Booklist* was too busy worrying about symbols even to smell the dung, much less accept it. As I reread *Charlotte* this time, I was impressed once more with what a marvelous balancing act White manages. On the one hand, he was adamant about showing barn life as it really was, but on the other hand, he set himself an utterly unrealistic goal: to keep Wilbur out of the pork barrel. As a farmer himself, White had killed his share of pigs—that's what farmers do—but he never liked it, and in *Charlotte's Web*, he wanted to find a way to let one live. To do so, he was obligated to mix fantasy and reality, which required the help of a spider who was capable of being "both a true friend and a good writer."

Introducing fantasy into a book intended to celebrate the reality of farm life was a dangerous move for White. In saving the pig, would he lose the barn? Will the manure still smell when the spiders become prose stylists? We know now that White's barn was plenty big enough for both Wilbur's manure and Charlotte's bons mots, and we are profoundly sorry *Booklist* didn't know it in 1952.

In the January 1948 issue of *Atlantic Monthly*, White published a powerful essay called "Death of a Pig" in which he described his unsuccessful attempt to save a sick pig on his farm. The pig dies, and White's grief, understated yet palpable, pours from the pages like sweat. *Charlotte's Web* gave White a chance to write a different ending. One could say that White feels about pigs as Robert Frost, another New England farmer, feels about walls. Pigs must die, either by their owner's hand or of natural causes, and walls are necessary devices on a working farm. But just as there is something that doesn't love a wall, so is there something that would save a pig.

Booklist, September 1, 2004

I HATE THESE
MEESES TO PIECES

MY FAVORITE DISNEY CARTOON character has always been Scrooge McDuck. No contest. I liked Donald, too, and Huey, Dewey, and Louie were tolerable, as long as they were causing trouble and not acting cute. Pluto was a bit too slapstick for my taste, though, and like so many others, I just couldn't get beyond Goofy's indeterminate-species problem. But most of all, I never liked Mickey Mouse—didn't like him in 1956 and don't like him any better now. Back then I just thought he wasn't as funny as Scrooge or Donald; today I think he's a smarmy corporate weasel, the ultimate conformist, shilling for the American way. I recently read that Mickey's favorite sayings are "Gosh!" "Oh, boy!" "Aw, Gee!" and "That sure is swell!" No, Mickey, it's not swell, and you're not swell either.

Don't get me wrong. I wanted to go to Disneyland as much as the next kid when the theme park first opened, but not to see Mickey. No, I was a Frontierland man all the way. There was nothing worse on a Sunday night than sitting down to an episode of *Disneyland*, praying for a new installment of Davy Crockett but getting Fantasyland instead. When you're expecting Davy killing bears or defending the Alamo, and you get Mickey squealing "Aw, Gee!" well—Gosh!—that stinks. I never made it to Disneyland as a kid, but I did go to Disney World once, sometime in the '80s, a family trip with my daughter, who was eight or nine at the time. I remember the gargantuan lines, of course, but I also remember running into Mickeys all over the place—big Mickeys, little Mickeys, every kind of Mickey, all of them trying to sell you something by playing up to your kid. In my mind, I see myself being a good sport, enduring the agony of the experience for the sake of my daughter, but I only recently learned that she offers an alternative interpretation, claiming that I was such a grouch all day that her Disney World trip was ruined and, further, that I snarled at every damned Mickey we encountered. She doesn't like Mickey either, but she contends it's because she was traumatized by what happened that day. One of the Mickeys I rebuffed apparently took umbrage, and my daughter was convinced the rodent was going to beat up her dad (it must have been one of the big Mickeys). I suppose I should feel bad about all of that, but frankly, I believe that whatever it takes to sour a kid on Mickey Mouse is probably well worth it.

As the decades have rolled on, I've managed fairly successfully to avoid further encounters with Mickey Mouse. But I'm afraid my luck has run out. As this column is being read, I'll be at the American Library Association's Annual Conference in Orlando, and I have a nasty feeling that the aisles of the exhibit hall are going to be crawling with mice. I'll only say this once, Mick: stay away from the *Booklist* booth.

Unfortunately, though, the Orlando trip is the least of my problems, Mickey-wise. As I'm sure you're aware, the mouse celebrated his 75th birthday in November, and the Disney folks like to get all the mileage they can out of a marketing opportunity (unless it involves a Michael Moore film). I had forgotten all about Mickey's birthday, of course (we don't exchange cards), but I was rudely reminded of it this morning on my walk to work. I was strolling down State Street, enjoying what promised to be Chicago's long-awaited one day of spring (it didn't pan out), when I noticed a six-foot Mickey Mouse on the corner smiling at me. "Aren't they great?" one of my fellow pedestrians asked. I was too stunned to answer so she went on to tell me the story of a mice infestation on Chicago's beloved Great Street. There are 15 of these monstrous Mickeys, each 700 pounds of polyurethane and designed by celebrities including Tom Hanks and Susan Lucci. Sure enough, as I glanced down the street, I saw a nightmare vision of enormous rodents. Slipping quickly over to Wabash Avenue, I made my melancholy way to the office.

But all the news isn't bad. It turns out that I'm not alone in my antipathy to M. Mouse. A recent *New York Times* article reported that even Maurice Sendak, who based his character Max in *Where the Wild Things Are* on Mickey, has turned against the Disney front man. "I was around six when I first saw him," Sendak says of Mickey, "and his character was the kind I wished I'd had as a child: brave and sassy and nasty and crooked and thinking of ways to outdo people. Not like the lifeless fat pig he is now." I never saw the "sassy and nasty" part, but I'll take Sendak's word for it. He's a little older than I am, after all. But thank you, Maurice, from the bottom of my heart, for that "lifeless fat pig" line.

The best news of all, shared by the *Times,* is that the Disney people are worried about Mickey, too. They deny it, of course, but it appears the minnows in Michael Eisner's think tank are trying to come up with a way to rejuvenate the mouse for the twenty-first century. Wisely assuming the Disney bureaucrats won't devise anything worthwhile, *Times* reporter Jesse Green looked elsewhere. Art Spiegelman, author of the *Maus* books, had the most interesting idea for giving Mickey some much-needed edge: "Make him gay." Nice try, Art, but I don't think it will work. Some corporate weasels are so straight that even a queer eye isn't enough to make them cool.

Booklist, June 1, 2004

HE'S STILL A LIFELESS, FAT PIG

THERE'S A SPORTSWRITER IN Chicago named Jay Mariotti who has made a career out of attacking White Sox manager Ozzie Guillen. Poor Ozzie needs only to drop an *f*-bomb, and his nemesis churns out another 800 words on why Chicagoans one and all should band together in a righteous crusade to get this moral reprobate fired at once. I'm an Ozzie fan myself—what's an *f*-word or 10 when your team is in first place—and

I despise sanctimonious writers in general. But most of all, I've always resented the way Mariotti manages to recycle his anti-Ozzie rants. It's as if he runs out of topics every few days and has no choice but to take another shot at good ol' Oz. That's a slap in the face at hardworking columnists everywhere, those of us who don't stoop to pummeling a convenient straw man whenever we find ourselves groping for something to write about.

Or so I thought until I found myself in the middle of every columnist's nightmare—staring into a dry well of ideas with a deadline less than 24 hours away. It was then that I came to admire Jay Mariotti for his resourcefulness. By God (excuse me, Jay, for that mild profanity), every columnist needs and deserves an Ozzie Guillen; we should think of it as a form of health insurance, a preventative measure designed to keep us from falling into dry wells and breaking our typing fingers.

But I still faced one problem: if I were going to emulate my new hero, Jay Mariotti, I would need to find my own Ozzie Guillen and find him quickly. Naturally, I thought first of Bob Greene, whose incredibly smarmy newspaper columns and books about the glories of coming-of-age as a dewy-eyed baby boomer have been savaged in *Booklist* repeatedly, but it's hard to pummel a straw man when he has already had the stuffing kicked out of him: Greene remains in pop-cultural limbo after a sex scandal cost him his *Chicago Tribune* job. If not Bob, who? Then it came to me: somebody every bit as smarmy as Mr. Greene, someone whom I attacked in this column four years ago, and someone who is definitely on tap for another bashing. I'm talking about Mickey Mouse.

It was June 2004, when Mickey was celebrating his 75th birthday, and the ALA Annual Conference was set to visit Orlando. It seemed the perfect opportunity to unleash several decades of animosity, which is what I did in a column called "I Hate These Meeses to Pieces." In researching that column, I was ever so pleased to learn that I wasn't alone in my antipathy for the little rodent. Even Maurice Sendak, who based the character of Max in *Where the Wild Things Are* on Mickey, had turned against the Disney front man. "I was about six when I first saw him," Sendak explained in the *New York Times*, "and his character was the kind I wished I'd had as a child: brave and sassy and nasty and crooked and thinking of ways to outdo people. Not the lifeless fat pig he is now."

Mickey is 79 now, and the ALA Conference is in Anaheim, just down a sterile four-lane highway from Disneyland, the mouse's first home. Unfortunately, he's the same lifeless, fat pig he was four years ago, when ALA visited the equally sterile Disney World. I never saw Mickey in his sassy period, but if Sendak is right about that, it makes the mouse's descent even more despicable. How could one little mouse be transformed from a Falstaffian, antiestablishment cutup into a squeaky clean, cloying corporate weasel, shilling for the American way?

Sure, one could blame the Disney suits for ruining Mickey, but I'm not buying that. Fictional characters need to stand firm against the ideals of their creators. Look at Milton's Satan, refusing to knuckle under to Milton's pieties and stealing *Paradise Lost* out from under its author. Mickey might at least have put up a fight when Uncle Walt began to clean him up. But, no, he was all too eager to shill for the boss, and before you could say sell-out, he'd become a disgusting cross between Andy Hardy and Eddie Haskell.

Unlike Ozzie Guillen, Mickey's favorite sayings are purported to be "Gosh!" "Oh, boy!" "Aw, Gee!" and "That sure is swell." Not an *f*-bomb in sight, of course, which is bound to please Jay Mariotti, but in my mind, there's nothing like an "Aw, Gee!" to earn an extra kick in the mousy groin (if, indeed, Mickey has a groin; Disney may well have removed that part of his anatomy).

Four years ago, I reported that the minnows in Disney's think tank were worried about Mickey's declining popularity and trying to come up with ways to rejuvenate the aging corporate symbol. Naturally, they didn't come up with anything. Here's an idea, guys: retire him, and bring back Scrooge McDuck, who was always my idea of an antihero. The stingy Scrooge might shill but only for himself, and you sure as hell will never hear him say, "Aw, Gee!"

Booklist, June 1 and 15, 2008

BARBARA DUREE
AND *BOOKLIST*

"ONCE UPON A TIME—BEFORE the age of computers, e-mail, and networking—when a mouse was still a furry, four-footed character often encountered in children's books, and the web belonged to a talking spider named Charlotte—that was when . . . I joined the *Booklist* staff more than 50 years ago, in May 1954, as a young-people's books assistant with an annual salary of $4,800."

That word-perfect paragraph began Barbara Duree's contribution to our 100th-anniversary issue, published in June 2005. Her essay, called "My 50-Year Association with *Booklist*," was one of the highlights of the entire anniversary celebration, and for those of us lucky enough to have worked at *Booklist* during some of Barbara's time here, it brought back swarms of fond memories. With the news of Barbara's death on January 5, those memories are on our minds again. During her tenure at *Booklist*, Barbara not only served as the magazine's first YA editor (when she arrived in 1954, the term YA had not yet been invented), but also, at various points, as interim editor of the children's and adult books sections.

By the time I arrived, in 1980, there was really no part of the *Booklist* operation that didn't have Barbara's stamp firmly affixed to it. That stamp was often invisible to the outside world, but it was there nonetheless. I don't know how many times in my 25 years with this magazine I've been asked a question along the lines of, "Do you really get paid for reading books?" Yes, we do, I always answer, but it isn't all reading. Someone has to figure out how to move 50,000 books in and out of a small office every year, recording what needs to be recorded, sending along the cream of the crop to be reviewed, and then editing and publishing those reviews. That "someone" who figured it all out was Barbara Duree. I'm confident Barbara never allowed the phrase work flow to fall from her lips, but she knew more about it than a phalanx of laptop-toting IBM consultants.

In the center of the *Booklist* offices, there sits a now-antique card catalog that holds records of books considered for review at the magazine from the early years through about 1987. That catalog was the hard drive behind our operations, and Barbara was its memory. In the years since Barbara's retirement in 1986, much of our non-reviewing time has been spent automating our publishing system and, more recently, developing an online version of *Booklist*, tasks that speak to a world far different from the one with which Barbara was familiar. And, yet, in many ways, she was the guiding light behind our whole process of automation. Whenever we encountered a sticking point—How do we move files around the way we used to move half-sheets of buff-colored paper?—we simply went back to Barbara's work flow and made the wonderful world of Windows accommodate to it. Barbara thought she retired in time to avoid computers, but she was wrong. We couldn't have done it without her.

But Barbara's real love wasn't work flow. It was words and books—YA books, in particular. Barbara's behind-the-scenes contributions to the growth of young-adult literature are impossible to calculate, but she was there when the genre was born, and she helped nurture it to maturity, building *Booklist*'s coverage of the field, making sure that we evaluated adult books for YA suitability as well as high-end "juveniles," working closely with publishers, and playing a key consulting role in the development of ALA's annual Best Books for Young Adults list. Every *Booklist* editor knows how easy it is to miss a classic-to-be as it flashes through the office in lockstep with 50,000 other, yet-to-be-published titles. Barbara was behind the YA desk in the 1960s and '70s when such landmark fare as S. E. Hinton's *The Outsiders* and Judy Blume's *Forever* arrived on the daily book trucks. They weren't missed.

As Barbara noted in our anniversary essay, *Booklist* reviews today are "longer, livelier, more critical" than they were in her day, when the idea was simply to describe the book and its intended readership in 150 words, or "about three good sentences." And Barbara knew good sentences. Those of us still on the staff who were hired or trained by Barbara—current Books for Youth Editor Stephanie Zvirin, contributing editor and former YA Editor Hazel Rochman, Media Editor and former YA reviewer Sue-Ellen Beauregard, and Adult Books Editor Brad Hooper—never quite lose sight of Barbara's red pencil when we connect a subject to a verb. Our sentences may not always be as good as Barbara wanted them to be, but they are always better than they would have been if we hadn't known her.

Booklist, February 1, 2006

THE BOOKS THAT GOT AWAY

MANY PEOPLE ARE SURPRISED when I announce that I hate book-stores. Admittedly, it sounds peculiar. I like to read, readers love books, and bookstores, like libraries, house what we love. So what's to hate? I should qualify my position just a bit. I don't hate the idea of bookstores, just the experience of going into them, at the least the ones that stock new books.

Call it an occupational hazard, but whenever I go into a bookstore, I dread finding a prominently displayed new book that *Booklist* hasn't reviewed. Because we do our reading and reviewing in advance of publica-tion, any book decorating the display space at your local Borders or Barnes and Noble should already have been reviewed in *Booklist*. So when I spot an interesting-looking new title that I don't immediately recognize, I automatically panic. What happened? Did we ignore the book? Is the galley proof lying forgotten on some editor's shelf? Did the publisher for-get to send us a review copy? My stomach tightening, I look closer at the display and see jacket blurbs from the other prepublication review jour-nals. *Library Journal* loved this book. Ditto *PW*. Good Lord, even *Kirkus* gave it a rave! It's the Full Catastrophe, as Zorba the Greek likes to say. The book is a sure-thing National Book Award winner, no doubt soon to be an Oprah selection, and every prepub journal except *Booklist* saw its genius and published a suitably early review. Quickly, I pull my coat tight around my face and slink out the door, scurrying back to the office to check the library listservs and see if word of our humiliation has already hit cyberspace. That's why I hate going to bookstores.

Fortunately, the Full Catastrophe doesn't occur all that often, but I'm never quite free of the fear of it. Usually, there's a good reason why we haven't reviewed Borders' big book of the week: it's been embargoed by the publisher, cutting off distribution of review galleys in hopes of gener-ating even more hype. Prepublication review editors deplore this practice, of course, but despite our grumblings, it seems here to stay. Frankly, most of the books that get embargoed—politicians' memoirs, for example—don't require much of a review anyway. Like all journalists, though, a book review editor dreads missing a story, whatever the reason.

Still, it's rarely the embargoed books that make my stomach tighten when I visit a bookstore. No, it's the less-hyped but more worthwhile titles, something like Charles P. Pierce's *Sports Guy*, which I happened to spot the other day in a Borders near my office (I was hurrying past the books on my way to the music section). I know Pierce's work from numerous magazines, and I've heard him on NPR. He's one of the best sports commentators in the business. But I didn't know he had a book out, and worse yet, I edit most of the sports reviews in *Booklist*. Back to the office I went, panic building. Calling up *Sports Guy* on our database, I learned the following facts: yes, we did receive a galley of the book—three months ago, in fact—and, yes, it was assigned to a reviewer promptly upon receipt. And who was that unreliable reviewer? "Bill Ott." A feverish search of my legendarily messy office revealed just what I was afraid it would: a pristine galley copy of the Pierce book, virtually untouched, lying under a few dozen budget spreadsheets, one black glove, and a loose-leaf binder labeled "Personnel Policy Manual."

An ethical crisis was at hand. One alternative was to return Pierce to his slumbers underneath the personnel manual (it might be decades before anybody picked that up), quietly expunge the database record, and hope the listservs wouldn't notice. Let me assure you, that's exactly what I intended to do, but I made one mistake. I started reading an essay in the book about playing on the Hooters Golf Tour, and I remembered why I liked Pierce so much. He finds the sports stories everyone else misses, and he reminds those of us who care about sports why we got hooked in the first place. A rag-tag golfer crashing and burning on the dead-end Hooters tour; what ice hockey means to the 1,600 residents of Warroad, Minnesota; why corkball is the sport that time forgot—those are typical Pierce stories, and they don't deserve to be buried under a personnel manual.

So sometimes it's best to face up to the Full Catastrophe: I missed it, I found it, it's fabulous. Fine, but I still hate going into bookstores.

Booklist, March 15, 2001

Life beyond Books

DIAGRAMMING SENTENCES

WE WERE TALKING THE other day at our *Booklist* coffee break about Sarah Palin's sentences. Well, maybe *sentences* isn't the right word, though her speech patterns do have beginnings and endings, places you might think to put a period, or so one might conclude from her occasional need to take a breath. But are those wandering convolutions really sentences? As we pondered this conundrum, someone asked, "Do you think you could diagram a Palin sentence?" We all agreed that this would be a good test, but none of us volunteered to give it a try. Then, shortly after I'd returned to my desk, intrepid Googler Ben Segedin e-mailed me an article from *Slate* in which Kitty Burns Florey demonstrated exactly how to diagram a Palin utterance.

Somehow, I found this instant access to the information I needed a bit depressing. Think about it. Every time you have an original thought or toss off a bon mot, someone at the table is likely to consult what George Bush calls *the* Google and prove that your thought wasn't original after all, or that your *mot*, however *bon*, wasn't really yours. In this case, though, I will gratefully use Florey's work to fill the empty space on this Back Page. She argues that a diagrammed sentence can tell you much about the mind of the writer or speaker: "The more the diagram is forced to wander around the page, loop back on itself, and generally stretch its capabilities, the more it reveals that the mind that created the sentence is either a richly educated one—with a Proustian grasp of language that pushes the limits of expression—or such an impoverished one that it can produce only hot air, baloney, and twaddle."

Well, let's put Florey's proposition to the test by comparing one of the diagrams she did of a Palin sentence with one from a writer who has a truly "Proustian grasp of language"—the great Anthony Powell, author of the 12-volume *Dance to the Music of Time*. First, let's look at Florey's masterful diagram of this much-quoted comment by Palin about, well . . . I guess it's about Mr. Putin:

> *It's very important when you consider even national security issues with Russia as Putin rears his head and comes into the air space of the United States of America, where—where do they go?*

Here's what Florey came up with:

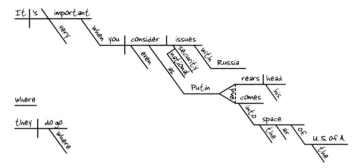

Now let's look at a sentence from the beginning of A *Question of Upbringing,* the first volume in Powell's *Dance:*

> *The image of Time brought thoughts of mortality: of human beings, facing outward like the Seasons, moving hand in hand in intricate measure: stepping slowly, methodically, sometimes a trifle awkwardly, in evolutions that take recognizable shape: or breaking into seemingly meaningless gyrations while partners disappear only to reappear again, once more giving pattern to the spectacle: unable to control the melody, unable, perhaps, to control the steps of the dance.*

Here's what *Booklist* Editor-at-Large and copy-editing supervisor Joanne Wilkinson came up with:

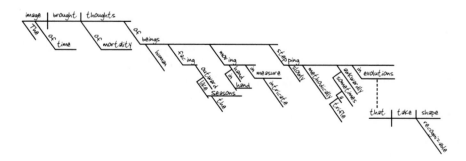

I'm sure veteran diagrammers will notice that Joanne didn't quite finish her assignment. Please don't hold it against her: this page is only so wide. Still, when we look at the two diagrams, a couple of things jump out: Powell's sentence works its way across the page horizontally, never dipping nearly as far downward as Palin's much shorter contribution. And, of course, there's that puzzling phrase of Palin's, "Where—where do they go?" Florey gave up on that one, finding no possible way to connect it grammatically to what came before. Powell's long, remarkably complex sentence is still anchored by one basic thought, expressed in a straightforward, subject, verb, object structure: "Time brought thoughts." The rest of the sentence simply expands on those thoughts in terms of the actions of human beings. In Palin's sentence, our attention is being drawn to something important, and it may have to do with Putin, but that's all we can say for sure. The verticality of the diagram suggests the lack of structure, even a randomness in the way one phrase attaches to another.

Have we learned anything here about "hot air and twaddle"? Hard to say, but I know I would rather listen to Powell than Palin. Don't take that as a political endorsement; Powell is a dead Brit, making him ineligible to run for office in the U.S. I'm writing this column three days before the election, so, unlike you, I don't know who won. I have a hunch, however, that even if the McCain-Palin ticket was defeated, we haven't heard our last Palin sentence. Just the other day, she uttered these relatively uncluttered words: "I'm not in this for naught." Let's see: is *naught* the object of *not* in that sentence? Guess not, but I like the symmetry.

Booklist, November 15, 2008

GOING ROGUE

SORTING THROUGH THE DETRITUS of the at-long-last-concluded presidential election, I keep coming back to the peculiar use of the metaphor "going rogue" to describe Sarah Palin's tendency to vary from the party line in her public utterances. Despite having proved in my last column, "Diagramming Sentences," that Palin's ramblings lack a certain, well . . . internal cohesiveness, I have to say that, in the matter of going rogue, I'm on the governor's side. Politicians and political commentators are always prone to hyperbole, but this notion of going rogue because you offered an opinion (even a lame one) that wasn't endorsed by a gaggle of pundits and campaign ombudsmen strikes me as bogus on multiple levels.

Not only is it the worst kind of hyperbole—campaign flunkies investing their less-than-adventurous lives with some James Bondish flair—it also sends the wrong message to both the candidate and the potential voter. I don't think I'm alone in enjoying a political candidate who doesn't always recite chapter and verse, and if winging it a little classifies one as a rogue, I guess the weasels have finally won. Either that, or we're a nation of rogues, and the weasels are hopelessly out of touch (I'm turning oddly optimistic as I age).

Most of all, though, the idea that Sarah Palin's babblings could ever possess enough substance to be categorized as rogue cheapens what, when used properly, can be a very vivid and meaningful notion. Gary Busey is what going rogue is all about, not Sarah Palin. To my mind, everything about Busey—the roles he plays, his public persona, his haircut, his bulging eyeballs—captures what rogue is supposed to mean. Take his role in Steven Seagal's so-bad-it's-wonderful *Under Siege*. I know, I know, you only watch PBS, and you've never seen a Steven Seagal movie, but even so, you must have heard about them: Seagal plays a special-forces superman turned cook who battles terrorists intent on hijacking various forms of conveyance (trains, planes, ships, etc.). *Under Siege* is the one about ships, and the lead terrorist is Busey, a former naval commander who has, yes, gone rogue and is now intent on taking over a battleship and launching a few missiles in the general direction of anyone who dissed him, all the while chewing as much scenery as possible and testing the hypothesis that you really can pop your eyes out of your own head. Now that's going rogue. Gary Busey and Sarah Palin don't belong in the same sentence, much less attached to the same metaphor. It's just wrong.

But going rogue isn't all bad. If you've read many thrillers, you know that often the hero makes a career out of going rogue—not in the sense of destroying the world, of course, but in the more socially acceptable sense of defying authority, abhorring institutional groupthink, and generally ignoring conventional wisdom wherever one encounters it. Often these rogue heroes were once part of an organization—the army, the police, the government—from which they were eventually expelled or simply quit. My favorite gone-rogue good guy is probably Miles Kendig in Brian Garfield's Edgar-winning *Hopscotch* (1975), played exquisitely by Walter Matthau in the 1980 movie version. Kendig is a CIA agent on the outs with his pencil-pushing chief, played by Ned Beatty, and rather than accept a demotion to a desk job, he decides to write a tell-all autobiography, a chapter of which he sends to the heads of the CIA, KGB, and MI6. Soon enough, all three are intent on killing Kendig, who, by going rogue, has endangered all their livelihoods. Humming Mozart all the while, Kendig leads the three stooges on a merry chase, outwitting and outmaneuvering the lot of them.

Like so much in life, going rogue is a matter of degree. Keep the game plan to confounding bureaucrats and showing up authority, and you'll probably do fine, at least in literature, if not at General Motors. Michael Connelly's Harry Bosch and Lee Child's Jack Reacher are just this side of going rogue, and it's that edge that makes us care about them and despise the bureaucrats who bedevil them. On the other side of every rogue, there's a soul-killing organization, or at the very least, a small-minded organization man. Who are you going to root for, the rogue or the organization? Even Sarah Palin can come across as a vaguely appealing character if she's defying her handlers and taking questions from the press. It's only when she answers the questions that she loses us. She's not smart enough to be Harry Bosch, and she lacks Gary Busey's style.

So, please, let's be careful about who we accuse of going rogue. It's a term that demands a certain scope. It's best if missiles are involved, especially if you're talking Gary Busey–caliber roguery, but even if you're hoping to be a good-guy rogue, do make it a point to defy the authority of an organization with missiles in its arsenal. Small-time defiance just doesn't cut it. Yes, the *Booklist* publishing assistant who, 30 years ago, protested against inhumane working conditions by hiding catalog cards in her desk rather than filing them did defy the authority of a book-review magazine, but she didn't go rogue. And neither did Sarah Palin.

Booklist, December 1, 2008

TRAVELIN' LIGHT (OR NOT)

HAVE YOU SEEN THE TV commercial in which the aging owner of an auto-repair shop announces to a customer that he's selling the business so he can "chase the dream before I'm too tired to do it"? Then we flash-forward to the same customer bringing his apparently persnickety Porsche back to the shop, where he encounters the new owner, also aging, who says that he bought the shop because he wants "to chase the dream before I'm too tired to do it." The point is obvious: we're supposed to nod knowingly at the truism that we should each pursue our own dreams even if they contradict what the next guy is doing. Yeah, sure, but I'd bet that nearly everyone who has seen that ad has asked, "What kind of a crazy-ass dream is owning an auto-repair shop?" Our sympathies naturally go to aging guy number one, whose dream seems to involve travel, heading out for distant ports and exciting adventures. That's what dreams are supposed to be made of.

Well, I'm having second thoughts. I'm about to set off on a long-awaited trip to Italy, and frankly, I'm thinking I might rather stay at home and clean out a carburetor or two (if I knew where exactly to find the carburetor after I opened the hood of my Nissan). My ambivalence about international travel stems, I suppose, from all the usual reasons: the horrors of air travel in the modern world, my hopelessly monolingual condition, the sort of nagging health concerns that plague anyone of a certain age, and, of course, my own general weariness. The other day a friend (to whom I was whining about getting ready for the upcoming trip) observed that I'd never really been all that much of a traveler. I took heated objection to this notion, citing the various jaunts I'd taken over the years, but on further reflection, I'm afraid she may be right. I'm the kind of guy who can always find a reason not to go somewhere—whether it's a movie or another continent.

To help myself feel better about this shocking realization, I started thinking about books and movies in which characters took ill-advised, even absurd, trips. Sometimes, damn it, there's nothing wrong with staying home. The motives of my crackpot travelers vary: some are in search of love, some of reconciliation, some of adventure, and one guy just plain stomped off. In every case, though, they might have been better off washing the car—or even going to Italy.

WORLD'S GREATEST OPTIMIST GETS BLUES AND RUNS BACK AND FORTH ACROSS U.S.

Yes, I'm talking about that "life is like a box of chocolates" boy, Forrest Gump, whose bubble of idiot-savant optimism is finally burst when his girlfriend leaves him. Forrest decides to run after her, literally, and when that doesn't work, he just keeps running—for a couple of years, or at least long enough to grow a major-league beard and attract a bunch of equally addlepated followers. I know it goes against the uplifting Gumpian spirit, but I can't help but think that a bottle of Scotch is a much better way to deal with being dumped than a two-year stomp off.

GOLFER WHACKS THREE-IRON ACROSS MONGOLIA

He hadn't heard of hybrid clubs? They're so much more forgiving when the fairway is a steppe. Club selection, though, is the least of the questionable decisions Andre Tolme made in deciding to hit three-iron shots across a country that had never seen a golf ball (*I Golfed across Mongolia*, 2006). The upside of his quest: on a par 10,000 course, you can afford to waste a few shots. The downside: let's mention only one small fact among so many. When you lose all your balls playing Mongolia National, you can't send your caddie back to the clubhouse for another sleeve of Titleist Pro-V1s.

OLD GUY RIDES LAWNMOWER ACROSS MIDWEST TO SAY HEY TO ESTRANGED BROTHER

Remember the Richard Farnsworth movie, *The Straight Story*, in which the Farnsworth character, 73-year-old Alvin Straight, rides a lawnmower from Iowa to Wisconsin in hopes of setting things straight with his 75-year-old brother? Admirable motive, terrible game plan. The moral here is simple: avoid all family upsets. If your parent or sibling is guilty of some horrendous insult to your person, don't stomp off. Take the high road, and mend fences quickly. Not because it's the right thing to do, but because, otherwise, you may one day find yourself sitting atop a lawnmower on the interstate when you could be at home watching *Project Runway*.

GREENWICH VILLAGE GAL WALKS TO RUSSIA TO GIVE COMMIE LOVER A BIG HUG

The movie *Reds* won an Academy Award for Warren Beatty (best director), but there's one big howler in the plot. John Reed (Beatty) has left his lover, Louise Bryant (Diane Keaton), and gone to Russia to join the 1917 Revolution. Bryant eventually decides she must follow her man (it's a love story), but she one-ups even Alvin Straight when it comes to unconventional methods of conveyance: she walks to Moscow, apparently hurdling the Bering Strait on the way. The plot jumps from Russia, where Reed encounters all sorts of troubles trying to be a good Communist, to somewhere on the road, where Bryant, wearing an Eskimo hat, trudges on through the snow (you keep waiting for Bing and Bob to join the trek). Louise finally gets her hug and then Reed dies. Idealists make lousy lovers.

LEGLESS LOVER SCOOTS OFF TO NEW YORK TO FIND GIRL

And you thought Louise Bryant was crazy. I've always had some problems with the plot of *Porgy and Bess*—especially the ending. Bess, hooked on cocaine ("happy dust") by the serpent of the piece, Sportin' Life, has left Porgy, abandoning the simple ways of Catfish Row, South Carolina, for the bright lights of the Big Apple. Porgy, who has no legs but moves about Catfish Row just fine by using his hands to push a sort of converted goat cart, is devastated. Blind to Bess' many flaws, he pushes off after her, apparently planning to use the blue highways for the thousand-mile scoot to New York. Sometimes, Porgy, you just have to let them go.

Booklist, October 15, 2006

BILL'S EXCELLENT ADVENTURE— AT THE WHITE HOUSE

"THE WHITE HOUSE, PLEASE," I was shocked to hear myself saying to a Washington, D.C., cab driver one sunny morning in June.

Give me your tired curmudgeons, your unashamedly apolitical pessimists yearning to just say no—give me, well . . . me—and see what happens when an invitation to attend the White House Conference on School Libraries turns up in the office mail. It's tough to admit that your hard-won grumpiness can't withstand one trip to the White House, but I'm afraid there's no hiding from the truth. I walked out of my D.C. hotel a world-weary naysayer, but by the time I had announced my destination to the cabbie, I was beginning to feel like a werewolf when the moon is full—except, in my case, I was being transformed into the kind of person who likes *Mr. Smith Goes to Washington.*

I blame at least some of my vulnerability on an unfortunate incident the previous night. Whenever I've been in Washington—usually to attend ALA conferences (where one's curmudgeonly ways are never in danger of being compromised)—I like to visit Kramer Books and Afterwords, both to browse the shelves and to enjoy a quiet meal in the store's charming restaurant. While I was standing in line to pay for the Bill Bryson book I was planning to read over dinner, I noticed another lone male in front of me buying a copy of *Dating for Dummies*. It must be a gag gift for a friend, I thought. I saw the man again as I was being led to a tiny table (designed for solo diners) at the back of the restaurant. He was seated across from me, and he was not only reading his new book, he was taking notes! Was that a smirk I noticed from our waiter after he took Dummy's order and then mine? Clearly he was treating us like outcasts at a fraternity rush party (à la *Animal House*). "Wait a minute," I wanted to shout. "I'm reading Bill Bryson, and I have a date—at the White House!"

I was in a fragile condition when I arrived at the East Entrance to the White House the next morning. How else can you explain the fact that I found myself admiring the crisp dress whites of the marines who escorted us to the dining rooms where continental breakfast was being served? I came of age in the '60s, damn it; nobody challenges my antiwar bona fides. Shaken, I tried to regain my composure by nibbling on some fruit cocktail, chatting with a few colleagues, stealing a napkin embossed with the White House seal, and generally acting the part of an awestruck patriot. (It was an act, right?)

Then it was time to be escorted to the East Room for the conference itself. A crisis loomed. Were there bathrooms in the White House, and were they available to born-again Mr. Smiths like myself? Nothing for it but to ask the marines. Yes, there was a men's room, and I could find it down the marble staircase and through the library. Ah, ha! My sense of irony lives, after all. I'm attending a conference on libraries at a house where the urinals are in the library! Refreshed spiritually and otherwise, I took time to check out the shelves. More irony! First I spied an autographed copy of that most subversive work of lit crit, *Love and Death in the American Novel*, by one of my literary heroes, Leslie Fiedler. Even better, down the row from Fiedler rested a tome called *Writers on the Left*, from the Communism in America series. I marched into the East Room confident that I could muster the ironic disdain necessary to resist whatever temptations awaited me. Wrong again.

First of all, Laura Bush's opening remarks were genuinely heartfelt, a moving tribute to her belief in the importance of school libraries and her commitment to the Laura Bush Foundation, which will support libraries and reading across the nation. The speeches that followed were nearly as impressive. I've heard my share of testimonials to the joys of reading over the years, and I like to think I've developed a strong allergic reaction to their piety-laden rhetoric. And yet I didn't sneeze once as a school superintendent from Medford, Oregon, described how reading scores in his system skyrocketed when school libraries were improved, or as a principal from Kentucky recounted similar success with a program designed to promote cooperation between teachers and librarians.

Perhaps it was the hands-on practicality of these speakers that won me over, but I knew I was putty in the hands of patriots when, during a break, we were directed to the Truman Porch, there to watch the president depart in his helicopter. I did restrain from offering up one of those hearty, full-armed waves that seem to be saying, "Hey, George, here I am, your pal Bill," but I can't say I wasn't impressed when the official helicopter hovered in front of the Washington Monument during its takeoff.

Then it was over, and I was out on the street, forced to deal with the crumbling of my worldview. If a trip to the George W. Bush White House could inflict such damage to my cherished cynicism, I can only shudder to think what might have happened if a president whose views I actually supported happened to have been in office. Still, as the days have passed since my excellent adventure, I can feel my old persona beginning to reassert itself. Perhaps my Mr. Smith period was only an aberration, a meaningless, one-time slip off my ideological wagon. That's my story, and I'm sticking to it, but what about that carefully preserved White House napkin, pressed so neatly into my copy of Bill Bryson?

Booklist, July 2002

CUPCAKES IN MY GO-PAK

WHY AM I AGAINST a war in Iraq? It's very simple. I don't want to wear a backpack. When I lived in Washington State, I liked to say that I was the only person in the Northwest who had never strapped on a backpack. Surrounded by outdoorsy types, I was determined to go a different way. I haven't lived in the Northwest for a long time, but I've stuck to my principles. No backpacks. Now the president tells me that, in the event of a terrorist attack, I should have a backpack at the ready at all times (one at home and one at work), filled to the brim with duct tape, water, and other essentials. When the guidelines on backpack preparedness were first announced on television, I misheard the instructions. Perhaps I wasn't paying much attention, but when one of our leaders was extolling the virtues of duct tape, I thought he was saying cupcakes. Imagine my confusion. After all these years of avoiding backpacks, I was being told that, as a loyal American, I was obligated not only to wear a backpack (now called a "Go-Pak") but also to fill it with cupcakes.

Clearly, I was going to be forced to make some big decisions. From the get-go, I stood firm on the backpack question. If I'd managed to avoid backpacks through all the years of the Vietnam War, I certainly wasn't going to sacrifice my principles now. (Oddly, I had some linguistic confusion in the '60s, too. At my first Vietnam protest march, I couldn't understand what football had to do with stopping the war, but fortunately, my friends Denny and Rob explained to me that the chant was "Ho, Ho, Ho Chi Minh, the NLF is gonna win," not the NFL, as I had been shouting enthusiastically.) This pattern of misheard slogans in times of national crisis caused me to experience an epiphany. Maybe it wasn't just a coincidence that I kept inserting my own malaprops into wartime rhetoric. Maybe there was a message there. After all, wouldn't the world be a better place if everyone kicked back on the couch, stuffing cupcakes in their mouths and watching football rather than inciting violence of one kind or the other? My course was clear. I would carry a Go-Pak—not a backpack but my old faithful shoulder bag—stuffed with cupcakes. Every successful antiwar movement must begin with one committed individual acting from his own conscience.

There were still more decisions. What about those crucial "other essentials" the president requires that we add to our Go-Paks? I would start with a bottle of Jack Daniels, of course, never having accepted the narrow-minded notion that whiskey and chocolate don't go well together. And let's not forget books. (Inexplicably, there was no mention of books in the official Go-Pak instructions—but what can you expect from a government whose chief executive cites *The Very Hungry Caterpillar* as his favorite book?) It seems only appropriate that my antiwar Go-Pak should include a selection of my favorite antiwar novels. But how to choose? I can only carry a few books in my bag without getting a knifing pain shooting down my left shoulder. (This is another advantage of the shoulder bag over the backpack. If you're wearing a backpack, which distributes its load evenly across your back, and you get a knifing pain down your left shoulder, it probably means you're having a heart attack. If you're wearing a shoulder bag, though, you can blame the pain on the bag and not bother about going to the doctor.) Still, you want to keep the pain within manageable limits, and to do that, I recommend no more than three books.

If we accept D. H. Lawrence's definition of the novel as the "book of life," then any novel about war is automatically an antiwar novel, since war is necessarily not on the side of life. We can narrow it down a bit, though, by eliminating from our Go-Paks all those wonderful novels portraying the ugly reality of the soldier's life (*All Quiet on the Western Front, The Naked and the Dead, The Thin Red Line, The Things They Carried*) and limiting ourselves to books whose antiwar message emerges in other ways. So here they are, the three titles constituting my essential Go-Pak collection:

> A *Farewell to Arms,* by Ernest Hemingway (1929). These two sentences contain the essence of all antiwar novels: "Troops went down by the house and down the road and the dust they raised powdered the leaves of the trees. The trunks of the trees too were dusty and the leaves fell early that year and we saw the troops marching along the road and the dust rising and leaves, stirred by the breeze, falling and the soldiers marching and afterward the road bare and white except for the leaves."

> *Going after Cacciato,* by Tim O'Brien (1978). Can a foot soldier, mired in the horror of Vietnam, leave his squad and walk 8,600 miles to Paris? Impossible, of course, utterly surreal, especially with the rest of his squad ordered to bring him back to stinking reality. And, yet, "What about Paris? What about the bistros and adventures and beautiful gardens? Have you forgotten the gardens?" Paul Berlin, one of the soldiers going after Cacciato, hasn't forgotten. "Paris is still a possibility. It is. It's still a live possibility." Thank God for that.

> *The Good Soldier Schweik,* by Jaroslav Hasek (1930). In this classic satire, Schweik, a Prague dogcatcher and seeming imbecile, is drafted into the Austrian army and sent to the Russian front during World War I. He

never disobeys an order yet somehow never manages to get to the front. I like to think that Schweik would immediately see the wisdom of carrying cupcakes in his Go-Pak.

Booklist, March 1, 2003

WHY I HATE CRAFTS

MOST OF THE BLAME for my allergy to all things crafty must fall on my only-too-obvious lack of talent, but even that formidable obstacle might have been overcome had it not been for the psychic damage done to me by my eighth-grade art teacher, who we'll call Mr. (Hannibal) Lecter. You don't run into too many sadistic art teachers, but this guy was the exception. You may understand his type better if I point out that, in addition to nurturing the artistic sensibilities of a gang of hormonal junior-high kids, Mr. Lecter was also the eighth-grade football and basketball coach and, in the summers, worked as a butcher.

I first encountered Mr. Lecter on the football field. Being a skinny, weak, and cowardly eighth-grader, I really didn't have much of a future on the gridiron. I saw it differently, of course, imagining myself as a rubber-armed quarterback in the Norm Van Brocklin mold. That illusion disappeared after the first day of practice. There was only one drill during that two-hour session, and it didn't involve throwing passes. No, Hannibal simply divided his troops into two lines that faced one another, with about 10 yards of demilitarized zone in the middle, and instructed us to knock our opposite partner on his ass. When the carnage ended, there were five broken arms and three broken collarbones on the day. (The rumor was that this total was not Hannibal's personal best; at his last school, he was said to have fractured 12 bones in one practice.) I survived the day without any damaged parts, but that was mainly due to a technique I'd perfected during somersault drills in gym class: you never quite get to the front of the line, pausing at crucial moments to tie a shoe, ask a question, cough, whatever it takes.

Being one of the taller kids in my class, I had always assumed that basketball was my sport. That was before I played for Hannibal, who saw the game as an indoor version of football. Admittedly, I was very slow and a terrible rebounder (skinny, weak, and cowardly, remember), but I could shoot the ball pretty well—a skill that not too many of my peers had mastered (this was long before the days of basketball camps). Unfortunately, for my career, Hannibal viewed the whole "put-the-ball-in-the-basket" thing as an unimportant and decidedly sissified aspect of the game, much preferring what he called "the battle under the boards," which could result in at least the occasional bloody nose if not a full ration of broken arms.

It may come as a surprise to learn that my most traumatic experience with Mr. Lecter took place not on any field of play but in art class. Yes, I had been flattened cartoon-style on the football field and elbowed into submission on the basketball court, but much worse, by far, was the humiliation I suffered when Hannibal got a look at my folded-paper creation. I don't think we called it origami back in 1959, but that was the general idea: fold a piece of paper into squares and then unfold it in such a way that it looked pretty. These days we think of origami as a peaceful art, sort of like the Japanese tea ceremony, but you wouldn't think peaceful if you'd ever seen Hannibal Lecter fold paper. He attacked a defenseless sheet of paper as if it were a quarterback left alone outside the pocket, and he was a linebacker with a clean shot.

Before going on to recount the full horror of my origami experience (I'm not quite ready to do that), I need to say a little bit more about how Hannibal came to be an art teacher. There was much discussion of this issue back in the day, and many theories were bandied about. The simplest explanation—and the one I've always liked—is that we already had a gym teacher, and art was the only other thing Hannibal could teach. (Many of us remain unconvinced that he was fully literate, which would rule out the more academic disciplines.) But why art? Because he was such a good butcher, of course. I have it on record from a grocery-store owner who was a friend of my father that Hannibal carved a pork shoulder like Michelangelo chiseled a hunk of stone. Significantly, painting was mysteriously absent from Hannibal's art curriculum. We were only taught arts and crafts in which the medium was either pummeled, twisted, or hacked into shape.

I'm sorry, but I'm still not ready to discuss my origami experience. Suffice it to say that what happened to me that day, in front of my peers in Hannibal's class, was worse even than the time my friend Jack was called out in Western Civ for having written on an exam that Sir Francis Drake was the first explorer ever to circumcise the globe. My therapist, if I had one, would surely support my decision to wait a little longer before fully confronting my memories of Hannibal, origami, and me. After all, I did give the green light to publishing *Booklist's* Spotlight on Crafts & Hobbies. It's true I might not have been so broad-minded had "hobbies" not been thrown in to soften the blow, but still, I think you'll have to admit I'm making real progress. Just don't ask me to fold any paper.

Booklist, December 15, 2003

PARSING THE PARADIGM SHIFT

I'VE ALWAYS HAD A difficult relationship with the words *paradigm* and *parse*. I first heard *paradigm* in the 1960s from the mouth of a college English professor I took to be an oracle of wisdom. You'll remember the type: longish hair, psychedelic ties, and a propensity for treating the Beatles' *Sgt. Pepper* album as worthy of the same scrutiny afforded the Victorian poets (my professor's area of formal expertise). Like most of what this prof said, I didn't really know what paradigm meant, but I thought it sounded cool when he said it. Over the years, my confusion increased when I somehow came to associate the word with two movies: *The Paradine Case*, a minor Hitchcock vehicle, and *The Parallax View*, an arty thriller about a right-wing conspiracy. So, gradually, my working definition of paradigm came to be something like this: a tricky sort of change that you had to be really smart and hip to understand and that helped explain both why Hitchcock was great and why right-wing conspiracies were omnipresent.

I've had to modify that definition a bit over the years, but as with so many first impressions, I've never quite been able to leave it behind. It gets more and more difficult, however, especially in an age when all the management consultants in the global village (all 14 billion of them) are issuing dire warnings about the need to adapt to the current paradigm shift. The men and women delivering these warnings at corporate retreats and on television news shows definitely don't wear psychedelic ties, and I'd wager most of them have never seen *The Parallax View.* So what in the hell are they talking about? It has something to do with change and with the digital age—that much I get. The way things used to work isn't the way they're going to work in the future. Fine, we should all take a crack at selling our products on the Internet, but why is that seemingly obvious insight so profound? Here's where paradigm comes in: If you just said, "things are going to change in the future," people would look bored and nod; no television networks would come calling; and you wouldn't be able to sell yourself to any companies holding management retreats. But when you substitute paradigm shift for the mundane "things change," your words instantly take on gravitas; you have become a consultant. What worked for my hippie professor works for today's MBA-toting, Armani-clad gurus: paradigm still sounds cool.

There's more. You might be able to argue with somebody's idea of how things will change, but you can't argue with a paradigm shift. Not in today's organizational culture. Think about it. You're 10 years old, and you're sitting around the dinner table. You have a brilliant argument as to why the virtues of a clean room have been utterly exaggerated by your parents and by the culture at large. If you're smart, though, you know you can't present that argument because, if you do, despite being right, you'll wind up in big trouble and probably find yourself cleaning your room just as much as if you'd kept your mouth shut.

It's the same with a paradigm shift. Say you're a junior executive with Oreo Cookies. A management consultant has just informed you that a paradigm shift is under way; the consumer of the future no longer wants his relationship with Oreos to be static. He or she wants the Oreo to be accessible in a variety of formats: open-faced or sandwich-style; with a variety of fillings, selected by the customer, who also may choose to design the contents of his own package. Further, the customer might want to order his glass of milk simultaneously and will expect links to several milk company databases. Perhaps you see this scenario as absurd, or perhaps, like me, you don't particularly like Oreos, and you absolutely despise milk. Either way, keep quiet. In organizational life, you don't want to be the guy with a reputation for not recognizing a paradigm shift. Besides, your technical people will never be able to get the two databases working together anyway.

Paradigms have much more power these days than they had back in the '60s, but I liked them a lot better when they still had something to do with Hitchcock. The word *parse* may not have all that much power today, but it definitely has a new cachet. The word used to belong only to grammarians (parse means "to break a sentence down into parts"), but it has recently been co-opted by programmers, who apparently parse up a storm in the course of "writing code." What has happened, then, is that a word belonging to the nerds of one era (grammarians) has been handed off to the nerds of another era (programmers). Yet, along the way, the term has been picked up by TV commentators and editorial writers, who are all parsing away as if it were the hippest possible thing to do. Since when do the Tom Brokaws of the world look to guys with penholders in their pockets for clues on how to sound cool? Clearly, there can be only one explanation: there's been a paradigm shift.

Booklist, December 15, 2000

IT WAS 40 YEARS
AGO TODAY . . .

THE FORTIETH ANNIVERSARY OF the Beatles' 1964 appearance on the *Ed Sullivan Show* elicited a startling outpouring of hyperbole from the sound-bite-crazed talking heads of the electronic media. While no one echoed John Lennon's infamous claim that the group was "bigger than Jesus" (religion, after all, is hot right now), there was no shortage of outrageous claims. The common theme seemed to be that, before the Fab Four belted out a few choruses of "She loves me, yeah, yeah, yeah," the sixties didn't exist. We were in the cultural doldrums, so the story goes, still shell-shocked by the assassination of JFK, still a mob of crew-cut ciphers content to read *Kids Say the Darndest Things* and listen to the song stylings of the Four Lads. Had the Liverpudlians not taken the stage that night, we were led to conclude, our hair would have refused to grow; *free* and *love* might never have been used in the same sentence; Ken Kesey wouldn't have painted his bus; and poor LBJ wouldn't have been driven from office in 1968.

I suppose we really shouldn't be too hard on our immaculately coiffed newsfolk. Few of them were born in 1964, to begin with, and more important, they were simply doing what we all tend to do when we attempt to make sense of history: create an iron-clad, cause-and-effect chronology where none exists. Certainly the emergence of the Beatles was a significant ingredient in the cultural stew that became the sixties, but it was just that: a piquant spice thrown into a pot already simmering with more than its share of hearty meats and tangy vegetables.

Would the Beatles have ignited a new spirit of rebellion in mainstream youth if Mario Savio hadn't prepared the soil with the Berkeley student revolt in the early sixties; if Bob Dylan, already a Greenwich Village hero by 1964, hadn't added a growly edge of protest to the folk-music scene; if the beat movement of the fifties (Ginsberg's *Howl* was published in 1956, and Kerouac's *On the Road* in 1957) hadn't created an underground for those inclined to resist the gray-flannel mainstream; and if, even further back, Charlie Parker, Dizzy Gillespie, Thelonious Monk, and the other bebop pioneers of the 1940s hadn't rescued jazz from the sameness of the swing era and provided the beats with an inspirational soundtrack?

It's clear that the sixties as we came to know them were blowin' in the wind by the time Ed Sullivan introduced the Beatles to America. Did the group turn the breeze into a pop-cultural hurricane? Maybe, but I'm guessing the big blow would have happened anyway. Let's take another look at those much-maligned early '60s. Take 1963, the year before the Beatles supposedly invented the decade. Edward Albee's *Who's Afraid of Virginia Woolf?* a seminal sixties' drama, won the Tony for best play, and just listen to this short list of books published that year: James Baldwin's *The Fire Next Time*, Betty Friedan's *The Feminine Mystique*, John Rechy's *City of Night*, Thomas Pynchon's *V*, John Updike's *The Centaur*, Kurt Vonnegut's *Cat's Cradle*, and Sylvia Plath's *The Bell Jar*. Sounds to me like a lot of the heavy lifting that would make the sixties the sixties had been done long before the Beatles crooned their first "yeah, yeahs" on American soil.

So, if we throw out the anniversary hyperbole, what are we left with? The Beatles didn't invent the sixties, but they definitely helped shape the decade by bringing the spirit of rebellion to the placid middle class. What about today? Is the group still a part of the pop-cultural mix? The music watchers at *Entertainment Weekly* think so; in an article called "Do the Beatles Still Matter?" (February 13, 2004), they argue that the once-Fab Four has become "America's hottest cult band." Attracting teenagers and twentysomethings, the Mop Tops are suddenly "the alternative to all the once-alternative stuff that has since become the mainstream."

Huh? This is all way too complicated for a guy who is old enough to have watched the Sullivan show. But I like the idea that the Beatles have come full circle on the musical wheel of fortune: from yesterday's trendsetter to today's alternative. Fans don't scream anymore; they pat themselves on the back for taking the long view. Listen to this 19-year-old quoted in *Entertainment Weekly*: "I'm going to be a Beatles fan for the rest of my life. I'm not sure I can say that about Jay-Z and OutKast."

Booklist, March 1, 2004

NO! IN THUNDER

I'M BORROWING THIS COLUMN'S title from a collection of essays published some 40 years ago by my favorite literary critic, the unquenchable maverick Leslie Fiedler, who spent his career saying no to whatever orthodoxy stood in his path. My topic, however, has nothing to do with either Fiedler or literary criticism. I'm here to sing the praises of another favorite of mine, Admiral James Stockdale, Ross Perot's vice-presidential candidate in 1992, the man who courageously made what I believe to be the most significant political gesture of the modern era: turning off his hearing aid in the middle of a nationally televised debate with his fellow vice-presidential candidates, Al Gore and Dan Quayle. Stockdale, who died on July 5, 2005, said no in thunder to the entire political process, and in doing so, he earned the undying respect of all of us who try to shut our ears to the incessant babble that passes for political discourse in this country.

Saying no to politics is not all that easy anymore. Thanks to cable television and the Internet, politicians are virtually ubiquitous in today's world; to tune them out completely would require turning off our hearing aids permanently. And, further, political involvement today, on either Left or Right, is seen by many as a moral obligation, right up there with promoting reading, preserving the environment, and supporting the troops. The ultimate futility of Stockdale's gesture makes it all the more attractive to me, all the more romantic, almost Gatsby-like in that "boats against the current" kind of way.

Let's stop right here for a moment. I'm guessing that if you haven't given up on this column already, you think I'm either trying to do a Jonathan Swift, or I've gone off the crackpot edge completely. So it was for Admiral Stockdale. His obituaries portrayed his actions during the debate as the work of a buffoon, demeaning the noble ideals of American politics. It wasn't just the hearing aid. Earlier, he had begun his opening remarks by asking, "Who am I? Why am here?" prompting numerous less-than-polite replies from the assembled talking heads, who assumed that the answers to such questions were obvious: to make news for us to analyze, you old fool. In fact, the talking heads and all of those who decried Stockdale's performance missed the allusion to Epictetus, the Stoic philosopher whose writings helped the admiral endure seven-and-one-half years of imprisonment in Vietnam.

Finally, though, I would argue that everyone got it wrong about Stockdale: the talking heads, of course, always get it wrong, convinced that politics has something to do with real life; loyalists on the Left and Right, appalled at the impiety of acting silly rather discussing the "issues," displayed the tunnel vision so often a by-product of misplaced piety. But what was Stockdale really up to on stage that night, asking the big philosophical questions, wandering away from the podium at one point for a stroll, and, of course, turning off the hearing aid? I have no idea what was in the man's mind, but I don't believe that matters much. Trust the tale, not the teller, D. H. Lawrence told us, and the episode of Stockdale's hearing aid plays out like a lyric poem in which the poet sees the folly of the world and turns away from it.

Those of us who harbor a profound antipathy to politics, and who, like Groucho Marx, would never join a group that would have us as a member, tend to be a lonely lot. Just try telling someone at a cocktail party that the only political philosophy you have much sympathy for is anarchy. Don't even bother trying to explain that, no, you don't mean the bomb-throwing anarchists, you mean the folks who don't like the whole idea of government and just try to ignore it. That tack won't work either because the next thing you know you'll be accused of being a survivalist or, if you happen to have a beard, of looking a bit like the Unabomber. No, you wind up screaming before the room clears, I don't want to change anything; I just want to hide from it all.

Where do lonely souls with such intemperate views go to find heroes? Literature offers some help: there's Falstaff, of course, our ultimate role model, and a handful of others, including the Good Soldier Schweik and, more recently, (ex-)Reverend Earley Hayes from Michael Malone's *Handling Sin*. And, since 1992, we have a politician of our own: Admiral James Stockdale, who looked into the eye of the political hurricane and screamed his version of "The Horror! The Horror!" Realizing he didn't want to be there at all but was unable to leave, he took the only course of action available to him: he turned off the sound. I do the same thing everyday. Thanks, Admiral, for showing me the way.

Booklist, August 2005

A NOT-SO-WONDERFUL LIFE

I'VE ALWAYS HAD A problem with *It's a Wonderful Life*. The thing is, it wasn't. As I see it—and, yes, I'm well aware that I'm taking the minority point of view here—George Bailey was the victim of a dirty trick, and he was too brainwashed to recognize it. George had a vision for his life: he wanted adventure; he thrilled to the sound of train whistles and the idea of ocean liners casting off for distant ports. And what happened? He got stuck in Bedford Falls, working at the Building and Loan, propping up his ne'er-do-well Uncle Billy, and seeing his limited resources squandered on a drafty old house with a staircase whose damnable banister knob wouldn't stay put. Sure, he kept old Mr. Gower, the pharmacist, from poisoning that kid, and he saved his brother's life, but—in a classic case of no good deed goes unpunished—his reward was to feel the noose of Bedford Falls cinched ever more tightly around his skinny neck.

And who put that noose there in the first place? The beloved Mary Bailey, that's who. I'm sorry to say it, but she is the real villain of the piece, not Mr. Potter. I can already hear the gasps from all you party-liners: Mary Bailey! Not the rock of the Bailey family, the all-American homemaker who would rather help the Martini clan move into their new bungalow (three rooms and a bath) than go to Florida with former suitor Sam Wainwright. But try to take your eyes off the family-values halo around Mary's head for a minute. Remember the scene in which George and Mary are on their way to the train station (finally, he gets to hear a train whistle with his name on it)? They're off to New York on their honeymoon, where George plans to paint the town ("the hottest jazz, the tallest buildings, the prettiest girls"). But, wouldn't you know it, the stock market has crashed, and Bedford Falls is panicking. George dutifully returns to the Building and Loan (think Dr. Zhivago trudging back to his wife) and does his best to talk the townsfolk out of selling their shares to Mr. Potter. He's giving it his best shot, but he's not handing out his own money—maybe they can still catch a later train for New York—when Mary offers up the honeymoon stash. How convenient! George misses his train forever, and Mary turns the key, locking him up in that drafty old barn of a house on Sycamore Street: the saddest scene in the movie, for my money.

And how about that money-guzzling house? Mary bought it without even consulting poor George, afraid, no doubt, that he might have wanted to save his cash and take a trip to Paris. Forget it, George! Mary wears the pants in the Bailey family, and your traveling days were over before you ever made it to the train station. Reverse George and Mary's genders, put Tracy and Hepburn in the roles, and you have the beginnings of a classic proto-feminist movie. No way does Hepburn stand for Tracy raining on her parade!

So Mary is the villain, no question, but George is hardly blameless. In the interests of space, I cite only two examples. First, what the hell is the matter with "ground floors"? You'll recall the scene in which Sam Wainright offers George the chance to "get in on the ground floor" of an emerging industry, and George defiantly declares he doesn't want any ground floors. Why not, George? Stay in Bedford Falls and marry Mary if you must, but why not have a little mad money in the bank to fund the occasional ocean voyage? No, George the sap prefers to tighten his own noose. And, finally, in perhaps the most stinging irony in the movie, George gets his trip to New York but is too far under Bedford Falls' thumb to know where he is. I refer to the fantasy scene in which the angel Clarence shows George what would have happened had he never lived. Bedford Falls has become Pottersville, and it is one swinging town, with everything George once looked forward to seeing in New York, including hot jazz and pretty girls. Does George pop into the Three Deuces, Pottersville version, to hear even one set? No, he's appalled at the disappearance of sleepy old Bedford Falls (where your musical choices are limited to a barbershop quartet on Sunday). So what's Frank Capra saying here? That George kept Bedford Falls pure or that his choices kept him from realizing his own dreams? Both, I think, which tells you something about the dark underbelly of purity.

All of which brings us to a frighteningly pure new book called *It's a Wonderful Life for Kids*, by Jimmy Hawkins, who happens to be the actor who played Tommy Bailey in the movie. The difference between this version and Capra's is that whereas the movie at least flirts with a double-edged view of George's life, Hawkins, predictably, ignores the dark side altogether. In his adaptation, an older Tommy is having his own George Bailey crisis: Tommy has misplaced his school's library fund, and he can't bear the humiliation, sending him off to George's bridge, contemplating suicide. Naturally, another angel second class turns up and shows him how one life touches other lives. Guess what?—the angel gets his wings in the end. Not surprisingly, Hawkins chooses to delete one of my favorite scenes in the original—the one in which the harried George, he of the mussed-up hair, looks over his brood on Christmas Eve and asks bitterly, "Why did we have to have all these kids?"

For those few troubled souls who find themselves sharing my jaundiced point of view, I recommend another book that draws on *It's a Wonderful Life*. Film critic David Thomson's little-known noir novel *Suspects* (1985), in which characters from various films turn up in later life, features George Bailey, transposed to a noir world, as the narrator. And get this: George reveals that he is the secret father of Travis Bickle, from *Taxi Driver*. All for want of a train whistle.

Booklist, September 15, 2006

ALAS, POOR XYWRITE, I KNEW HIM WELL

THIS ISSUE OF *BOOKLIST* is the first in the electronic era to be produced without the help of XyWrite word-processing software. Yes, we realize we're late to climb aboard the Microsoft bandwagon, but for a lot of boring, technological reasons involving the way we transfer files from editor to editor and the elaborate system of macros we use to make these transfers easier, it was just too much trouble to give up XyWrite, which has formed the backbone of our electronic infrastructure for more than a decade. We all knew that change was inevitable, however, and just as we are forced from time to time to discard that much loved pair of jeans, so now we have begrudgingly made the transition to what computer geeks call the Windows environment. Because the air in this new environment is far too refined for XyWrite to be able to breathe, the ubiquitous Word has become our word processing system.

During the last year at the American Library Association, new systems have been installed on what sometimes seemed like a daily basis: a new membership database, a new accounting system, a new phone system, even new toilets in some of the restrooms. Along with all the new technology, we have also been subjected to a barrage of rhetoric about dealing with change in the workplace: change is good; the healthy organization must remain on the cutting edge; we need to reinvent ourselves for the new millennium—you've heard it all, I'm sure. Certainly, I'm not here to argue with change or even to debate organizational theory; no, I'm here merely to say good-bye to a friend. Just as Hamlet's chance discovery of poor Yorick's skull occasioned a moment of melancholy (change wasn't very damn good for Yorick), so I can't help but feel a little blue about the passing of poor XyWrite.

In the merry days of DOS, before Bill Gates strutted onto the stage, XyWrite was a major player. Most newspapers and many magazines were written with XyWrite because it was widely regarded as the most powerful word processor in the business. XyWrite had muscles, to be sure, but you had to know where to look for them. Perhaps the most unfriendly piece of software ever written, XyWrite demanded that its users learn thousands of commands and execute them perfectly. There were no drop-down windows, no explanatory notes, no multiple-choice options. If you didn't learn the commands, you looked at a blank screen forever. It's no wonder why XyWrite failed in the home-computer marketplace, but for professional writers who had no choice but to learn the system, it could be a thing of beauty—not of the warm, cuddly variety, mind you, but coldly efficient beauty (think of one of those Margaret Bourke White photos of giant generators or the innards of a steel mill). When you mastered XyWrite, you felt like you'd really done something, given that old left brain the kind of workout it rarely gets when it's trapped in the body of a mere book reviewer.

And, oh, those commands! Learning the XyWrite commands was easier if you made up stories to function as memory keys. My favorite was the SAD command. SAD stood for "save as defined," but I could never remember that. Usually, I used the SAD command when I was blocking off a chunk of lame prose that I was about to cut from a review. I remembered the right command by reminding myself that this cruel act I was about to perform would be certain to cause SADness, both to the words themselves, exiled to cyberspace, and to the author, who inexplicably seemed to believe that it was the finest line he or she had ever written. It's simply untrue, as some have suggested, that a little smile crossed my face every time I typed SAD on the screen and summarily deleted the offending phrase.

I also loved XyWrite's error messages. Harking back to an era of stern taskmasters who refused to tolerate sloppiness, XyWrite had little sympathy for those who did it wrong. If you typed the wrong command, there would be no friendly offers to help. No, XyWrite laid it on the line: "Bad Command." You did it wrong, and there's no use doing it again until you figure out how to do it right. My favorite XyWrite error message (borrowed from DOS) occurred when you tried to save or copy a file in a bogus manner. XyWrite didn't even bother telling you'd done it wrong; it simply said, "Access Denied." The message was clear: you don't know enough to do what you're doing; practice harder and try again. So refreshingly undemocratic! So flagrantly in violation of the Library Bill of Rights!

Learning XyWrite was a lot like learning the multiplication tables. There were no shortcuts, no programmed positive reinforcement, no rhetoric whatsoever. But when you learned what seven times three was, you didn't forget. (I remembered that one by telling myself that seven times three equaled when I would be old enough to drink.) I doubt if I'll ever know Word as well as I knew XyWrite because, a mere click away, there's always a menu ready to nurse me through the problem. I'm sure most people are thrilled to be living in a drop-down world, and I wish them well. For my part, I'll try my best to get with the program (although I make no promises about reinventing myself for this or any other millennium). I reserve the right, however, to offer the occasional toast to my old friend, the ever-crotchety XyWrite. After all, I knew him well.

Booklist, September 1, 2000

BOOKS RUINED MY LIFE

MOST PEOPLE THINK OF sabbatical leaves as perks for professors: take a semester off from the little buggers and punch up that scholarly article on what Wordsworth and Coleridge had for breakfast—allowing time, of course, for a field trip to the Lake District. So what is a workaday editor doing turning off his computer and turning a 97-year-old magazine over to his capable colleagues for four glorious, deadline-free months?

If the American Library Association is magnanimous enough to offer its worker bees a sabbatical after a few decades of service, who am I to say no? The application form says something about engaging in a "meaningful project." I gave this one careful thought. What about that sensitive coming-of-age novel, the one we all have buried deep within us, the one that proves that our misunderstood outsider years were somehow different from, yet poignantly similar to, the misunderstood outsider years of every other living organism that ever strutted and fretted its hour upon the stage? Or, failing that, how about a crime novel, set in the world of public-links golf—allowing time, of course, for extensive field research on the mysteries of the lob wedge? And let's not forget travel. There is a Tuscan villa out there with my name on it. Or perhaps a stone cottage just across an unpaved road from the only still-undiscovered links course in all of Scotland?

OK, maybe I'm dreaming; maybe, as every *Seinfeld* fan knows, there are no Tuscan villas left to rent in Tuscany, and as any reviewer of golf books certainly knows, the last undiscovered links course in Scotland was discovered in last week's sensitive, midlife-crisis memoir by a guy on sabbatical who found his game in the heather. Forget the novels and the travel; I could always clean the basement, a "meaningful project" by anyone's standards.

The truth of the matter, though, is that the only thing keeping me from doing any of those things is me. I won't have time to write novels or take trips or clean basements because I have too much reading to do. If I did have time to write a book, it would be an angry, post–midlife crisis memoir called *Books Ruined My Life*. Don't think I'm exaggerating here. The difference between me and all those smiley-faced book lovers with T-shirts that say "So many books, so little time" is that I realize what my addiction to reading has cost me. I won't go so far as to claim I could have been a contender, but at the very least, I might have a functioning lower back today if I hadn't spent so much time lugging boxes of books from house to house as I made my peripatetic way through life. In college, after I bought a copy of *Bound for Glory*, the autobiography of Woody Guthrie, my friend Rob bet me one dollar that I'd never read the book no matter how long I kept it. Well, I haven't read it yet, more than 30 years later, but I still have it, and I've lugged it to approximately 20 different abodes over the decades. (If only I'd known that in the twenty-first century there would be a new children's book about Woody Guthrie published every 35 minutes.)

Yes, books ruined my back, and now they're going to ruin my sabbatical. You'd think someone who reviews books for a living would be taking a sabbatical to get away from reading, but the shocking truth is that when I contemplate what I'm going to most enjoy over the next four months, it's the books I'm going to read that I think of first. That's sick, and I'm the first to admit it.

Like any drug addict, I must shoulder most of the blame for my ruined life. Nobody makes me keep turning the damn pages; I turn them all by myself. But there are others at fault, too. I blame Knopf's Everyman Library for publishing Raymond Chandler's *Collected Stories* (more than 1,000 pages) to coincide with my sabbatical; I blame Little, Brown, George Pelecanos' publisher, for distributing galleys of his new crime novel before I was able to get out of the office; and, perhaps most of all, I blame Al Gore. Allow me to explain. I've wanted to read Stendhal for years—almost as long as Woody Guthrie has been my own personal albatross. But in the year 2000, I was ready to take the plunge. I bought a new copy of *The Red and the Black* (the print in my old Penguin Classic had shrunk), and I had big plans to read the book and then write a Back Page about having finally done it. Then Al Gore told the world his favorite book was *The Red and the Black*. Rather than being accused of jumping on a presidential bandwagon, I immediately reshelved my new Stendhal, where it has languished ever since. (George Bush, incidentally, presented no such problems for me; his favorite book is *The Very Hungry Caterpillar*.)

So there you have it. I'm going to read Chandler and Pelecanos and Stendhal on my sabbatical, and maybe I'll catch up on Margaret Drabble, too. And if I manage any traveling, I'll probably do it by reading Bill

Bryson. Who knows, maybe I'll even read that Woody Guthrie book. The dollar I'll collect from Rob just might be the start of something big in my life. Or maybe books really do make failures of us all.

Booklist, August 2002

CATFIGHT IN THE NEWSROOM

ONE OF THE SUBJECTS that has kept this column wheezing along for the last 20 years has been literary feuds. I can't get enough of them. There's something so deliciously low, as Henry Higgins liked to say, about writers sniping at one another, often in the style more commonly associated with pimply teenagers snapping towels in the locker room. Usually, though, when I've written about literary feuds, I've been obligated to revive sparring matches from the past: John Ruskin noting that "Thackeray settled like a meat-fly on whatever one had got for dinner and made one sick of it," or Mark Twain taking dead aim at Jane Austen ("Everytime I read *Pride and Prejudice* I want to dig her up and beat her over the skull with her own shinbone").

Ouch. But what I really crave is a literary feud happening in real time. Yes, there have been skirmishes: Martin Amis has been attacked by British critic Terry Eagleton, who accused Amis of being an "Islamaphobe" and appended a slam at Martin's late father, Kingsley, whom he labeled "anti-Semitic and a homophobe," but while this brouhaha was big news in Britain, the storm had dissipated by the time it crossed the Atlantic. For a good American literary feud, you really need to go back to the era of Norman Mailer, Gore Vidal, and William F. Buckley. Ah, those were the days: Vidal labeling Buckley a "crypto-Nazi" at the 1968 Democratic Convention, and Buckley responding by calling Vidal a "queer," or Mailer head-butting Vidal in the green room before a taping of *The Dick Cavett Show* in 1971, and Vidal responding with an uppercut to Mailer's stomach. But what about today? Has political correctness or, even worse, genuine civility, ruined the literary feud?

Well, maybe so, if you limit your universe to the high end of literature. But if you're willing to drop down to daily journalism, and then even further, to the sports page, boy, have I got a feud for you. The scene is the *Chicago Sun-Times*, and the featured player is Jay Mariotti, formerly one of the paper's two lead sports columnists. Readers of the Back Page may remember that back in June I took a mild swipe or two at Mariotti myself, pointing out that whenever he was without a topic, he mustered yet another hollow attack on White Sox manager Ozzie Guillen. The other day Mariotti haters all over Chicago, myself included, were thrilled to read that, just after signing a fat new contract, Jay suddenly quit, claiming that newspapers were a thing of the past, and he wasn't going to go down with the ship. No, it's off to the Internet for our boy Jay, a venue where lame insults, perpetual flip-flops, and adolescent whining—all key components of any Mariotti column—have found a permanent home.

This was good news, certainly, but we all craved the rest of the story. It didn't take long to get it. Mariotti's colleagues at the *Sun-Times* were chomping at the bit to get back at the guy who trashed his fellow sportswriters for being "homers." Beat reporters like Chris De Luca, who spend time in the White Sox locker room on a daily basis, were particularly incensed with Mariotti, as they were the ones obligated to interview the sports figures whom Mariotti regularly lambasted. (Jay was famous for never showing his face in Chicago sports teams' locker rooms.) De Luca hit first, calling Mariotti a flip-flopper to the end for his embracing of the Internet after repeatedly belittling bloggers, but the heavy hitters came next. Roger Ebert, in an open letter to Mariotti, defended his colleagues— "The rest of us are still at work, putting out the best paper we can"—and then offered Jay some advice: "On your way out, don't let the door bang you in the ass."

Now that's more like it, especially coming from the notoriously charitable Ebert, who gives out an extra star or two to every movie he sees these days. But the best was yet to come from Rick Telander, Mariotti's fellow *Sun-Times* columnist. (Telander enjoys much more national recognition than Mariotti and is also the author of numerous books, including a fine YA novel called *String Music*.) Rumors were rampant a few months ago that Telander and Mariotti had come to blows over the latter's attack on his fellow writers at the paper, so it was no surprise to hear Telander open up on Mariotti in an interview in the *Chicago Reader*. It turns out that Mariotti quit because Telander got the go-ahead to write a column Jay wanted to write about Barack Obama disparaging Cubs fans. Mariotti resigning, we learn in the *Reader*, was a common occurrence at the *Sun-Times*, something that happened whenever little Jay didn't get his way. Only this time his resignation was accepted. "Finally, hopefully forever, they called this person's bluff," Telander says. "You can only hold your breath and lie on the floor and pound your fists and kick your feet so many times."

Now I know that I'm vulnerable here to being accused of boring *Booklist*'s national audience with a story of mainly local interest. I also realize that the stereotypical librarian isn't supposed to be a sports fan, but even without getting into the unfairness of that characterization, let me just say that even stereotypical librarians read newspapers and work in offices. How can any red-blooded reader and office worker not feel just a little bit connected to a story about how the gang at the office finally turned on the little weasel who had been making their lives miserable. It's not Twain beating on Jane Austen's skull with her own shinbone, but I bet if somebody gave Telander a spare shinbone, he'd be happy to take a few swings at any exposed part of Mariotti's body. Let's hope he sells tickets.

Booklist, September 15, 2008

JURY DUTY

A FEW YEARS AGO, I testified in this column that books had ruined my life. I was referring to the fact that, on the eve of a four-month sabbatical, the only thing I was looking forward to doing in my time away from the office was reading more books. Who knows, I bemoaned, what a rich real-world life I might have enjoyed had I not spent so much time shirking reality in favor of its literary alternative. That all remains true to this day, but recently something happened to make me rethink my position on reading. Books may have ruined my life, but they also got me out of serving on a jury, and in my view, a ruined but jury-free life may well be preferable to the alternative.

I've been dodging summons to do my civic duty throughout my adult life, but I guess I always knew that my streak had to end sometime. Finally, a few months ago, I was caught in the crosshairs of the legal system and found myself trudging off to a county courthouse in suburban Chicago. My colleagues at *Booklist* had provided me with ample advice on how to avoid landing on a jury. One faction felt that my range of crackpot opinions on all things political guaranteed that I would offend someone and thus get booted off any jury that might otherwise have me. Just find a way to mention that you think of yourself as an anarchist, this group counseled, and you're home free. (I should clarify here, as I'm so often forced to do, that I have no truck with those bomb-throwing anarchists. I don't want to change our revered institutions; I merely want to ignore them.)

Other *Booklister*s, however, warned that my unquestioned crackpottiness might not help. Look at Ray Olson, they reminded. Hadn't Ray, widely known to be every bit the crackpot I am, not only been selected to a jury but also appointed its foreman? True enough, but I took solace in the fact that beneath Ray's crackpot ideas lurks a good citizen. Thankfully, I possess no such stain on my integrity. Simply being myself should do the trick, I thought, as I ambled confidently through the courthouse's metal detector (emptying my pockets and keeping mum on the whole anarchist issue).

Nothing went quite as planned. I spent the morning reading a terrific new crime novel set in Oslo (*The Redbreast*, by Jo Nesbo) and waiting to hear my number called. Fortunately, it wasn't, despite my complete failure to employ the appropriate creative-visualization strategy. Just try *not* imagining the number 283 being intoned by the formidable bureaucrat standing before you. In the afternoon, however, all those 283s I was trying not to send to Ms. Bureaucrat found their undesired target, and I was instructed to muster for duty.

Into the courtroom we marched, myself and 30 other citizens, all girding our loins to be of service to democracy. *Loins* turned out to be the operative word, too, as the case before us involved what the judge demurely described as "indecent solicitation." Some of my fellow prospective jurors gasped audibly when it turned out that we might wind up on a jury trying a middle-aged defendant accused of using the Internet to seduce a minor. Nothing like a sex crime to jolt even a cynical citizen into paying attention.

Naturally, juror number 283 was the third person called by the judge to be interviewed. Before I set foot in the courtroom, I had pondered what I would say if I made it to this stage. I saw myself taking no nonsense from weasely lawyers or supercilious judges. No, I would shoot from the hip, like Norman Mailer did when questioned by Judge Hoffman during the Chicago Seven trial. "Mr. Mailer, please stick to the facts," the judge cautioned, interrupting Stormin' Norman in full rant. "But your Honor," Mailer replied, "facts without nuance are nothing." Maybe I'd even have occasion to quote Mailer.

Well, readers, I wimped out. It wasn't just the seriousness of the crime that undid me, I'm sorry to say. No, I turned to jelly as soon as I sat down in the courtroom and got a look at the judge. There's something about a guy wearing a big, flowing Old Testamenty robe, sitting a few feet above everybody else, and occasionally banging a gavel that makes you feel like a nine-year-old who forgot to clean his room. I dutifully testified to my ability to view erotic pictures and listen to explicit e-mails without letting either affect my ability to render an impartial verdict, and I even politely explained to the judge what was involved in being the editor of a book-review journal. No mention of anarchy; no Mailer quotes.

Then came the prosecutor, who opined that I must read a lot in my job and proceeded to ask what I liked to read. "Crime fiction," I replied, honestly. "And have you ever read a novel about a case similar to this one?" "Many," I admitted, thinking of, among others, the novels of John Harvey and Michael Connelly, which have included plotlines concerning sexual abuse. "And did any of the novels you've read ever make you sympathetic to the defendants in these cases?" "Some did, and some didn't." "What was the difference?" "Context."

It wasn't exactly "facts without nuance are nothing," but it was enough to get me excused from the case. The juror interviewed before me was also "excused," seemingly because she testified that her belief in the Bible would make it difficult for her to treat the defendant objectively. It occurred to me as I left the courthouse—free at last—that one of us had been excused for reading too many books and the other for having read only one. Whatever works.

Booklist, August 2007

Quizzes

TRUST YOUR INSTINCTS—NOT

WE'VE ALL BEEN TOLD at some point or other to trust our instincts, go with our first choices, don't second-guess ourselves. Former *Booklist* Adult Books Editor Martin Brady called this timeless advice the Sister Catherine Agnes Rule, after his second-grade teacher who inculcated her charges early on with the wisdom of following their initial vibes, though she may not have used the word *vibes*. Well, we can only hope that graduates of the Sister Catherine Agnes school of decision making didn't go into the movie business. Even a cursory glance at Jeff Burkhart and Bruce Stuart's *Hollywood's First Choices: How the Great Casting Decisions Were Made* (Crown) shows that, when casting movie roles, first choices are often disastrous. Cary Grant and Ingrid Bergman swapping obscenities in *Who's Afraid of Virginia Woolf?* Now there's a plan in serious need of second-guessing.

The list below includes a few more really bad casting ideas hatched by misguided producers and directors. Try matching them with the actors in the second column, who actually got the parts. For the story of how it all happened, consult the anecdote-rich book. And somebody, please send Sister Catherine Agnes a copy.

Booklist, April 15, 1994

FIRST CHOICES

1. Claudette Colbert as Margo Channing in *All about Eve*
2. Mae West as Norma Desmond in *Sunset Boulevard*
3. Marlon Brando as T. E. Lawrence in *Lawrence of Arabia*
4. Cary Grant and Ingrid Bergman as George and Martha in *Who's Afraid of Virginia Woolf?*
5. Eli Wallach as Maggio in *From Here to Eternity*
6. Laurence Olivier as Don Corleone in *The Godfather*
7. Doris Day as Mrs. Robinson in *The Graduate*
8. Bob Hope as Mortimer Brewster in *Arsenic and Old Lace*
9. Ali MacGraw as Evelyn Mulwray in *Chinatown*
10. Noel Coward as Humbert Humbert in *Lolita*

FINAL CHOICES

a. Richard Burton and Elizabeth Taylor
b. James Mason
c. Bette Davis
d. Frank Sinatra
e. Cary Grant
f. Faye Dunaway
g. Peter O'Toole
h. Anne Bancroft
i. Marlon Brando
j. Gloria Swanson

ANSWERS: 1-c; 2-j; 3-g; 4-a; 5-d; 6-i; 7-h; 8-e; 9-f; 10-b

157

WORKING TITLES

DO BOOK TITLES MATTER? According to a recent article by Caroline Baum in *The Age* (Melbourne), they certainly do. No, I'm not a regular reader of Australian newspapers, but fortunately, there are a handful of Web surfers at *Booklist* who have a real knack for smelling out a possible Back Page topic as it drifts its way through cyberspace. Ben Segedin, our production director, spotted the Baum article and knew right away it was Back Page gold. A lot of the title changes Baum discusses will be of interest mainly to Australian readers, but she devotes a couple of fascinating paragraphs to a writer with the reputation of being a titling genius: Julian Barnes. Not too many writers can claim to have launched a title trend, but Barnes' *Flaubert's Parrot* (1985) has spawned a shelf-full of imitations (*Pushkin's Button, Audubon's Elephant, Wittgenstein's Poker*, and, of course, the whole Galileo family: *Galileo's Daughter, Galileo's Treasure Box, Galileo's Finger, Galileo's Mistake,* and *Galileo's Pendulum*). Barnes, Baum notes, had the good sense not to imitate himself. His book *Staring at the Sun* had a working title of *Lindbergh's Sandwiches*, but wisely, the author resisted the temptation to go to the well one more time.

Working titles open up a world of goofiness, along the lines of original casting choices (Ronald Reagan to play Rick in *Casablanca*). But whereas weird casting ideas usually can be traced to the folly of producers, book titles often go awry in that not-always-amicable struggle between author and editor. As Raymond Chandler famously remarked to Alfred Knopf, "I'm trying to think up a good title for you to want me to change." Ah, but more times than not, it's the author with the dopey ideas. F. Scott Fitzgerald, for example, just wouldn't give up on the notion that his book about a lovestruck bootlegger should be called *Trimalchio in West Egg*. Even after the novel was published as *The Great Gatsby*, Fitzgerald kept complaining to his editor, Maxwell Perkins, that the book would have done better if they hadn't dropped *Trimalchio*. (Apparently, Fitzgerald was convinced that readers would understand that Trimalchio was the rich patron in Petronius' *Satyricon.*)

Drawing from Baum's article and from a nifty literary trivia book called *Now All We Need Is a Title,* by André Bernard, I've come up with a list of titles that might have been—had the books' authors or editors not had the wisdom to think twice. On the assumption that most things in life are more fun in the form of a quiz, I've scrambled my lists of working titles and real titles. It's up to you to put them back together again. Be warned: there is a movie title thrown in with the books.

Booklist, February 15, 2004

WORKING TITLES

1. *The Kingdom by the Sea*
2. *First Impressions*
3. *Pansy*
4. *Four-and-a-half Years of Struggle against Lies, Stupidity and Cowardice*
5. *The Sea Cook*
6. *Mindless Pleasures*
7. *The Dignity of Man*
8. *Anhedonia*
9. *Three Tenant Families*
10. *Zounds, He Dies*
11. *At This Point in Time*
12. *Before This Anger*
13. *They Don't Build Statues to Businessmen*
14. *The Saddest Story*
15. *The Poker Night*

REAL TITLES

a. *Pride and Prejudice*
b. *Gone with the Wind*
c. *Roots*
d. *All the President's Men*
e. *Gravity's Rainbow*
f. *The Good Soldier*
g. *A Streetcar Named Desire*
h. *Lolita*
i. *Mein Kampf*
j. *Treasure Island*
k. *Annie Hall*
l. *Farewell, My Lovely*
m. *Valley of the Dolls*
n. *Let Us Now Praise Famous Men*
o. *The Old Man and the Sea*

ANSWERS: 1-h; 2-a; 3-b; 4-i; 5-j; 6-e; 7-o; 8-k; 9-n; 10-l; 11-d; 12-c; 13-m; 14-f; 15-g

SWAN SONGS

LAST NOVELS GET NO respect, and it's only partially because they tend to be fairly bad. Part of the problem is bibliographic: How do you tell which novel is a writer's last when he or she keeps churning them out long after death? We have a standing rule at *Booklist* that forbids describing the work of any recently deceased novelist as that writer's "last" book. The "dead-guy rule," as it's known around the office, went into effect after I received an irate letter from the widow of a midlist genre novelist who had died just as the galleys of one of his thrillers had arrived at *Booklist*. In our review, we cavalierly deduced that, given the author's demise, this work would be his last. Not so, claimed the entrepreneurial widow; she had at least eight more finished manuscripts in her drawer and was planning on publishing them at the rate of one per year. How dare we jeopardize her sales by supposing that her dead husband was through writing?

Even without the energetic efforts of greedy heirs, the swan songs of most novelists, both literary and commercial, are usually not their best efforts. There are a few perfectly good books on the list below, but overall, they are a middling crew at best. Still, you can't help but feel sorry for last novels as they shuffle off to the inevitable remainder table. Attention must be paid to these Willy Lomans of literature, and so we'll tip our Back Page glasses to a few less-than-famous finales. Show your respect by matching the authors, their last novels, and the books' publication dates. And don't forget the dead-guy rule: some of these pub dates come after the authors' death dates.

Booklist, November 15, 2001

TITLES	AUTHORS	YEAR OF PUBLICATION
1. *The Winter of Our Discontent*	A. Agatha Christie	a. 1965
2. *Oh, What a Paradise It Seems*	B. Robertson Davies	b. 1994
3. *The Cunning Man*	C. Ian Fleming	c. 1972
4. *The Reivers*	D. John Cheever	d. 1982
5. *The Holy Sinner*	E. Bernard Malamud	e. 2000
6. *Between the Acts*	F. Evelyn Waugh	f. 1978
7. *God's Grace*	G. Joseph Heller	g. 1962
8. *The Man with the Golden Gun*	H. Marjorie Kinnan Rawlings	h. 1925
9. *The Ewings*	I. John O'Hara	i. 1994
10. *The Captain and the Enemy*	J. George V. Higgins	j. 1976
11. *The Blue Hammer*	K. John Steinbeck	k. 1982
12. *Recessional*	L. Edith Wharton	l. 2000
13. *Basil Seal Rides Again; or, The Rake's Regress*	M. William Faulkner	m. 1938
14. *The Secret River*	N. Sir Arthur Conan Doyle	n. 1988
15. *Portrait of an Artist, as an Old Man*	O. Ross Macdonald	o. 1976
16. *The Land of Mist*	P. Graham Greene	p. 1951
17. *At End of Day*	Q. Virginia Woolf	q. 1963
18. *Sleeping Murder*	R. James Jones	r. 1941
19. *The Buccaneers*	S. James Michener	s. 1955
20. *Whistle*	T. Thomas Mann	t. 1961

ANSWERS: 1-K-t; 2-D-k or d; 3-B-b; 4-M-g; 5-T-p; 6-Q-r; 7-E-d or k; 8-C-a; 9-I-c; 10-P-n; 11-O-j; 12-S-i; 13-F-q; 14-H-s; 15-G-e or l; 16-N-h; 17-J-l or e; 18-A-o; 19-L-m; 20-R-f

LIBRARIES AND LIBRARIANS IN THE MOVIES

A FEW YEARS AGO I did a quiz about librarians in the movies. This time, while still paying attention to the librarians, I'm focusing on the libraries themselves. Libraries pop up more often than you would think in movies—they make a great place for that transitional scene where the hero does a little research or whispers to his lover—and, of course, the old-fashioned library made a wonderful symbol for mindless rigidity (not that one would ever find rigidity @ your library these days). Along with the buns and the "Quiet" signs, though, there are more than a few "positive images" of libraryland floating around on film. The quiz below only scratches the surface. For more information, consult a wonderful Web site I used extensively. It's called Librarians in the Movies, maintained by Martin Raish at David O. McKay Library, Brigham Young University–Idaho.

And, now, on to the quiz. Your assignment is to match a description of what happened at each cinematic library with the movie where it happened. For extra credit, you can also identify the actor or actress who played the librarian.

Booklist, April 15, 2003

THE LIBRARIES

1. A television network's Reference Center, filled with reference books and hard-working librarians, is invaded by one of those room-filling midcentury computers.
2. A turn-of-the-century library in Iowa, where a librarian does a little research into her would-be boyfriend's bona fides.
3. The New York Public Library, complete with card catalogs, librarians who say "Sh'hh," and a board with numbers that are illuminated when your book is ready.
4. Working at this dreary-looking library, which she closes up at night while the rest of the town parties, is a fate worse than death for a timid, bun-wearing spinster.
5. An exciting chase takes place at the San Francisco Public Library, where one particularly fetching librarian helps an unconventional sleuth.
6. With the help of a librarian, socialite Tracy Lord learns to appreciate the writings of Macaulay Connor, an aspiring novelist from South Bend ("It sounds like dancing").
7. A former Pinkerton agent turned writer, in the process of trying to find a San Francisco cabaret performer, repairs to the library, where he encounters a sexy librarian.
8. An Egyptologist and librarian has trouble with the shelving in a Cairo library, but she's more than capable of Indiana Jones–style derring-do.

9. A Holocaust survivor in New York requests a book by the American poet "Emil Dickens." The reference librarian breaks every rule in the book by ridiculing his patron and informing her that Charles Dickens was neither an American nor a poet.

10. A prisoner needs to do some determined fund-raising before he's able to build the collection at his woefully understocked prison library.

11. The Newark Public Library offers less-than-satisfying work to an aspiring author involved in a romance with a country-club beauty.

12. In the early '60s, at a small library in England devoted to the occult, a librarian, who is also a Communist, falls in love with a library clerk, who is also a double agent. An ill-advised trip to East Berlin comes to no good.

13. A library page who works at NYPL has some difficult coming-of-age to do, thanks to his overprotective mother and his rare-book librarian father. There's only one solution: steal Dad's Gutenberg Bible.

14. After a mysterious death in a Benedictine abbey in 1327, a Franciscan monk turned sleuth follows the trail to the monastery librarian.

15. In 1956, a small-town librarian is branded as a Communist when she refuses to remove a book called *The Communist Dream* from the collection.

16. With the help of a librarian at the Hollywood Public Library, a hard-boiled private eye does a little research on rare books.

THE MOVIES

a. *Breakfast at Tiffany's*
b. *Hammett*
c. *Desk Set*
d. *You're a Big Boy Now*
e. *Shawshank Redemption*
f. *The Spy Who Came in from the Cold*
g. *The Music Man*
h. *The Big Sleep*
i. *Foul Play*
j. *Goodbye, Columbus*
k. *The Mummy*
l. *The Philadelphia Story*
m. *The Name of the Rose*
n. *It's a Wonderful Life*
o. *Sophie's Choice*
p. *Storm Center*

THE LIBRARIANS

A. Hilda Plowright
B. Elvia Allman
C. Rachel Weisz
D. Claire Bloom and Richard Burton
E. John Rothman
F. Katharine Hepburn, Joan Blondell, and Dina Merrill
G. Carole Douglas
H. Goldie Hawn
I. Richard Benjamin
J. Volker Prechtel
K. Shirley Jones
L. Bette Davis
M. Tim Robbins
N. Marilu Henner
O. Peter Kastner and Rip Torn
P. Donna Reed

ANSWERS: 1-c-F; 2-g-K; 3-a-B; 4-n-P; 5-i-H; 6-l-A; 7-b-N; 8-k-C; 9-o-E; 10-e-M; 11-j-I; 12-f-D; 13-d-O; 14-m-J; 15-p-L; 16-h-G

"ROSEBUD"

The tongues of dying men enforce attention like deep harmony.
　　　—John of Gaunt, from Shakespeare's *King Richard II*

———————————

A COUPLE OF ISSUES ago, the Back Page celebrated dead lovers in literature, and ever since I put together that tribute, I haven't been able to get dead guys in books out of my mind. Now I've moved on from how they died to what they said before they died. Famous last words of real people have been collected in numerous books and on numerous Web sites, but the farewells of fictional characters don't get nearly as much attention. This seems wrongheaded. After all, fictional characters don't have to think of their own last lines; they have an author behind the scenes to do all the work. It should stand to reason, then, that the last words out of the mouths of soon-to-be-dead people in books would be more memorable than the feeble offerings of their real-but-just-barely-alive counterparts. It's true, but not as true as you'd think. Too often, in books, the nearly dead guy just lies there while the live guys around him do all the jabbering. Only in Shakespeare is death guaranteed to bring an opportunity to say a few words to the fans. And, thus, you won't be surprised to find a healthy smattering of Shakespearean characters listed below in my fictional finale matching quiz. (You won't find "Rosebud," which is the only last word ever to drive the action of an entire movie but is still a pretty silly thing to be mumbling on your deathbed.) Even the best of these last words, though, must take a backseat to these lines from Dylan Thomas, which remain my personal favorite exit speech: "I've had 18 straight whiskeys. I think that's the record."

Booklist, March 15, 2003

LAST WORDS

1. "The horror! The horror!"
2. "It is a far, far better thing that I do, than I have ever done; it is a far, far better rest I go to, than I have ever known."
3. "Man's happiest hours are pictures drawn in shadow. Then ill fortune comes, and with two strokes the wet sponge wipes the drawing out. And grief itself's hardly more pitiable than joy."
4. "Well, I'll be damned! It didn't even hurt. Wait'll I tell Nell."
5. "Thanks, Ollie."
6. "Long live Captain Vere!"
7. "Don't worry, darling. I'm not a bit afraid. It's just a dirty trick."
8. "Towards thee I roll, thou all-destroying but unconquering whale; to the last I grapple with thee; for hate's sake I spit my last breath at thee."
9. "O happy dagger! This is thy sheath; there rust, and let me die."
10. "I got a bullet in my left-hand side,
    Great God, it's hurtin' so.
    I was her man, but I done her wrong."

11. "The blind man!"
12. "Why should a dog, a horse, a rat, have life!
    And thou no breath at all? Thou'lt come no more,
    Never, never, never, never, never!
    Pray you, undo this button: thank you, sir.
    Do you see this? Look on her, look, her lips,
    Look there, look there!"
13. "Oh, banish me, my lord, but kill me not!
    Kill me to-morrow; let me live to-night!
    But half an hour!
    But while I say one prayer!"
14. "And now what?"
15. "The rest is silence."
16. "Thy drugs are quick. Thus with a kiss I die."
17. "Which is better—to have rules and argue, or to hunt and kill?"
18. "Mother of Mercy! Is this the end of Rico?"
19. "Made it Ma! Top of the world!"
20. "I'm melting! Melting! Oh, what a world! What a world! Who would have thought a good little girl like you could destroy my beautiful wickedness."

DYING CHARACTER

A. Captain Ahab
B. Cesare Enrico Bandello
C. Catherine Barkley
D. Billy Budd
E. Hamlet
F. Sula Peace
G. Cody Jarrett
H. Captain Kurtz
I. Piggy
J. Romeo
K. Gregor Samsa
L. The Wicked Witch of the West
M. Sidney Carton
N. Cassandra
O. Jenny Cavilleri
P. Johnnie
Q. Juliet
R. Desdemona
S. Emma Bovary
T. King Lear

SOURCE

a. *Lord of the Flies*
b. *Love Story*
c. *Othello*
d. *Moby Dick*
e. *Agamemnon*
f. *Romeo and Juliet*
g. *King Lear*
h. *Tale of Two Cities*
i. *Billy Budd*
j. *White Heat*
k. *"Frankie and Johnnie"*
l. *Madame Bovary*
m. *Heart of Darkness*
n. *Hamlet*
o. *Little Caesar*
p. *The Metamorphosis*
q. *Sula*
r. *A Farewell to Arms*
s. *The Wizard of Oz*
t. *Romeo and Juliet*

USELESS INFORMATION, POORLY ORGANIZED

"IT IS A VERY sad thing that nowadays there is so little useless information."

When Oscar Wilde wrote those words, the Internet hadn't been invented, and I hadn't begun writing the Back Page. Even so, I believe Wilde was right to bemoan the paucity of truly useless information, and despite the noble effort I make every two weeks to help the cause, I also believe that we continue to suffer from a distinct shortage of uselessness in the world. The thing about the Internet, you see, is that the information stored there, while largely useless, purports to be useful—and, worse, there is, among the useless bits, the occasional disgustingly useful nugget. Hence, the Internet is searched (often futilely) in hopes of exploiting its utility, not to wallow in its uselessness, a much healthier endeavor to my (and Wilde's) way of thinking. In fact, my New Year's resolution is to do one purely useless thing each and every day.

This is not as easy a task as it sounds. We are surrounded by technology—search engines, for example—that is designed to bring utility to our lives. Yes, there is still television, but careless clicking of your remote is likely to land you in the middle of a cooking show or, God help us, the home-improvement channel. Don't be fooled: to accept the role of a twenty-first-century Diogenes, in search of uselessness rather than honesty, is to invite frustration. Sure, you can read the Back Page, but that appears only twice a month. What about all those other days?

Sometimes help comes from unlikely places—under your Christmas tree, for example. This year, lurking among the socks and sweaters, was a truly useless gift: a copy of a little book called *Schott's Original Miscellany*, by Ben Schott. I'm told this book was all the rage in England when it appeared in 2002, and I'm not surprised. The English have always appreciated the purity of a useless moment; Jane Austen devoted a career to writing about what might be called the uses of uselessness. Schott takes her one glorious step further: uselessness for its own sake. As he says, the book's purpose is to "gather the flotsam and jetsam of the conversational tide." And so he does, but thankfully, not in any organized way; organization, after all, is one domino away from utility. Excerpting from such a purely useless miscellany is difficult. Where do you start? With the size of a sheet of Double Foolscap writing paper, perhaps? Or how about a list of all the voices created by Mel Blanc? Either would do fine, of course, but instead, I've come up with a little quiz: below you'll find three lists of seemingly random names. The trick is to find the common denominator. (Be specific; it doesn't count to say, "They're all women.") If you're inclined to take the wussy way out and turn this challenge into a multiple-choice test, consult the scrambled answers; if you scoff at the need for training wheels, figure it out on your own. You're then free to consult the unscrambled answers. The whole process should take you at least five useless minutes.

Booklist, February 1, 2004

GROUPS

Random Group #1: Britt Ekland, Jill St. John, Barbara Bach, Maud Adams, and Halle Berry

Random Group #2: Cheryl Ladd, Barry Manilow, Anita Bryant, Aaron Neville, and the Backstreet Boys

Random Group #3: Joseph Stalin, Jeff Bezos, Wallis Warfield Simpson, Ted Turner, and American Women

Random Group #4: Lenny Bruce, Fred Astaire, Sonny Liston, Tom Mix, and Aleister Crowley

SCRAMBLED ANSWERS

Time Person of the Year winners

actresses who played "Bond girls" in a James Bond movie

among those pictured on the cover of the Beatles' Sgt. Pepper album

singers of the National Anthem at the Super Bowl

UNSCRAMBLED ANSWERS
#1: actresses who played "Bond girls" in a James Bond movie
#2: singers of the National Anthem at the Super Bowl
#3: Time Person of the Year winners
#4: Among those pictured on the cover of the Beatles' Sgt. Pepper album

THEIR SIDE OF THE STORY

CHARACTERS IN FICTION OFTEN seem to have lives of their own. As readers, we routinely imagine our favorite characters as existing apart from their creators. Usually, though, this phenomenon is limited to protagonists. But what of secondary characters? They deserve their own lives, too, especially if they are portrayed in less than flattering terms, or if they are limited to small roles in the books that give them life. This installment of the Back Page turns over the podium to seven such characters, who, if they really could talk on their own, might have said the words I've put in their mouths below. Your job is to figure out who's talking. The speakers and the books in which they appeared are listed on the following page.

Booklist, December 15, 1991

1. Frankly, I don't miss her one bit. It's nice to attend a psychiatric convention and not worry about which one of the panelists your wife is sleeping with—or trying to sleep with, I should say. And what about her life since she left me? I'm just a poor shrink, but if you ask me those last couple of books were real stinkers. The only good book she ever wrote was the one I was in.

2. It broke my heart to read that book. I only tried to be a good mother to him. If I'd just watched him closer. I should have known something was wrong; no normal boy spends that much time in the bathroom. His baseball glove was one thing, but a perfectly nice piece of liver!

3. These rich kids! You take them under your wing, try to show them a thing or two about real life, give them a taste of sack, and what happens? They turn on you every time. All in the name of honor. Stick with your own kind, that's what I say.

4. I should have known there was more on Miss Mayella's mind than just bustin' up that chiffarobe, but I felt down-right sorry for her, even if she was white. I had a good lawyer, too, but it didn't help me one bit.

5. I know, I know, I should never have gotten involved with him again. He was fine for a wartime fling, but anybody could see he was unstable. Still, it was so damn hot that summer, and my husband was playing around with that tramp. She lived in a garage, for God's sake. The thing that did it, though, that really made me swoon, was his shirts. He had all these beautiful shirts. There were so many of them. And every color you could think of! And, you have to admit, he gave great parties.

6. I'll admit my choice of lovers wasn't the best as far as national security was concerned, but you can't say I didn't have cause. My husband may have understood ambiguity, but he was damn dull. I mean, for fun he read eighteenth-century German theologians. And all that Bach . . .

7. What kind of a man would turn his girl into the cops? Since when is knee-jerk rule-following an admirable trait? Especially for a tough guy. These so-called hard-boiled types, they're all just marshmallow idealists if you ask me. So what if I did kill his partner? The guy was a sap anyway. Just my luck, getting stuck in a book about a gumshoe who's more interested in the law than he is in love.

....

ANSWERS: 1. Dr. Bennett Wing (*Fear of Flying*); 2. Sophie Portnoy (*Portnoy's Complaint*); 3. Falstaff (*Henry IV, Part One*); 4. Tom Robinson (*To Kill a Mockingbird*); 5. Daisy Buchanan (*The Great Gatsby*); 6. Ann Smiley (*Tinker, Tailor, Soldier, Spy*); 7. Brigid O'Shaunessey (*The Maltese Falcon*)

....

LITERARY REAL ESTATE

"LOCATION, LOCATION, LOCATION." IT'S the cliché of choice in the real-estate business, but does it hold true in literature? Would Sherlock Holmes have been as popular if his office had been on Marylebone Road, a few blocks away from 221B Baker Street? Well, maybe so, but his address didn't hurt. (It's hard to imagine a fan club being called the Marylebone Road Irregulars.) Maybe the addresses of some fictional characters are so memorable because they provide a link between imaginary and real worlds. We make our pilgrimages to 221B Baker Street because it plants Holmes on a particular piece of terra firma and makes him just a little more real. It takes more than an address to give a novel a vivid sense of place, but a street name wraps the package very nicely.

Currently, a hot trend in the investment world is something called REITs (Real Estate Investment Trusts)—mutual funds made up of real estate rather than stocks. Here's your chance to invest in a BLIT (*Booklist* Literary Investment Trust), but first you have to display your own sense of place by matching the literary addresses listed below with the appropriate residents and the books from which they fame. Dividends will be paid to BLIT shareholders who visit all the locations in the trust (including Neverland).

Booklist, March 15, 2002

ADDRESSES

1. Wragby Hall
2. West Egg
3. Thornfield
4. Thrushcross Grange
5. Howards End
6. 27A Wimpole St.
7. River St., St. Botolphs
8. Macondo
9. Klickitat St., Portland
10. Slip F-18, Bahia Mar, Fort Lauderdale
11. West Thirty-fifth St., NYC
12. 9 Bywater St., Chelsea
13. Sutter St. near Kearney, San Francisco
14. Cahuenga Building, Hollywood Blvd.
15. 8411½ Sunset Blvd.
16. Quai des Orfevres, right wing, second floor, room 202
17. 110A Piccadilly
18. St. Mary Mead
19. 57th St. and 8th Ave.
20. East Eleventh St., between Broadway and University Place
21. No. 4, Privet Drive
22. "Second to the right and straight on till morning"
23. No. 17 Cherry-Tree lane

PROPERTY

A. Mr. Rochester's manor
B. Nero Wolfe's home and office
C. Lord Peter Wimsey's office
D. The Banks family manse
E. Sam Spade's office
F. Heathcliff's estate
G. Inspector Maigret's office
H. Matthew Scudder's office
I. Neverland
J. Location of both Ramona Quimby's and Henry Huggins' house
K. Sir Clifford and Lady Chatterley's house
L. Jay Gatsby's mansion estate
M. Home of Travis McGee's houseboat, *The Busted Flush*
N. Henry Higgins' home and office
O. The Dursleys' home
P. The Wapshot family's house
Q. Philip Marlowe's office
R. Margaret Schlegel Wilcox's country house
S. Barnegat Books, Bernie Rhodenbarr's book shop
T. Home of the Buendia family
U. Lew Archer's office
V. Miss Marple's village
W. George Smiley's townhome

TITLES

a. *A Tan and Sandy Silence*, et al.
b. *Howards End*
c. *Mary Poppins*
d. *The Nine Tailors*, et al.
e. *A Dance at the Slaughterhouse*, et al.
f. *The Great Gatsby*
g. *Peter Pan*
h. *Fer de Lance*, et al.
i. *The Long Goodbye*, et al.
j. *The Wapshot Chronicle*
k. *The Zebra-Striped Hearse*, et al.
l. *Jane Eyre*
m. *Harry Potter and the Sorcerer's Stone*, et al.
n. *Ramona the Pest*, et al.
o. *Maigret Hesitates*, et al.
p. *Lady Chatterley's Lover*
q. *The Maltese Falcon*, et al.
r. *Wuthering Heights*
s. *Murder at the Vicarage*, et al.
t. *One Hundred Years of Solitude*
u. *Tinker, Tailor, Soldier, Spy*, et al.
v. *The Burglar Who Thought He Was Bogart*, et al.
w. *Pygmalion*

ANSWERS: 1-K-p; 2-L-f; 3-A-l; 4-F-r; 5-R-b; 6-N-w; 7-P-j; 8-T-t; 9-J-n; 10-M-a; 11-B-h; 12-W-u; 13-E-q; 14-Q-l; 15-U-k; 16-G-o; 17-C-d; 18-V-s; 19-H-e; 20-S-v; 21-O-m; 22-I-g; 23-D-c

ART IMITATES LIFE

FOR EVERY ATHLETE WHO has professed a desire to "take it one game at a time," there is an author who has denied all biographical links from the characters in his or her work to anyone in real life. To both athlete and author, any sensible person replies, "Yeah, right." We know the ballplayer is looking ahead to the Big Game just as we know the author's "work of pure imagination" stinks like last week's roman à clef. Sometimes, though, as headlines fade and memories dim, it's hard to remember who is based on whom. The quiz below is designed to reconnect art and life. We've tried to pick fictional characters whose real-life counterparts were reasonably well known or who acquired a certain notoriety in the process of being fictionalized. The trick is to match fictional character with real-life counterpart with the author who wrote the book (or play or movie) in which the character appeared. The titles are not listed (too many of them give away the characters' names), but they do appear in the answers at the bottom of the page. Take an extra credit point for each one you get right. Don't be surprised to see some authors' names turn up twice, or to see the same names turning up in two columns. It's a tangled web these authors weave from the stuff of real life, and we're happy to help sort it out for you.

Booklist, April 1, 2002

FICTIONAL CHARACTERS

1. Willie Stark
2. Youngblood Hawke
3. Gudrun Brangwen
4. Henry Drummond
5. Maggie
6. Ralph Crawford
7. Frank Skeffington
8. Tobias Oates
9. J. J. Hunsecker
10. Abe Ravelstein
11. Dean Moriarty
12. Jack Stanton
13. Dill
14. Henry Burton
15. Matthew Harrison Brady
16. Grady Tripp
17. Neely O'Hara
18. Carlo Marx
19. John Foster Kane
20. Von Humboldt Fleisher
21. Sheridan Whiteside

REAL-LIFE COUNTERPARTS

a. Katherine Mansfield
b. Clarence Darrow
c. Neal Cassady
d. Allan Bloom
e. Walter Winchell
f. Truman Capote
g. Allen Ginsburg
h. Judy Garland
i. William Randolph Hearst
j. James M. Curley
k. Charles Dickens
l. Chuck Kinder
m. Delmore Schwartz
n. Marilyn Monroe
o. Raymond Carver
p. William Jennings Bryan
q. Alexander Woolcott
r. Bill Clinton
s. George Stephanopoulos
t. Thomas Wolfe
u. Huey Long

AUTHORS

A. Chuck Kinder
B. Jack Kerouac
C. Herman J. Mankiewicz
D. Peter Carey
E. Michael Chabon
F. Jacqueline Susann
G. Jack Kerouac
H. Robert Penn Warren
I. Saul Bellow
J. Edwin O'Connor
K. Jerome Lawrence and Robert E. Lee
L. Joe Klein
M. Harper Lee
N. George S. Kaufman and Moss Hart
O. Ernest Lehman
P. Herman Wouk
Q. Joe Klein
R. Jerome Lawrence and Robert E. Lee
S. Arthur Miller
T. Saul Bellow
U. D. H. Lawrence

ANSWERS: 1-u-H (All the King's Men); 2-t-P (Youngblood Hawke); 3-a-U (Women in Love); 4-b-k or R (Inherit the Wind); 5-n-S (After the Fall); 6-o-A (The Honeymooners); 7-j-J (The Last Hurrah); 8-k-D (Jack Maggs); 9-e-O (Sweet Smell of Success); 10-d-T or I (Ravelstein); 11-c-B or G (On the Road); 12-r-Q or L (Primary Colors); 13-f-M (To Kill a Mockingbird); 14-s-L or Q (Primary Colors); 15-p-R or K (Inherit the Wind); 16-l-E (Wonder Boys); 17-h-F (Valley of the Dolls); 18-g-G or B (On the Road); 19-i-C (Citizen Kane); 20-m-I or T (Humboldt's Gift); 21-q-N (The Man Who Came to Dinner)

GETTING AND SPENDING

IN THE LATE 1960s, influenced by the books I had read and the society I was a part of, I took a decidedly negative view of business as a career. Business majors were crew-cut jocks biding time in college before taking over their father's plumbing companies (like Brenda Patimkin's brother, Ron, in Philip Roth's *Goodbye, Columbus*). "Why don't you take some business classes along with all that poetry crap?" was my father's refrain whenever the topic turned, as it did with some frequency, to the impractical nature of my education. (Little did I know that a few decades later I would be saying to my daughter, "Why don't you take some Shakespeare along with Introduction to the Japanese Tea Ceremony?" but that's a story for a different Back Page.)

I certainly didn't imagine back then that, in a few short years, businesspeople (led by Bill Gates) would become philosopher-gurus to a generation of disciples, and the M.B.A. would be transformed from an educational oxymoron to the glamour degree of the nineties. There is one arena where business hasn't resurrected itself, however, and that is literature. Most businesspeople in literary fiction remain either objects of satire or symbols of wrongheadedness. In genre fiction, you will occasionally find positive portrayals of caterer/sleuths (in mysteries) or jet-setting perfume executives (in romances), but most literary fiction celebrates, in one form or another, the inner life, and business will always be a convenient metaphor for the outer life, what Margaret Schlegel, in E. M. Forster's *Howards End*, calls the world of "telegrams and anger." With nostalgia for a simpler age, therefore, we offer a roll call of bad-guy businessman, the characters in nineteenth- and twentieth-century English and American fiction who have given business such a bad name. (A few of these folks turned out to be good guys in the end, but that was only after they saw the error of their ways, usually prompted by a woman who recognized the supremacy of the inner life.)

I still like books better than business, but I've softened my youthful, hard-ass stance on businesspeople themselves. How you make your living is your business, as Don Corleone once said, but if you can match the characters listed below to their business and authors, you've probably read too many novels to succeed in business without really trying.

Booklist, November 1, 1999

THE CHARACTERS

1. Paul Dombey
2. Frank Cowperwood
3. Kenneth Widmerpool
4. Rabbit Angstrom
5. Mr. Wilcox
6. George F. Babbitt
7. Martin Dressler
8. Silas Lapham
9. Sherman McCoy
10. Tom Rand

THE BUSINESSES

a. industry
b. real estate
c. investment banking
d. shipping
e. paint manufacturing
f. advertising
g. restaurants and hotels
h. banking
i. used cars
j. finance

THE AUTHORS

A. Anthony Powell
B. William Dean Howells
C. Tom Wolfe
D. Theodore Dreiser
E. Steven Millhauser
F. Charles Dickens
G. Sloan Wilson
H. John Updike
I. Sinclair Lewis
J. E. M. Forster

ANSWERS: 1-d-F (*Dombey and Son*); 2-j-D (*The Financier*); 3-a-A (*A Dance to the Music of Time*); 4-i-H (*Rabbit Is Rich*); 5-h-J (*Howards End*); 6-b-I (*Babbitt*); 7-g-E (*Martin Dressler*); 8-e-B (*The Rise of Silas Lapham*); 9-c-C (*The Bonfire of the Vanities*); 10-f-G (*The Man in the Gray Flannel Suit*)

MORE THAN THE FACTS, MA'AM

IT'S ONE THING FOR a novelist to invent characters and place them in a recognizable historical moment; it's quite another to dramatize the lives of famous historical figures. For history-reading purists, the idea of sullying fact with mere storytelling is never more troublesome than when novelists presume to get inside a real-life person's head and report on their so-called findings. We profane types, however, unconcerned about purity in any of its forms, would much rather encounter historical figures in the pages of a novel than in the pages of a history text. We respond to story, whether fact or fiction, and we like our characters to have inner lives. It's not an argument likely to be won by either side, but for those who prefer to meet historical figures in a narrative context, here is a quiz to rekindle memories and perhaps prompt a quick trip to the library. The trick is to match the historical figures with the novelists who wrote about them. Beware: some of these authors have written about more than one of the historical figures listed, but there is only one way to finish the quiz with 25 correct answers. We're not telling you the titles of the novels in question since most of them give away their subject. We expect you to know them, however, and we'll give you extra credit for each one you can name. Answers, including titles, are listed below, but no peeking, no matter how impure you profess to be.

Most of the books included in this quiz were selected by Brad Hooper, who is *Booklist*'s resident historical fiction expert and that rare individual who reads both history and historical novels with equal relish.

Booklist, May 15, 2005

HISTORICAL FIGURES

1. Aaron Burr
2. Albert Einstein
3. Vermeer
4. Marie Antoinette
5. Charles Lindbergh
6. Abelard and Heloise
7. Simon Bolívar
8. Meriwether Lewis
9. Bix Biederbecke
10. Henry VIII
11. Vincent van Gogh
12. Claudius
13. Elizabeth I of England
14. Henry Morgan
15. Sappho
16. Mary, Queen of Scots
17. John Brown
18. Alexander the Great
19. Pretty Boy Floyd
20. Thomas Paine
21. Anne Boleyn
22. William Shakespeare
23. Jesus Christ
24. Raphael Trujillo
25. Roman emperor Hadrian

HISTORICAL FICTION AUTHORS

a. Irving Stone
b. Marguerite Yourcenar
c. Robert Nye
d. Robin Maxwell
e. Patricia Finney
f. John Steinbeck
g. Mario Vargas Llosa
h. Erica Jong
i. Mary Renault
j. Margaret George
k. Gore Vidal
l. Tracy Chevalier
m. Philip Roth
n. Antoine Audouard
o. David Nevin
p. Robert Graves
q. Nino Ricci
r. Howard Fast
s. Bill Brooks
t. Frederick Turner
u. Chantal Thomas
v. Jean Plaidy
w. Russell Banks
x. Gabriel García Márquez
y. Alan Lightman

ANSWERS: 1-k (Burr); 2-y (Einstein's Dreams); 3-l (Girl with a Pearl Earring); 4-u (Farewell, My Queen); 5-m (The Plot against America); 6-n (Farewell, My Only One); 7-x (The General in His Labyrinth); 8-o (Meriwether); 9-t (1929); 10-j (The Autobiography of Henry VIII); 11-a (Lust for Life); 12-p (I, Claudius); 13-e (Firedrake's Eye); 14-f (Cup of Gold); 15-h (Sappho's Leap); 16-v (The Captive Queen of Scots); 17-w (Cloudsplitter); 18-i (The Persian Boy); 19-s (Pretty Boy); 20-r (Citizen Tom Paine); 21-d (The Secret Diary of Anne Boleyn); 22-c (The Late Mr. Shakespeare); 23-q (Testament); 24-g (The Feast of the Goat); 25-b (Memoirs of Hadrian)

WRITERS IN LOVE

IMAGINE LITERARY HISTORY AS one big writers' conference at which novelists and poets work by day and make love with one another by night. If that seems a bit far-fetched to you, try reading a few chapters in John Booth's *Literary Lovers*, which catalogs the amorous activity of a particularly randy group of nineteenth- and twentieth-century writers. Somehow it's comforting to know that, in affairs of the heart, writers—even very good ones—tend to behave like junior-high kids. If you care about literature but aren't interested in literary gossip, read no further. If, on the other hand, you aren't above wondering which French writer claimed to have made love to more than 10,000 women, you'll want to try your hand at the quiz below. Please match the bedroom vitae with the list of names; note that there are often multiple names associated with each description. That's what makes it interesting—for participant and voyeur alike.

Booklist, September 15, 1999

BEDROOM VITAE

1. Notorious for her flamboyant affairs with women (her husband preferred men), this English aristocrat was described by one of her lovers, a rather famous novelist usually concerned more with affairs of the head than heart, in these uncharacteristically ribald terms: "Her real claim to consideration is, if I may be so coarse, her legs. Oh, they are exquisite— running like slender pillars up into her trunk, which is that of a breastless cuirassier. . . but all about her is virginal, savage, patrician."

2. This small, bespectacled, plumpish bachelor not only wrote novels (including one that many believe launched a genre) but also maintained two separate households presided over by respective mistresses. At 63, the randy Victorian wrote to a friend: "I think the back view of a finely formed woman the loveliest view and her hips the more precious part of that view."

3. She maintained a 55-year relationship with one of the leading intellectuals of the twentieth century but found passion in the arms of a blue-collar novelist from Chicago. He called her "little frog"; he was her "crocodile."

4. Although he wrote about sex with remarkable power, he was a poor lover— at least in the opinion of his wife (a woman of gargantuan appetites). This fastidious fellow, who was 23 before he kissed a woman on the mouth, strongly disapproved of promiscuity and remained faithful to his wife despite her dalliances with numerous younger men.

5. As proud of his sexual exploits as his literary success, this French writer, who died of syphilis at 42, had witnesses present in a Paris brothel when

he made love to six women in one hour. He bragged of his performance to his mentor, an older French author who wrote a novel about adultery that many thought was immoral.

6. The author of nearly 400 novels, this indefatigable Frenchman claimed to have made love to more than 10,000 women in his life. His conquests included wives, friends of wives, maids, and celebrities, including a dancer who occasionally dressed in bananas. The most famous character in his fiction was his very opposite: deliberate, thoughtful, and abidingly faithful to his wife.

7. Perhaps one of literature's most unlikely romances was this one between a portly author of prophetic novels and feisty feminist writer, who was 20 when she met and fell hard for the squeaky-voiced 46-year-old. "His company was like seeing Nureyev dance," she recalled.

THE WRITER/LOVERS AND ONE OF THEIR CHARACTERS

A. Vita Sackville-West
B. Harold Nicholson
C. Wilkie Collins
D. Nelson Algren
E. H. G. Wells
F. Jean-Paul Sartre
G. Freida Lawrence
H. Simone de Beauvoir

I. Josephine Baker
J. Georges Simenon
K. Guy de Maupassant
L. Inspector Maigret
M. D. H. Lawrence
N. Rebecca West
O. Gustave Flaubert
P. Virginia Woolf

ANSWERS: 1-A-B-P: Vita, married, to Harold, had a brief affair with Virginia, who apparently liked long legs on a gal; 2-C: Wilkie Collins created the English detective story when he wasn't admiring the female posterior; 3-D-F-H: Simone de Beauvoir talked existentialism with Sartre, made love with Algren; 4-G-M: D. H. Lawrence wrote about sex; his wife, Freida, practiced it, sometimes with her husband; 5-K-O: De Maupassant knew Flaubert wouldn't believe anything without multiple sources; 6-I-J-L: Georges Simenon was the French Wilt Chamberlain; his character, Maigret, stayed home with his wife; Josephine Baker was one of Simenon's 10,000 conquests; 7-E-N: H. G. Wells wooed and won Rebecca West, despite squeaking his sweet-nothings.

QUIZZES ■ 179

FIRST FIRSTS

THE FIRST 20 PAGES or so of every January issue of *Booklist* are devoted to our annual Editors' Choice lists. The writers honored on those pages vary from rookies to seasoned veterans, but the majority of them have been toiling at what Dylan Thomas called "my craft or sullen art" for long enough to remember when sitting down to write didn't require loading software. Still, everyone was a rookie once, and it's intriguing—especially at the beginning of a new year—to look back at the first efforts of established authors. Below you will find the first sentences from the first novels of some major players in twentieth-century literature, some of whom are contemporary enough to have graced previous *Booklist* Editors' Choice lists. Your task is to match sentences with books; for extra credit, supply the writers. Then contemplate whether their careers lived up to their first sentences or whether it was all downhill after that first period hit the page.

Booklist, November 15, 2000

FIRST SENTENCES

1. I first heard Personville called Poisonville by a red-haired mucker named Hickey Dewey in the Big Ship in Butte.

2. If you really want to hear about it, the first thing you'll probably want to know is where I was born, and what my lousy childhood was like, and how my parents were occupied and all before they had me, and all that David Copperfield kind of crap, but I don't feel like going into it, if you want to know the truth.

3. They're out there. Black boys in white suits up before me to commit sex acts in the hall and get it mopped up before I can catch them.

4. Nobody could sleep. When morning came, assault craft would be lowered and a first wave of troops would ride through the surf and charge ashore on the beach at Anopopei.

5. Amory Blaine inherited from his mother every trait, except the inexpressible few, that made him worth while.

6. A green hunting cap squeezed the top of the fleshy balloon of a head.

7. There were 117 psychoanalysts on the Pan Am flight to Vienna and I'd been treated by at least six of them.

8. You are not the kind of guy who would be at a place like this at this time of the morning.

9. When he finished packing, he walked out onto the third-floor porch of the barracks brushing the dust from his hands, a very neat and deceptively slim young man in the summer khakis that were still early morning fresh.

10. To someone like myself, whose literary actives have been confined since 1920 mainly to such pedestrian genres as legal briefs (in connection with my position as a partner in the firm of Andrews, Bishop & Andrews) and Inquiry-writing (which I'll explain presently), the hardest thing about the task at hand—viz., the explanation of a day in 1937 when I changed my mind—is getting into it.

11. It was about eleven o'clock in the morning, mid October, with the sun shining and a look of hard wet rain in the clearness of the foothills.

TITLES

A. *Fear of Flying*
B. *The Big Sleep*
C. *The Far Side of Paradise*
D. *Red Harvest*
E. *The Floating Opera*
F. *The Catcher in the Rye*
G. *A Confederacy of Dunces*
H. *The Naked and the Dead*
I. *One Flew over the Cuckoo's Nest*
J. *From Here to Eternity*
K. *Bright Lights, Big City*

ANSWERS: 1-D (Dashiell Hammett); 2-F (J. D. Salinger); 3-I (Ken Kesey); 4-H (Norman Mailer); 5-C (F. Scott Fitzgerald); 6-G (John Kennedy Toole); 7-A (Erica Jong); 8-K (Jay McInerney); 9-J (James Jones); 10-E (John Barth); 11-B (Raymond Chandler)

HARD-BOILED KISSERS

I HAVE SOME BAD news: the classic hard-boiled heroes were not very good kissers. I know this flies in the face of conventional wisdom: What about Bogey and Betty in *The Big Sleep*, you ask? Fine, but that was the movies. If you go back to the books as I did, hoping to put together a Valentine Back Page, you find a different story altogether. Many of our most memorable hard-boiled heroes, from the thirties into the seventies, tend to use the kiss as an expression of power, violence, and control but rarely as a vehicle for romance. This approach is certainly not going to wash with most women of the nineties, but even on a purely aesthetic level, it seems to fall short. One looks for adjectives like *soft* or perhaps *lingering* when it comes to describing kisses, but if you do a little perusing in the hard-boiled canon, you'll be amazed at how often the heroes' attempts at osculation are described with words like *hard* or *tight* and, further, how the kisses themselves seem to prompt angry reactions in the recipients. Many might argue that if you were kissed by someone who smoked as much as Philip Marlowe, you'd vote for *quick* and *tight* over *soft* and *lingering* any day. On the other hand, if you were walking around in the pages of a Marlowe novel, you were probably smoking as much as the hero. Different kisses for different kissers, I suppose, so check out the passages below and decide for yourselves. Then try your luck at matching kiss with kisser. Happy Valentine's Day!

Booklist, February 1, 1997

THE KISSES

1. "I put my arms around her loosely at first. Her hair had a harsh feeling against my face. I tightened my arms and lifted her up. I brought her face slowly up to my face. Her eyelids were flicking rapidly, like moth wings. I kissed her tightly and quickly."

2. "'This is goodbye,' she said, then tilted her cheek toward me again. 'To hell with that,' I said as I grabbed her shoulders and kissed her on the mouth so hard that it blurred the careful lines of her lips, mussed her hair, and made her drop her carry-on bag. 'You bastard,' she muttered. . . . She reached up to wipe my mouth, repeating, 'You bastard. That was the last one.'"

3. "He moved his shoulders a little and said: 'Well, a lot of money would have been at least one more item on the other side of the scales.' She put her face up to his face. Her mouth was slightly open with lips a little thrust out. She whispered: 'If you loved me you'd need nothing more on that side.' [He] set the edges of his teeth together and said through them: 'I won't play the sap for you.' She put her mouth to his, slowly put her arms around him, and came into his arms. She was in his arms when the doorbell rang."

4. "It seemed to come slowly, the way sleep does when you're too tired, the gradual coming together of two people. Slow, then faster and all of a sudden her arms were around me and my hands were pressing into her back and my fingers curled in her hair. I looked at that mouth that wasn't just damp now, but wet and she said, 'damn you,' softly and I tasted the hunger in her until the fury of it was too much and I let her go."

5. "I mashed out my cigarette, so I could get up and go. I was going to get out of there, and drop those renewals and everything else about her like a red-hot poker. But I didn't do it. She looked at me, a little surprised, and her face was about six inches away. What I did do was put my arm around her, pull her face up against mine, and kiss her on the mouth, hard. I was trembling like a leaf. She gave it a cold stare, and then she closed her eyes, pulled me to her, and kissed back."

THE KISSERS

a. C. W. Sughrue (*The Last Good Kiss*, by James Crumley)
b. Mike Hammer (*Kiss Me, Deadly*, by Mickey Spillane)
c. Walter Huff (*Double Indemnity*, by James M. Cain)
d. Sam Spade (*The Maltese Falcon*, by Dashiell Hammett)
e. Philip Marlowe (*The Big Sleep*, by Raymond Chandler)

ANSWERS: 1-e; 2-a; 3-d; 4-b; 5-c

PUPPY LOVE

VALENTINE'S DAY APPROACHES ONCE again, and as we've done in the past, the Back Page salutes love and lovers. This time, though, we're doing it a little differently: our subject is love between animals. No, we're not talking about PBS documentaries ("The Mating Habits of the Osprey"), nor are we alluding to anything even slightly kinky. The lovers on parade below happen to be animals in children's books. Who's to say, after all, that a couple of bears or spiders or hippopotamuses, for that matter, can't be just as romantic as Cary Grant and Katharine Hepburn in *The Philadelphia Story*? Read the descriptions and then guess the identities of the lovers. And remember to buy your favorite puppy a box of candy on February 14.

Booklist, February 1, 1996

1. Two bears in love: when he, a self-sufficient fisherman (you know, a real bear's bear kind of guy), spots her, a graceful, society sort of bear, doing a few pirouettes around the skating pond, it's time to launch a full-scale campaign. And this bear knows how to impress a gal: hot chocolate, blueberry pie, skiing, star-watching. One question: Aren't bears supposed to be hibernating in the winter?

2. She certainly had no intention of falling in love with him. After all, she's a middle-age, slightly dowdy lady, and he's, well . . . an alligator. You just can't keep some couples apart, however, and this duo was meant for one another. As usual, the outside world puts up a struggle, but our lovers stay the course.

3. There's this poet, see, who happens to be a dog. He's a New Yorker, but he lives in Paris now, and his poems are all the rage. But success rings hollow; our poet is lonely. Then one night he stumbles into a nightclub and hears a certain pianist named Crepes Suzette ("You played the legato, my heart went staccato"). Fortunately, Crepes happens to be a dazzling Dalmatian, so there is nothing to stand in love's way. Thank heaven for little dogs.

4. It's an operetta in paradise when a certain owl falls for a certain pussycat. A shipboard romance on the gently rolling Caribbean seas is what's called for (just imagine Frank and Kathy Lee on a Princess cruise), but obstacles keep getting in the way, and the somewhat hoity-toity owl winds up overboard (too bad he couldn't take Frank and Kathy Lee with him). Like any traditional romance, it all ends in marriage, with a slightly sleazy, beachcombing pig providing the ring.

5. Two sheepdogs have it all: good jobs, nice home, sweet kids, much love shared by everyone. So what could possibly get in the way? A pig, that's what. And not just any pig, but a Pig of Destiny, a presumptuous porker with the big idea that pigs ought to be able to hang with sheepdogs if they are so inclined. Mr. Sheepdog, nice guy though he is, has trouble with this multicultural concept, and his failure to embrace diversity causes tension in his marriage. Don't despair, though; the pooches don't wind up in divorce court, and the porker finds his destiny.

6. Ah, domesticity! The special intimacy shared by long-term lovers is on display in this story of two happily-ever-aftering hippopotamuses. Not that the couple doesn't encounter difficulties: he pours her split-pea soup in his loafers; he has a problematic fondness for peeking in other people's windows; she is just a teensy bit vain (and there's nothing like a vain hippo). Still, they muddle through together, celebrating the dailiness of mature love.

7. Never listen to your friends when it comes to finding a mate. Take poor Miss Spider, who lets her nosy pal May turn her against Mr. Holley, a perfectly nice spider but not exactly a hunk. May disses Holley terribly ("that pantywaist"), and soon Miss Spider is being courted by the slick but villainous Spiderous Reeves. Well, the good suitor wins in the end, and Miss Spider looks ravishing at the wedding, sporting a particularly stylish spiderweb veil.

....

ANSWERS: (1) The Wedding of Brown Bear and White Bear, by Martine Beck, with illustrations by Marie H. Henry; (2) Elizabeth and Larry, by Marilyn Sadler, with illustrations by Roger Bollen; (3) Ooh-La-La (Max in Love), written and illustrated by Maira Kalman; (4) The Owl and the Pussycat, by Edward Lear, with illustrations by Jan Brett; (5) Babe: The Gallant Pig, by Dick King-Smith; (6) George and Martha, written and illustrated by James Marshall; (7) Miss Spider's Wedding, written and illustrated by David Kirk

....

TOO MANY MORALS

TOO MANY MORALS IS what I thought I'd find when I began to examine a nice little gift book called *What the Dormouse Said: Lessons for Grown-Ups from Children's Books*, by Amy Gash. I was right, there were too many morals—pious aphorisms on the wonders of the imagination and the strength of the individual—but it wasn't all pieties. One of the challenges I set for myself as the compiler of trivial quizzes ("You've got to be able to make those daring leaps or you're no-where," says Russell Hoban's muskrat) is to find something subversive, or at least kind of mean, in the most seemingly inspirational quote books. I've found the dark underside in would-be poignant quotations about writers and about mar-riage, so why not children's books? ("So many things are possible just as long as you don't know they're impossible"—*The Phantom Tollbooth*.) I must report only limited success, but I don't think you can blame children's literature for that. As anyone who has read Alison Lurie's *Don't Tell the Grown-Ups* knows, there's plenty of subversion to be found in kids' books. Gash's selection, unfortunately, tends toward the wholesome, but she slips up now and then. Even the most up-right of compilers usually can't resist setting aside a chapter or two for the mean stuff; here it's a section called "Defiance." (Interestingly, some of the most "defi-ant" statements come from classics like *Mary Poppins*.) To my mind, grown-ups could learn a lot more from these defiant quotes than they could from the tired chestnuts in the section called "Growing Wise." ("Sometimes one must travel far to discover what is near." Thanks, Uri Shulevitz, for reiterating something I've heard, oh, maybe a thousand times.)

If all the quotes below aren't truly subversive, or even all that mean, they at least haven't appeared on too many Hallmark cards. And some of them really do offer valuable lessons: check out the one about getting machines to work; I'd argue that it tells you far more about life than Madeleine L'Engle does when she informs us that "a poet friend of mine told me that his poems know far more than he does, and if he listens to them, they teach him." Don't you just hate it when poets go off like that?

Booklist, April 1, 2000

THE QUOTES

1. And now, cried Max, let the wild rumpus start!
2. I *hate* being good.
3. When I grow up I'm going to stay up all night every night until I die.
4. I detest relatives even more than regular people.
5. Believe me, young friend, there is nothing—absolutely nothing—half so much worth doing as simply messing about in boats.
6. Without a doubt, there is such a thing as too much order.
7. Too much learning breaks even the healthiest.
8. I've learned what a nuisance bravery can be, So a coward's life is the life for me.
9. It is not too often that someone comes along who is both a true friend and a good writer.
10. Sometimes if you hit a machine a couple of times you can get it going again.
11. After dinner, Harry fell asleep in his favorite place, happily dreaming of how much fun it had been getting dirty.
12. This sharing business is for the birds.
13. Persons attempting to find a motive in this narrative will be prosecuted; persons attempting to find a moral in it will be banished; persons attempting to find a plot in it will be shot.

THE TITLES

A. *Fables* (1980), by Arnold Lobel
B. *Top Banana* (1997), by Cari Best
C. *Charlotte's Web* (1952), by E. B. White
D. *Pippi Longstocking* (1950), by Astrid Lindgren
E. *Where the Wild Things Are* (1963), by Maurice Sendak
F. *Custard the Dragon and the Wicked Knight* (1961), by Ogden Nash
G. *Thimble Summer* (1938), by Elizabeth Enright
H. *The Wind in the Willows* (1907), by Kenneth Grahame
I. *Worse Than the Worst* (1994), by James Stevenson
J. *Harry the Dirty Dog* (1956), by Gene Zion
K. *The Adventures of Huckleberry Finn* (1884), by Mark Twain
L. *Mary Poppins* (1934), by P. L. Travers
M. *Freaky Friday* (1972), by Mary Rodgers

ANSWERS: 1-E; 2-L; 3-G; 4-I; 5-H; 6-A; 7-D; 8-F; 9-C; 10-M; 11-J; 12-B; 13-K

GOIN' HOLLYWOOD

TALES OF WRITERS FORCED to sell themselves to Hollywood in order to pay the bills are legion. The archetypal version of the story usually has the writer forced to endure all manner of humiliation at the hands of cinematic philistines who respect neither the written word nor the writer's imagination. Yes, but. The movies also kept many a between-the-wars writer alive to write the novels for which they would later become famous (Faulkner is the classic example). In addition, a funny thing happened every now and then: a famous literary author would stop moping about the indignity of it all long enough to write or cowrite a pretty decent movie. The quiz below, borrowed from a soon-to-be-published trivia book called *And You Thought You Knew Classic Movies!* by John DeLeo, brings together scrambled lists of writers and the films they wrote. (In Sidney Sheldon's case, at least, the movie was considerably better than any of his books.) Match the writer to the film for which he/she wrote or cowrote the screenplay.

Booklist, November 1, 1998

THE WRITERS

1. Aldous Huxley
2. Truman Capote
3. Dorothy Parker
4. Sidney Sheldon
5. John Steinbeck
6. Gore Vidal
7. F. Scott Fitzgerald
8. William Faulkner
9. James Agee
10. Ray Bradbury

THE MOVIES

a. *Suddenly, Last Summer*
b. *Easter Parade*
c. *Beat the Devil*
d. *Moby Dick* (1956)
e. *To Have and Have Not*
f. *Pride and Prejudice*
g. *The Night of the Hunter*
h. *A Star Is Born* (1937)
i. *Three Comrades*
j. *Viva Zapata!*

ANSWERS: 1-f; 2-c; 3-h; 4-b; 5-j; 6-a; 7-i; 8-e; 9-g; 10-d

POETIC LAST LINES

WHO SAYS REFERENCE BOOKS can't be fun? Take *Last Lines: An Index to the Last Lines of Poetry* by Victoria Kline. This Facts On File book, reviewed in the January 15 *Booklist*, makes great browsing, whether you land in the last-line section itself or in the equally fascinating keyword index. (*Love* and *death* are the big winners, with more than 15 pages of entries between them.) There are certain kinds of books that seem to have been published for the express purpose of helping a weary editor beat a fast-approaching Back Page deadline. Thank you to both Kline and Facts On File for producing just such a book and conspiring to have it land on my desk in the nick of time. As you read the last lines below and attempt to connect them to the scrambled authors and titles, it's even money you'll find yourself pulling that dusty *Norton Anthology* down from your shelf and reading the poems in their entirety. Keep *Norton* at the ready; there's a poetic first-lines quiz in the works.

Booklist, April 15, 1992

LAST LINES

1. Till human voices wake us, and we drown.
2. Had somewhere to get to and sailed calmly on.
3. To strive, to seek, to find, and not to yield.
4. In the foul rag-and-bone shop of the heart.
5. a savage servility / slides by on grease.
6. Though I sang in my chains like the sea.
7. Where is it now, the glory and the dream?
8. I measure time by how a body sways.
9. Where ignorant armies clash by night.
10. Is what to make of a diminished thing.

AUTHORS

A. Robert Lowell
B. Matthew Arnold
C. T. S. Eliot
D. Theodore Roethke
E. Alfred, Lord Tennyson
F. W. H. Auden
G. Robert Frost
H. Dylan Thomas
I. W. B. Yeats
J. William Wordsworth

TITLES

a. "The Circus Animals' Desertion"
b. "Musee de Beaux Arts"
c. "Fern Hill"
d. "Intimations of Immortality"
e. "For the Union Dead"
f. "Dover Beach"
g. "I knew a woman"
h. "Ulysses"
i. "The Oven Bird"
j. "The Love Song of J. Alfred Prufrock"

ANSWERS: 1-C-j; 2-F-b; 3-E-h; 4-I-a; 5-A-e; 6-H-c; 7-J-d; 8-D-g; 9-B-f; 10-G-i

GREAT LINES

ARE MOVIES BETTER THAN real life? The risk of dying from some lingering disease must be about 500 percent higher on screen than it is in real life (look at poor Julia Roberts), and the possibility of being shot, even for those in violent lines of work, is similarly inflated (most real-life cops go years without firing a gun). On the other hand, there is one area where movies have it all over daily life: dialogue. In the movies, people always say the right thing, the characteristic thing, the symbolic thing, the romantic thing, at just the right moment. In my experience at least, this almost never happens in the real world. Great lines in life tend to be spoken in silence, to yourself, long after the right moment has come and gone. That's why the movies are so much fun: you might get bumped off in the third reel but not before a cavalcade of great lines has rolled from your lips like arpeggios off Art Tatum's fingers. With the help of a delightful little book, *Great Movie Lines*, by Dale Thomajan (Fawcett), I've listed a few personal favorites below. Match them with the larger-than-life performer who uttered them. Then pretend you spoke them at all the appropriate moments in your life.

Booklist, November 15, 2000

GREAT LINES

1. I've been waiting all my life to fuck up like this.
2. Was you ever bit by a dead bee?
3. I never dreamed that any mere physical experience could be so stimulating!
4. Last night I dreamt I went to Manderley again.
5. Nobody loses all the time.
6. You have no idea what a long-legged gal can do without doing anything.
7. The psychiatrist asked me if I had a girl and I said no and he said, well, do I think that sex is dirty and I said it is if you're doing it right.
8. We all go a little mad sometimes.
9. You were extremely attractive . . . but you were a little worse, or better, for wine—and there are rules about that.
10. When it comes to dying for your country, it's better not to die at all.
11. It's a hard world for little things.
12. I've done my time with one cold-blooded bastard. I'm not looking for another.
13. When women go wrong, men go right after them.
14. What Jefferson was saying was "Hey! You know, we left this England place 'cause it was bogus, so if we don't get some cool rules ourselves—pronto— we'll just be bogus too."

15. You're not too smart—are you? I like that in a man.
16. What I really want to do with my life, what I want to do for a living—I want to be with your daughter. I'm good at it.
17. A guy'll listen to anything if he thinks it's foreplay.
18. One morning I shot an elephant in my pajamas. How he got into my pajamas I don't know.
19. I was born when she kissed me. I died when she left me. I lived a few weeks while she loved me.

PERFORMERS

a. Walter Brennan in *To Have and Have Not,* 1945
b. Groucho Marx in *Animal Crackers,* 1930
c. Katharine Hepburn to Humphrey Bogart after shooting the rapids with him in *The African Queen,* 1951
d. Lew Ayres to a classroom of children in *All Quiet on the Western Front,* 1930
e. Susan Sarandon in *Bull Durham,* 1988
f. Anthony Perkins in *Psycho,* 1960
g. John Cusack in *Say Anything,* 1989
h. Kathleen Turner to William Hurt in *Body Heat,* 1981
i. Patricia Neal to Paul Newman in *Hud,* 1963
j. Sean Penn in *Fast Times at Ridgemont High,* 1982
k. Woody Allen in *Take the Money and Run,* 1969
l. Humphrey Bogart in *In a Lonely Place,* 1950
m. Mae West in *She Done Him Wrong,* 1933
n. Warren Oates in *Bring Me the Head of Alfredo Garcia,* 1974
o. Lillian Gish in *The Night of the Hunter,* 1955
p. Joan Fontaine in *Rebecca,* 1940
q. James Stewart explaining his previous night's restraint to Katharine Hepburn in *The Philadelphia Story,* 1940
r. Claudette Colbert in *The Palm Beach Story,* 1942
s. Michael Moriarity in *Who'll Stop the Rain,* 1978

POEMS FOR A SUNDAY
AFTERNOON

I AM NOT ONE of those people who memorizes poems, or who remembers the poems he memorized 30 years ago. Many would see this as a character flaw. You know the type: stuffed shirts who attribute the sorry state of education today to three sources—kids don't take Latin anymore, they don't diagram sentences, and they don't memorize poems. Well, I didn't take Latin, my sentence-diagramming skills were average at best, and the only poem I ever successfully memorized was "Casey at the Bat." Somehow I've survived in spite of these failings. I do wish I knew a little more about the pluperfect tense, but I haven't missed Latin, and in a way, I'm glad I didn't manage to memorize more poems. Since I don't know all my favorite poems by heart, I occasionally need to look them up, which prompts me to read them again, and that, in turn, prompts me to read the poem on the next page, which reminds me of still another poem in a different book, which leads me down to the basement in search of the missing book. At that point, I'm distracted by my cat Homer's litter box—in dire need of attention—and the string of associations is broken. Still, if I hadn't needed to look up that first poem, I wouldn't have spent a pleasant Sunday afternoon reading poetry, although perhaps the mental discipline of memorizing poems would help me remember where I put my car keys.

The reason I was rereading poems on this particular Sunday afternoon was to put together the column you're now reading. As so often happens, my original idea didn't really work out. I'd hoped to construct a quiz of famous first lines from poems of all kinds—highbrow and low, ancient and contemporary, profound and nonsensical. The more I got into the reading, however, the less interested I became in the quiz, and the more interested I became in rereading poems I liked. What you have below may look like a quiz, but it's really more of a report on how I spent my Sunday afternoon. If the column was more fun for me to prepare than for you to read, I make no apologies—at least this time. A man needs to spend a relaxing Sunday every now and again. In fact, if this collection of opening snippets from some of my favorite poems strikes you as boring, I recommend you spend the next hour or two browsing your own bookshelves. You're sure to find something interesting. Just don't memorize it.

Booklist, March 15, 2000

THE LINES

1. The old south Boston Aquarium
   stands
   in a Sahara of snow now.
2. It is 12:20 in New York a Friday
3. You might come here Sunday on a
   whim.
   Say your life broke down. The last
   good kiss
   You had was years ago.
4. About suffering, they were never
   wrong,
   The Old Masters
5. It little profits that an idle king,
   By this still hearth,
   among these barren crags,
6. Here I am, an old man in a dry
   month,
   Being read to by a boy, waiting for
   rain
7. Now as I was young and easy
   under the apple boughs
8. While my hair was still cut
   straight across my forehead
   I played about the front gate,
   pulling flowers
9. I knew a woman lovely in her
   bones
   When small birds sighed, she
   would sigh back at them;
10. That is no country for old men
11. We stripped in the first warm
    spring night and ran down into
    the Detroit river.
12. Life, friends, is boring. We must
    not say so.
13. Five years have passed; five
    summers, with the length
    Of five long winters!
14. The sea is calm tonight.

THE POEMS

A. "Belle Island, 1949"
B. "For the Union Dead"
C. "Gerontion"
D. "Sailing to Byzantium"
E. "Dream Song—14"
F. "Tintern Abbey"
G. "Degrees of Gray in Phillipsburg"
H. "The Day Lady Died"
I. "Musee de Beaux Arts"
J. "Dover Beach"
K. "Fern Hill"
L. "Ulysses"
M. "The River Merchant's Daughter:
   A Letter"
N. "I Knew a Woman"

THE POETS

a. Richard Hugo
b. Philip Levine
c. Matthew Arnold
d. W. H. Auden
e. Alfred, Lord Tennyson
f. Frank O'Hara
g. John Berryman
h. Dylan Thomas
i. Ezra Pound
j. Robert Lowell
k. William Wordsworth
l. W. B. Yeats
m. Theodore Roethke
n. T. S. Eliot

ANSWERS: 1-B-j; 2-H-f; 3-G-a; 4-I-d; 5-L-e; 6-C-n; 7-K-h; 8-M-i; 9-N-m; 10-D-l; 11-A-b; 12-E-g; 13-F-k; 14-J-c

SEX WITH DEAD PRESIDENTS

TO MY MIND, THOSE Sunday-morning pundits who have tied their undies in such a bunch over the doings of President Clinton sound a lot like Captain Renault. You remember him, the prefect of police in Casablanca who ordered the closing of Rick's Café American because he was "shocked, shocked to see that gambling is going on in this establishment." (Then a teller handed the captain his roulette winnings.) Though nowhere near as charming as Captain Renault, the pundits (or "sabbath gasbags," to quote Calvin Trillin) know a thing or two about profiting from righteous indignation. As long as the gasbags keep emitting their noxious fumes, the ballad of Bill and Monica will remain fixed in our brains like a jingle we can't stop singing.

Like many Americans, I'm sick of the whole mess. But unlike some of my fellow citizens, it's not the sleazy sex that wearies me. I like that fine. It's the high seriousness that I find so offensive. The problem, really, is how to enjoy the juicy details of presidential sex without it all being ruined by high-mindedness. I think I have the answer. We only treat ourselves to sex with dead presidents. That way, the noble majority (including all gasbags), who say they care about such things as effective government and national image, won't have anything to get riled up about. The rest of us, on the other hand, will be free to enjoy all the tabloid tidbits that have been stored up while the various prexies were still living. To get this new system off and running, I offer a brief quiz taken from a lovely, low-minded book called *Presidential Sex*, by Wesley O. Hagood (Citadel). Remember: Bill Clinton is not among the answers. We play by the rules here.

Booklist, October 15, 1998

THE DEEDS

1. Which president repeatedly made love to a young girl from his hometown in a White House coat closet when, on at least one occasion, his wife was prevented from beating down the closet door by a Secret Service agent?
2. Which president married a woman who was not yet divorced from her first husband and was later labeled an "adulterer" during his reelection campaign?
3. Which future president wrote love letters to his neighbor's wife while he was engaged to another woman?
4. Which president smoked marijuana with a young, nude playgirl and joked about being incapacitated when it came time to "push the button" in the event of a nuclear attack?
5. Which vice president became angry because he felt his record of actual sexual conquests was far greater than the then existing president's reputation for the same?
6. Which president has a song written about his alleged illegitimate child that was often chanted at parades and political rallies?
7. Which president had numerous caustic poems written about his sexual dalliance and published in the major newspapers of the day.

THE DEAD PRESIDENTS

A. Andrew Jackson
B. John F. Kennedy
C. Warren G. Harding
D. George Washington
E. Grover Cleveland
F. Thomas Jefferson
G. Lyndon B. Johnson

ANSWERS: 1-C; 2-A; 3-D; 4-B; 5-G; 6-E; 7-F

DENTISTS AND MOVIE STARS

THERE JUST AREN'T MANY dentists in literature. That insight occurred to me earlier today while I was sitting in a dental chair waiting for an oral surgeon to pull an infected tooth. Knowing I had a Back Page to write by the end of the day, I decided to distract myself from the various ripping and cracking noises that were coming from my mouth by composing a list of memorable dentists in fiction. Unfortunately, I ran out of dentists long before the ripping stopped.

First, you have McTeague, the hero of Frank Norris' novel of the same name; McTeague doesn't really love his work and throws it over in the pursuit of gold, which leads to a decidedly bad end. Then there's Doc Adams, the only oral-surgeon hero in the entire crime-fiction canon. Rick Boyer's series is thoroughly entertaining, and Doc Adams makes a fine Everyman hero, but most of the action, not surprisingly, has little to do with oral surgery. Now the pickings get slim. There's the dentist in *M*A*S*H*, who was determined to kill himself but didn't; there's the dentist/Lothario in Susan Isaacs' *Compromising Positions*, who gets bumped off on page 1; and, of course, there's the evil Nazi dentist in *The Boys from Brazil*, who practices his own variety of oral surgery. (It's best not to think about Nazi dentists while you are sitting in a dental chair.) Without more extensive research, that's the best I can come up with on the topic of literary dentists. Clearly, it's not enough to make a column. Not to worry. Over many years, I have developed one immutable rule about composing this column. When all else fails, find some lists about movie stars. So, with no attempt at any kind of segue, I give you a three-cornered quiz about actors playing writers. It's a shame the dentist thing didn't work out, but right now I need another pain pill.

Booklist, October 15, 2000

STARS WHO HAVE PLAYED WRITERS IN BIOPICS

THE ACTORS	THE WRITERS	THE MOVIES
1. Gregory Peck	a. Christy Brown	A. *Shadowlands*
2. Daniel Day-Lewis	b. Eugene O'Neill	B. *Beloved Infidel*
3. Gregory Peck	c. Agatha Christie	C. *My Left Foot*
4. Jack Nicholson	d. C. S. Lewis	D. *Old Gringo*
5. Vanessa Redgrave	e. Lillian Hellman	E. *Fear and Loathing in*
6. Olivia de Havilland	f. Joe Orton	*Las Vegas*
7. Gary Oldman	g. Charlotte Brontë	F. *Julia*
8. Anthony Hopkins	h. F. Scott Fitzgerald	G. *Prick Up Your Ears*
9. Jane Fonda	i. Hunter S. Thompson	H. *Devotion*
10. Johnny Depp	j. Ambrose Bierce	I. *Reds*
		J. *Agatha*

ANSWERS: 1-j-D; 2-a-C; 3-h-B; 4-b-I; 5-c-J; 6-g-H; 7-f-G; 8-d-A; 9-e-F; 10-i-E

INDEX

Note: This index includes authors and titles of books, periodicals, and films discussed or mentioned in the text. Page numbers with asterisks indicate allusions to authors.

You may also be interested in

The Librarian's Book of Quotes: Celebrate librarianship and the love of libraries with this charming collection of quotes! Tatyana Eckstrand has compiled nearly two hundred of the most insightful, thought-provoking, and inspiring aphorisms about the library profession.

The Readers' Advisory Guide to Genre Fiction, Second Edition: Legendary readers' advisor Saricks offers a groundbreaking reconsideration of the connections between genres, providing key authors and themes within fifteen genres, an explanation of how the different genres overlap, the elements of fiction most likely to entice readers, and more.

The Library: In this remarkable story, Stuart A. P. Murray traces the history of the library from its very beginnings in ancient Babylon and Alexandria to some of the greatest contemporary institutions—the Royal Society of London, the Newberry Library, the Smithsonian Institution, and many others. Nearly two hundred color and black-and-white photos illustrate the fascinating progress of the institution we know today as the library.

Fundamentals of Collection Development and Management, Second Edition: In this fully updated revision, expert instructor and librarian Peggy Johnson addresses the art in controlling and updating your library's collection. Each chapter offers complete coverage of one aspect of collection development, including suggestions for further reading and a narrative case study exploring the issue. Johnson also integrates electronic resources throughout the book, covering topics on organization and staffing, policymaking and budgeting, and purchasing and weeding.

For more information, please visit www.alastore.ala.org.

LaVergne, TN USA
21 October 2009

161621LV00008B/139/P